GAME FOR ALL

'Netsuke' — tiny Japanese carvings used as a toggle to enable a small box to be worn on a belt (kimonos have no pockets). Eventually became an art form in their own right.

2 stags at rest 18th.

no guinea fowl or pheasant netsukes so here's a guinea fowl feather

Pigeon on a clay roof tile.
— Some Japanese believed that the pigeon is the only animal to care for its parents, hence court veterans were presented with a pigeon-headed staff.

2 quails on a head of millet — on a straw hat. Popular motif.

Dried salmon 18th. made of lacquered wood & fishskin

GAME FOR ALL

with a flavour of Scotland

NICHOLA FLETCHER

LONDON
VICTOR GOLLANCZ LTD
in association with Peter Crawley
1987

TO

Ian Thomson of Taygame in Perth,
who gamely answered all my questions
and cheerfully parted with so much
from his larder

AND

David Auchterlonie of Auchtermuchty,
a fisherman of remarkable talent
and very great generosity

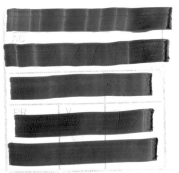

First published in Great Britain 1987
by Victor Gollancz Ltd
14 Henrietta Street, London WC2E 8QJ

British Library Cataloguing in Publication Data
Fletcher, Nichola
  Game for all: with a flavour of Scotland.
  1. Cookery (Game)
  I. Title
  641.6'91   TX751

  ISBN 0-575-03787-3

Photoset in Great Britain by
Rowland Phototypesetting Limited, Bury St Edmunds, Suffolk
and printed in Great Britain by St Edmundsbury Press Limited,
Bury St Edmunds, Suffolk

Contents

Acknowledgements

I could not possibly have written this book without the kind help and forbearance of a great many people. First and foremost come John, Stella and Martha, who put up with periods of great neglect and then had to eat the results. And to the rest of my family and friends who have contributed recipes, suggestions, tastings, opinions, advice and valuable time, thank you. Suzanne and Nicky can rest their aching fingers after mammoth typing sessions. Alfie and Barry will now, I hope, welcome my help on the farm once more. If you like this book, thank Jan Fladmark, who first told a charming man called Peter Crawley that there are writers as well as musicians and burghers in Auchtermuchty.

I should like to thank the Scottish Salmon Information Service for their generous help; Jennie Shapter from Toshiba for giving microwave advice; and Pat Sherren of the N.Z. Kiwi Fruit Board for explaining the wondrous properties of kiwi fruit.

I am most grateful to the Trustees of the National Library of Scotland, not only for providing a peaceful haven for studying, but also for granting permission to reproduce the 17th-century engravings in this book.

Last, but by no means least, I should like to acknowledge the many authors whose writings, both culinary and historical, have given me such delight over the years. My first cookery book was one of Elizabeth David's; Mrs David, Jane Grigson and Edouard de Pomiane instilled in me the sheer pleasure of cooking. For techniques and clear explanations I have for years turned to *Mastering the Art of French Cooking* by Simone Beck, Louisette Bertholle and Julia Child. Michel Guérard, Alexis Soyer and Escoffier have also left their mark. William Scrope, Evelyn Shirley, Jonathan Couch, Osgood MacKenzie, William Radcliffe, F. Marian McNeill, Bruce Banwell, Charles Trench, Roger Longrigg and Barbara Wheaton are among the historical writers whose books I have found fascinating and invaluable. There are many more, and to them all I remain profoundly grateful.

Introduction

To some people, the word 'game' means the pursuit of quarry, close seasons and high meat. Others define it as a bird or beast with certain characteristics. And to some it implies a cheerful willingness to 'have a go', in the expectation that something good will happen. My interpretation focuses on the last two meanings, though of course the first is an integral part. This theme is an expansion of one started off a few years ago. That subject, venison, is dear to my heart as we farm these delightful creatures, and I am interested in the differences and similarities between wild and reared venison. All the species covered in this book are reared for the table as well as being available wild, although some (pheasants for example) are mostly set free before being shot, while others (guinea fowl and quail) are largely only available in their reared form in this country. Game farming means that it is not now essential to participate in the sporting aspect, or even befriend those who do, in order to procure these delicious ingredients. They are to be found in increasing numbers in our shops and supermarkets. I hope this book will serve for laird and layman alike.

So much for All, now for Game. A characteristic feature of my chosen subjects is that by and large, these animals are extremely lean and healthy. They are also packed with good honest flavour—another ingredient sadly lacking in many modern foods. What appropriate subjects they make, therefore, for today's health-conscious cook, as well as the consumer whose palate is sated with blandness.

I may be criticised for my inclusions as well as exclusions. To the former I say that I know quails, guinea fowl and pigeons have no close season, and that in sporting terms are not considered game. But in culinary terms they are, and I am by no means the first to have so listed them. The exclusions? Rabbits, perhaps, should feature, but I have never got over a most divine meal in Morocco consisting of just rabbit and mashed potato. Try as I will, I have never been able to recreate it and I have given up in pique. Perhaps it wasn't rabbit. Ducks and geese should be here too, although the reared type do not fit so snugly into the fat-free image.

Given my book's title, one might reasonably expect to find partridges featuring and, considering the subtitle, one could present a case for grouse. But, historically, they have not had such close involvement with man; and, in any case, my pheasant and guinea fowl recipes will work admirably with grouse or partridge. I have given a little guidance in the appropriate section.

I do hope that you will enjoy reading this book as well as cooking from it. A lot of the most helpful information is in the general explanations at the start of some sections. You will find the book's repertoire enormously expanded if you read them. Now, with your cheerful willingness, have a go and expect something good: that is Game for All.

N.F.
Auchtermuchty, November 1986

BONING FISH — METHOD A - QUICK BUT NOT SO NEAT AS B.

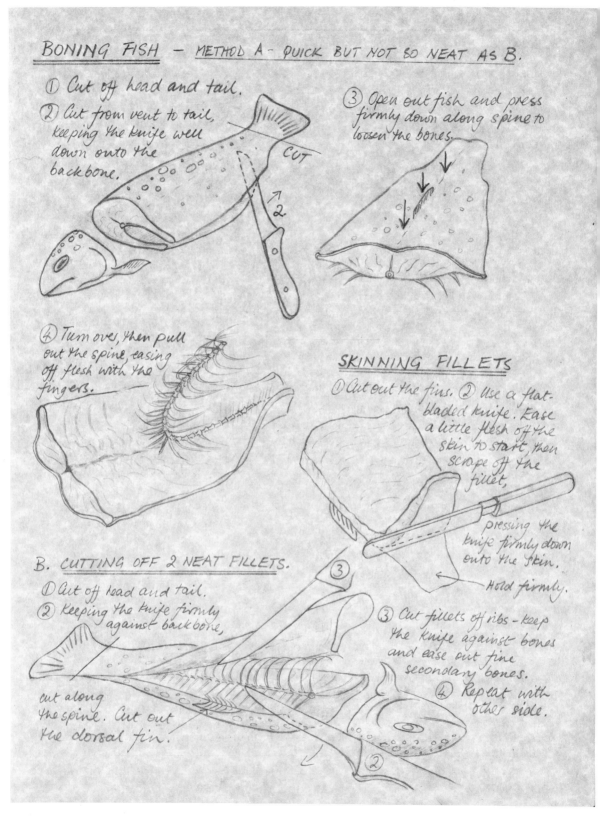

① Cut off head and tail.

② Cut from vent to tail, keeping the knife well down onto the backbone.

③ Open out fish and press firmly down along spine to loosen the bones.

CUT

↗ 2

④ Turn over, then pull out the spine, easing off flesh with the fingers.

SKINNING FILLETS

① Cut out the fins. ② Use a flat-bladed knife. Ease a little flesh off the skin to start, then scrape off the fillet,

pressing the knife firmly down onto the skin.

← Hold firmly.

B. CUTTING OFF 2 NEAT FILLETS.

① Cut off head and tail.

② Keeping the knife firmly against backbone, cut along the spine. Cut out the dorsal fin.

③ Cut fillets off ribs - keep the knife against bones and ease out fine secondary bones.

④ Repeat with other side.

③

②

1
Basics

A Note on Health

I have already extolled the virtues of game—with few exceptions it is healthy and extraordinarily free from fat. If not carefully cooked it will dry out and, although unnecessary, this can and does occur. The obvious and traditional foils to a potentially dry meat are butter and cream. They are also extremely delicious when not used to excess.

Because most of the meat in our household is game, I feel quite justified in enjoying the occasional dollop of butter and cream, but I appreciate that excessive use nullifies the healthiness of the original subject, and I am aware that nowadays some people are worried by these ingredients. Should this be the case, look first for the recipes and methods which do not use animal fats to excess. Fish should be lightly steamed, poached, or baked with stock instead of butter. Grilling and frying must be done speedily with minimal fat. When cooking for health, meat should be roasted or grilled quickly, since slow roasting requires fat of some sort. Alternatively, poach or stew it. But there are some exceptions, particularly with poultry. Browning can be achieved in some measure by using a non-stick pan with a thin brushing of oil, and some of the most flavoursome sauces are made from a well-reduced stock. Wine is frequently optional but, in any case, most alcohol will be driven off in the cooking.

When you are tempted, as I hope you will be, by the other recipes, you can very often substitute low-fat ingredients. Oil or margarine, as long as they are not needed in large proportions, can be used in place of butter. Instead of flour, butter and cream, sauces can be thickened with a vegetable purée, yoghourt, or a low-fat soft cheese. The last two, though, cannot be boiled and reduced as cream can. Because of their slight acidity they can curdle when overheated, so add these ingredients at the last moment and warm them through gently.

Health is important, nay vital, but I may as well say that we thoroughly enjoy cooking with cream, butter and cheese—we wouldn't squelch through the mud to milk our Jersey cow if we didn't. I have written the recipes the way we and our friends enjoy them; I hope that when substitutes are necessary you will bear my suggestions in mind and enjoy them too.

Game—Succulent and Tender

Succulence and tenderness are two qualities which, combined with perfect flavour, represent the height of culinary success. But how can they be achieved?

Succulence With the exception of quails, which seem to be remarkably resistant to desiccation, everything in this book is susceptible to drying out if treated unsympathetically. But there is no reason why they should not be juicy. The answer lies, whether fish, fowl or flesh, in choosing one of two cooking systems. By far the best results are had by *either* cooking quickly at a high temperature (grilling, sautéing or hot roasting), *or* cooking for a longer period at a low temperature (poaching, slow-roasting, stewing etc). In the first case the fish or meat is not heated for long enough to harden, giving rare or medium results. In the second, the temperature never

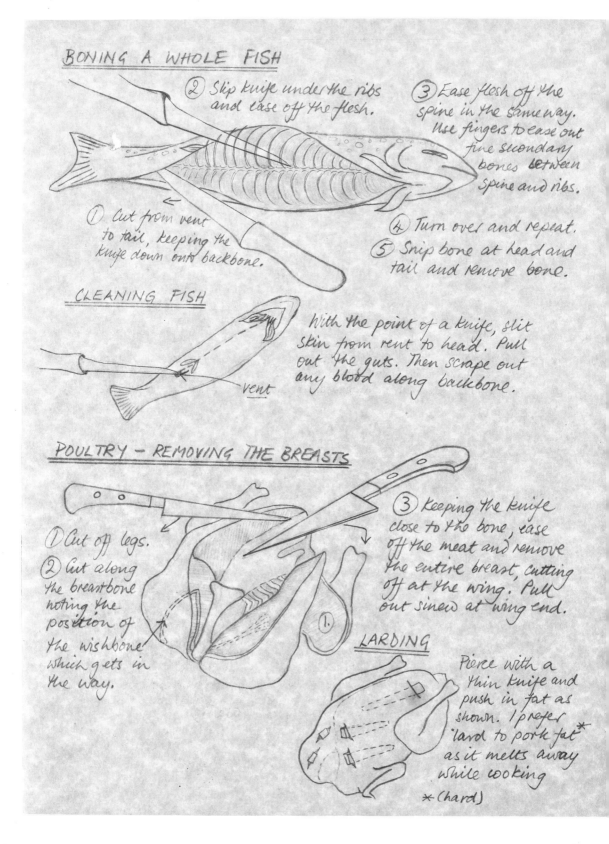

BONING A WHOLE FISH

② Slip knife under the ribs and ease off the flesh.

③ Ease flesh off the spine in the same way. Use fingers to ease out fine secondary bones between spine and ribs.

① Cut from vent to tail, keeping the knife down onto backbone.

④ Turn over and repeat.
⑤ Snip bone at head and tail and remove bone.

CLEANING FISH

With the point of a knife, slit skin from vent to head. Pull out the guts. Then scrape out any blood along backbone.

vent

POULTRY — REMOVING THE BREASTS

① Cut off legs.
② Cut along the breastbone noting the position of the wishbone which gets in the way.

③ Keeping the knife close to the bone, ease off the meat and remove the entire breast, cutting off at the wing. Pull out sinew at wing end.

(1.)

LARDING

Pierce with a thin knife and push in fat as shown. I prefer "lard to pork fat* as it melts away while cooking

* (hard)

reaches the point at which the meat toughens. Even the smallest creature will be dry if incorrectly cooked, and older ones need even more careful treatment. Cooking fish and venison in these ways is covered in the appropriate sections, but the same principles apply to the other subjects.

With the slow method, *larding* is appropriate, especially when there is no liquid to keep the meat moist. Traditionally, 'lardoons' are strips of hard pork fat, which are inserted into the meat. In some cases (such as pâtés, terrines and galantines) the fat is desirable in the end-result. In others where it serves merely to keep the meat moist, I would advise using a soft fat such as lard or butter, since this will seep through and out of the meat during cooking, leaving little residue—a desirable state when health is being considered.

Tenderness is produced by the cooking methods just described, but also by hanging and marinating meat. Those subjects are covered in detail on pp. 11 and 159. But one method of inducing tenderness in tough meat is quick and ludicrously simple. Just slice or pulp some kiwi fruit and spread it over the meat. Kiwi fruit, along with pineapples and papaya, contains an enzyme called papain which breaks down the fibres in meat. Allow half an hour for every inch (2.5 cm) thickness of meat. Really tough meat needs more time, but avoid leaving it too long or the meat can become mushy. A very thick chunk can have slits cut into it and the fruit pulp pressed deep inside.

Another simple tenderising technique, applicable to steaks or poultry breasts is to beat them, hard. A spiky steak bat is the best utensil, but anything that can partly pulverise the meat will do. I always beat pigeon breasts before sautéing them nowadays, and it makes a lot of difference.

Hanging Game

There is no need to read this section unless it interests you, since all the subjects covered in this book can be bought plucked, drawn, butchered and hung. But hanging game is a topic which leads to much snarling and words of abuse and, since this is my book, I shall have my say.

Meat is hung, or matured, for various reasons. First, meat becomes more tender as enzymes break down the fibres. Secondly, but no less important, hanging strengthens the characteristic flavour of the meat. Given time, this flavour changes from an initial mildness to a more mature taste, finally becoming gamy or 'high'. As I have mentioned, tenderness can be imparted artificially (and often is in the meat trade) by injecting an enzyme called papain. And tenderising can be speeded up by vacuum-packing meat. But as far as I know, the natural change in flavour can only occur with hanging.

I recently heard that a convention of some of Britain's most illustrious chefs pronounced that the best venison was procured from wild deer which have been hung for a week with the skin and guts left intact. This is an utterly meaningless statement. I am astonished and disappointed that any chef, who may take the trouble to fly to France in order to handpick every tomato, should take such an absurdly inflexible stance when it comes to game. Wild game in particular is so variable that, in order to reach perfection, each individual has to be assessed separately. Even with farmed game, which starts off by being a more consistent product, huge differences can be obtained by changing the hanging conditions. There is obviously something about the word 'game' that reduces some people's power of reasoning, and, as you can see, it irritates me profoundly. Exactly how long a bird or beast should be hung is a question of taste. Do not be

BONING OUT POULTRY

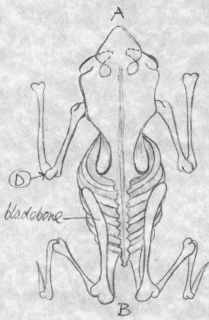

A

D

bladebone

B

CARCASE SEEN FROM UNDERNEATH

Points to note ① It's not impossible!
② Read through the instructions first.
③ Always keep the sharp edge of the knife firmly against the bones to avoid slitting the skin.
④ Start with a bird that has its skin intact and leave plenty of neck skin to ease the sewing up.

Start from the underneath. Cut from A–B and scrape the flesh off the bones. Note the position of the bladebones and wishbone. When you come to the leg, bladebone or wing joints, stop and sever the bones. Continue round ribcage till you reach the top edge of the breastbone (c.) Repeat with the other side.

Now lift up the frame, and very carefully cut along the ridge of the breastbone © – avoid splitting the skin (note 3.)

Then remove the thighbones by scraping back the meat. Sever the bone at the drumstick ⓓ

The wings and drumsticks are often left on as there is not much meat on them and boning out is fiddly.

The boned bird can now be stuffed and sewn up, or be rolled and tied, in which case cut off the drumsticks and wings, leaving behind as much skin as possible.

That's it! Lay the untidy heap skin-side downwards and rearrange the flesh.

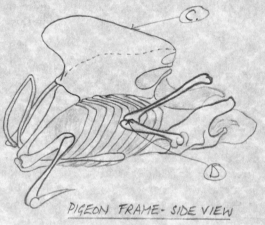

C.

D

PIGEON FRAME· SIDE VIEW

PHEASANT FRAME – note different shape of breastbone & wishbone.

browbeaten by anyone into hanging game until very high if you don't like it that way. Equally, if you do like a gamy flavour, demand that it be hung in a cold airy place until it has acquired the desired strength. They are your taste-buds and you may surely do as you please.

The time required to hang game (or any other meat for that matter) depends on a host of variables, personal taste being only one of them. Others are: temperature; humidity and air circulation; whether the animal itself is dry or rain-soaked; whether or not it is hung in fur or feather; whether or not the carcase has been punctured or bruised; and of course the age of the beast.

Ideally, meat is hung in cool and, more important, not humid conditions. A certain amount of heat will not necessarily make meat go bad; think of Italian prosciutto or African biltong. Although hung in warm conditions, if the air is sufficiently dry, raw meat will become partially desiccated and keep for months. All other things being equal, every 10°C increase in temperature halves the time required to achieve the same result.

Humidity and air circulation have a most dramatic effect. In chilly November, if it is teeming with rain, venison carcases can reach ample maturity in six or seven days, but, if the weather is dry, those same carcases will happily mature for three weeks or more. In warm weather the process is speeded up and the times may need to be halved. Exactly the same goes for pheasants, pigeons, or anything else.

Venison is always hung by the back legs to give the haunches a good shape. Game birds are usually hung by the neck, though some people hang them by the feet for lengthy hanging so that the abdomen doesn't become too black. In this case, tie a polythene bag round the head to prevent drip.

Venison from a game-dealer is not generally skinned before hanging; farmed venison always is. I believe that venison matures to a superior flavour when it is skinned first—the surface dries and the meat inside is sublime. When hung in the skin, it never sets so well and is more difficult, often impossible, to skin and butcher properly.

Venison carcases are eviscerated at once, not only to relieve the stalking pony of a considerable weight, but because it allows the carcase to cool down quickly. A red deer carcase left intact can take 24 hours to cool down, hardly ideal conditions for producing well-matured and set meat. Game birds, being smaller, are not appreciably affected, but some of you may already have made the unfortunate discovery that pheasants from a great pile left overnight never taste as good as those hung up on return from the shoot. Here again, the carcases could not cool quickly.

There is a good case for hanging game birds undrawn and in feather—it helps to keep flies off. Unless you can pluck the bird, leaving the skin intact, while still warm so that the outside dries off (flies are not interested in dry surfaces), it is better left intact. And whereas to eviscerate neck-shot venison without contamination is easy, it is not so with poultry—their size and anatomy are not helpful.

Wild game is frequently shot in inconvenient places. The carcase and maybe the guts are pierced and sometimes the wrong sort of bacteria get to work. This as well as bruising make the meat mature quicker and in a different way. An acrid taste develops, quite a different flavour from that of well-matured gamy meat. What can you do to improve such a situation? Humid weather

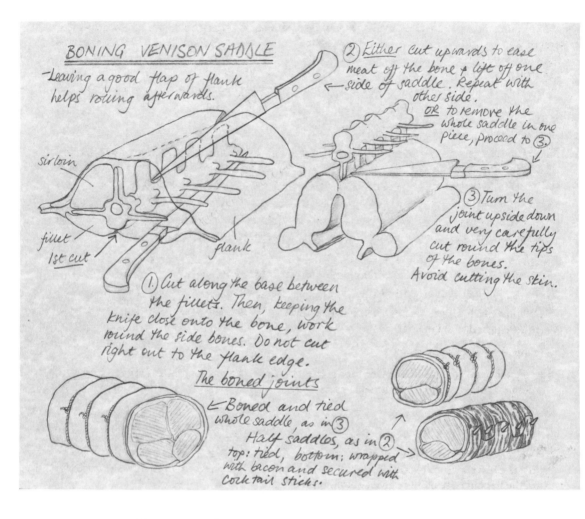

BONING VENISON SADDLE

Leaving a good flap of flank helps rolling afterwards.

sirloin

fillet
1st cut

flank

① Cut along the base between the fillets. Then, keeping the knife close onto the bone, work round the side bones. Do not cut right out to the flank edge.

② Either cut upwards to ease meat off the bone & lift off one side of saddle. Repeat with other side.
OR to remove the whole saddle in one piece, proceed to ③.

③ Turn the joint upside down and very carefully cut round the tips of the bones. Avoid cutting the skin.

The boned joints

← Boned and tied whole saddle, as in ③
Half saddles, as in ②
top: tied, bottom: wrapped with bacon and secured with cocktail sticks.

may cause moulds to grow—these can be inhibited by wiping with a mild acid such as diluted vinegar or the traditional soured buttermilk. A cold fan will greatly improve matters. Cut surfaces and wounds can be patted with ground ginger. This dries the meat, inhibits flies, and gives rather a good flavour.

Here is a summary, bearing in mind my previous comments. In summertime, poultry will be adequately hung in 2–4 days if weather is humid, 4–7 if it is dry; venison, 4–6 days if humid, 6–10 if it is dry. For a stronger flavour, increase by a few days. In winter or in a chill, for both poultry and venison, 4–7 days if humid; 10 days if dry, for a good flavour; 10 days and up to three weeks respectively for a stronger taste.

If a tail feather can be pulled easily from a game bird, it is fairly ripe. If a venison carcase becomes sticky, either butcher it or treat as described before.

To be sure, a competent cook can work wonders with the most inauspicious ingredients. In the eighteenth century, M. Marin recalls that 'a renowned cook (lacking other meats) served to some gentlemen an old pair of buffalo leather gloves, shredded and stewed, with onions, mustard and vinegar, which they found excellent while they knew not what they ate.' But how very much more is our enjoyment when imaginative cooks use flawless ingredients in the first place.

Quantities

This is a *very* general guide! Appetites vary enormously according to age, activity and weather. The quantities required will also depend upon the number of courses in a meal, whether the dish is a first or main course, and its style. Are you feeding a hungry worker or having a chic *cuisine minceur* dinner? And so on.

Salmon and Trout. Less head, tail and bones: 3–4 oz/80–100 g for a starter; 6–8 oz/170–225 g for a main course. Allow up to 20 per cent extra for head, tail and bones.

Venison Main course. Off the bone: 6 oz/170 g. On the bone: 8 oz/225 g for middle cut haunch, 12 oz/350 g for top-cut haunch, saddle and shoulder which have proportionately more bone.

Pheasant and Guinea Fowl, plucked and drawn, weigh 1¼ lb/550 g–2¼ lb/1 kg. Allow one small bird for 2–3 people and one large or two small for 4. It depends whether you are going to eat the legs or discard them.

Pigeon. Allow one per person.

Quail, unboned and unstuffed: One for a starter, two for a main course. Boned and stuffed: One sometimes suffices but the enthusiastic prefer two.

Ingredients

It is often necessary to substitute, but in preparing these recipes I have used, unless otherwise stated: free range size 2 eggs; unpasteurised Jersey double cream; golden granulated sugar; plain flour; fresh breadcrumbs; and fresh herbs. Substituting dried herbs for fresh can dramatically alter the flavour. Use half the given quantities if dried.

Beurre manié is made of equal quantities of butter and flour mashed to a smooth paste. It is very useful for thickening gravy and sauces without giving a floury taste. It is always added at the last moment.

Crème fraîche—stir 1 dessertspoon of sour cream into ¼ pt (150 ml) double cream. Warm to blood heat and let it stand in a warm place until thickened. This can take from 8 to 24 hours. It will keep for four days in the fridge.

Avoid cast-iron utensils where wine, vinegar or other acids such as lemon and fruit juice are used, as the iron reacts to give a metallic taste. Very strong acids will react with aluminium as well, but enamelled utensils are fine as long as they are not chipped.

Chinese fishing reel.
1st. examples made
500 years before
European
ones.

cock salmon
has hook

used turtles
as bait.

also frogs

Salmon fly

David Auchterlonie's
trout flies —
(actual size)

brown

Shiny gold
beads

fuzzy red

orange

Hardy's Gold

green
fuzz

greybrown

orange,
black tips

Birleigh

Wild herbs for
trout & The Times
— try wood sorrel —
Scots lovage, wild celery
wild garlic

△ stem

THE

PRIVATE EYE

2
Salmon and Trout

There must be something very fundamental about catching fish that strikes the heart of man, whether he be struggling with the seas for his livelihood, or leisurely forgetting the cares of the world with rod and line. The testament of writers and the wealth of advice flows back into antiquity.

Pliny enthuses about such bucolic delights on the shores of Lake Como, where his villa jutted out over the water so that he could fish from his bedroom window, a luxury which pleased him no end. His urbane contemporaries enthusiastically built vivaria (ornamental fish ponds) instead, which became very elaborate. Although originally built as stew ponds to provide fish for the table, latterly they became fashionable status symbols. The fish were given gold earrings to wear, and taught to come and be fed and stroked when called. The most brutal punishments were exacted on the poor chap who actually tried to eat one.

But salmon and trout are predominantly natives of colder waters, so we will leave the Romans to their pampered red mullet and travel northwards, where we find the Norsemen with a particular fondness for the tail-piece of their salmon as explained by this mythical story: Loki, god of fire, was being hotly pursued by a throng of angry gods, and to save himself, plunged into a foaming pool and changed into a fish. He chose to be a salmon on account of its fiery red flesh, but to Loki's chagrin, Thor caught him by the tail. After this unfortunate incident, the salmon's tail became thin and sleek, albeit retaining its steely power, and thus was revered by Norse Warriors.

Early Scottish Celts avoided eating fish, which seems odd since there was such an abundance. But they were worshippers of springs and water, a practice which has not entirely disappeared on some Scottish islands, and therefore considered it sacrilegious to harvest the inhabitants. Christianity, with its plethora of fast-days, changed all that, and soon the sanctuaries were raided and their denizens eaten with positively cat-like alacrity. Many pagan superstitions linger on, sometimes with Christian overtones. Women were and still are frequently connected with ill-luck in fishing: 'If a woman wade through the one fresh river in the Lewis, there shall no salmon be seen there for a twelvemonth after.'

In view of this, it is gratifying to note that the earliest angling book *A Treatyse of Fyshynge Wyth an Angle* was written by Dame Juliana Barnes. Her descriptions of the peaceful delights of angling, the stateliness of certain fish, and recommendations as to procedure, started off a perfect deluge of piscatorial writing.

Before the advent of fly fishing, worms and various forms of paste were used as bait, some of them bizarre in the extreme. Powdered mummies, cat fat, man's fat and powdered skulls (for purging worms) were all recommended. Thomas Barker, an expert on both culinary and angling affairs, pronounced salmon roe to be the perfect bait for trout. If you don't wish to eat this delicacy you could, like Barker, dry and sell it as a useful little side-line. Especially if, as Mr Jesse asserted, a hen-salmon will produce 20 million eggs.

Conservation was an issue at quite an early stage, close seasons and size limits being imposed. As long ago as 1598 Thomas Bastard was lamenting: 'But now the sport is marred, and wot ye why? Fishes decrease and fishers multiply.' One can't help feeling that his worries were a little premature; for the next two centuries salmon were netted by the hundred, sometimes thousand, in the larger rivers, and vast numbers of trout were hauled from river and loch.

General Wade's roads opened Scotland's comparatively untouched countryside to visiting English sportsmen who wrote enthusiastically about their spartan experiences. My particular favourite is William Scrope who was an inveterate deer-stalker as well as fisherman. A friend of Sir Walter Scott's, he often visited Abbotsford on his fishing trips to the Borders where he revelled in pitching himself against the elements. No Damarts or welly warmers for Scrope, far from it, his advice is as follows: 'Should you be of a delicate temperament, and be wading in the month of February, when it may chance to freeze very hard, pull down your stockings, and examine your legs. Should they be black or even purple, it might, perhaps, be as well to get on dry land; but if they are only rubicund, you may continue to enjoy the water.' Considering that he wore leather seaboots with holes to let out the water, and recommended wading in above the waist, I fancy he was made of sterner stuff than many of us.

Fish farming

In order to stock his ponds, streams and rivers, man has been rearing fish for centuries. There was a large and lucrative trade in fish eggs in China as early as the 5th century B.C. Some of their hatchery methods were a little involved to say the least. The fish spawn was put into empty eggshells and placed under hens for a few days to mature. The eggs were then broken into warm fresh water where they would, surprisingly, hatch out.

Most early breeders simply hatched fertilised eggs collected from river bottoms, and these primitive methods kept the Roman vivarium, the Elizabethan stew pond, and many rivers conveniently stocked. But two illiterate French peasants finally cracked the secret of artificially fertilising eggs by mixing the milt and spawn together. They also realised the importance of diet, rearing non-carnivorous fish and frogs whose spawn fed the fry.

This made life a lot easier for fish breeders, but, nothing daunted, men made further attempts at rearing them in difficult conditions. At the turn of the century, two brothers called Mitchell imported frozen brown trout eggs into India from Scotland and finally succeeded in hatching them out. This was difficult in rivers below 5,000 feet because of the heat. When they hatched, they wouldn't breed. So they experimented with rainbow trout eggs instead, also imported from Scotland. The first two consignments hatched successfully, but all had a kink in their spines, due, it was suggested, to the jolting of the bullock cart as it lumbered up from the railway station. So in 1908, a fresh tank of eggs was carefully brought up the road by one of the first motor cars. Success! The rainbow trout has thrived ever since.

Nowadays, trout farms supply our shops and supermarkets, and provide easy fishing for those who eschew Scrope's methods, stocking many ponds and rivers with rainbow trout. With their characteristic pink flesh, they are very different from our native brown trout. Some people dismiss the rainbow as being muddy and tasteless, but I have enjoyed a plump rainbow caught in a loch, and equally found brown trout living in muddy places that taste pretty boring. Diet does affect them, and one cannot pretend that a seething mass of four thousand trout, living on tinted pellets and the odd dose of antibiotic are ever going to be quite the same as the kind that blows an inviting bubble in the river. However, they make good eating and should not be spurned. When I have a choice, I tend to use the farmed variety for robustly flavoured dishes, and reserve brownies or 'wild' rainbow for the more delicate ones.

With salmon, it is less easy to make a comparison, for the wild species is the same as that farmed. The best salmon I have ever eaten was a freshly caught wild one, just running in from the sea, 'with the sea-lice still on it'. But I wonder how much of that enjoyment was in the telling of the tale and the excitement on our friend's face as he related it? I have a sneaking suspicion that if a farmed salmon had been quietly slipped into the fish kettle we would have enjoyed it just as much.

For the fact is, most culinary experts agree that it is very difficult to tell the difference. The treatment of the fish after catching, not to mention the cooking of it, will affect the flavour and texture far more than anything that happened beforehand. A wild salmon could be lovingly carried from river bank to kitchen, or it could sit in the back of a car all day with the sun beating down on it, to be bumped down to the game-dealer and plonked (ungutted) into a freezer without so much as a piece of cling film round it. Those are the extremes, of course, and farmed salmon is at least consistent. There is an understandable suspicion of modern techniques and their use of chemicals. Salmon farmers, dealing with a valuable commodity, have taken more pains to emulate a natural diet (salmon too are given dietary fibre), and I am assured that the pigment used is of natural origin. But pest control treatments have given cause for concern. Some of the early types had most unpleasant environmental effects, but thankfully legislation has been passed to ban them now. I am quite sure that it is in the interests of salmon farmers to ensure that their farming methods bear scrutiny. In any case, who knows what pollution a wild salmon may have passed through on its long sea voyage? Enjoy your salmon, and be glad that so many more of us can savour the King of Fish.

Cooking them

Salmon and trout are at their best when rather simply and gently cooked so that their delicate flavour is not lost. The only art in this approach is making sure that both the cooking method and the accompanying sauce and vegetables are chosen and executed to perfection. The basic methods, in combination with the chapters on sauces and vegetables, provide scope for endless permutations, so don't restrict yourself to the set recipes.

However, there are times of glut and times of scarcity. The recipes I have chosen include some for preserving, some for ringing the changes to basic methods, and some for stretching a small amount to feed the five thousand.

I have divided the chapter into sections, starting each with an explanation of the basic method and an example or two to give you the general idea. Then there are the inevitable exceptions to every rule, some of which slither happily between sections, as, for example, when fish is poached/baked in a sauce. The common thread knotting these sections together is a point which needs stressing time and again. It is that fish is infinitely more delicious, not to mention more nutritious, when it has not been dried up by overcooking.

gravadlax

Gravadlax is a Scandinavian method of curing salmon, though a large sea or rainbow trout will be virtually indistinguishable. Gravadlax is far easier to make than smoked salmon, the curing of which is quite a delicate art. I actually prefer Gravadlax because the fresh taste of salmon is not drowned.

Jens Berg gave me his recipe for Gravadlax, and also one for mustard and dill sauce which he was given by a famous Swedish chef. Actually, the proportions of salt and sugar are not critical. If you double the amount of salt, it becomes Rimmedlax (salted salmon) which is harder and drier and without, I think, such a delicate flavour, though being less sweet some prefer it. Also, there is no need to use a whole fish—pieces will cure just as successfully.

For every 1 lb (450 g) boned flesh
2 tablesp salt
2 tablesp sugar
1 dessertsp white
    peppercorns
heaped tablesp dillweed

Remove the head, tail and bones of the fish, but not the skin. Weigh the peppercorns and chop the dill very fine. Fresh dill is by far the best, is easy to grow and can be frozen for later use. Use less if dried.

Find a dish that will just contain the fish. If all yours are too wide, then make a foil container inside a baking tray. Spread a layer of the salt mixture over the bottom, cover this with a good layer of dill, and lay one fillet on top, skin side down. Press another layer of salt and dill on to the flesh, scatter on the crushed peppercorns, and place the second fillet on top, skin side upwards this time. In other words you reassemble the fish. Completely cover this with the rest of the dill and then the salt mixture. Cover with foil and lay a board with a weight on top.

Leave like this in a cool place for a day before turning the whole fish over and pressing for another 24 hours. Then scrape off the salt, but do not wash. That's it. You can freeze it if need be, though I think it is much better fresh.

Serve Gravadlax cut on the slant, with Jens Berg's Dill Sauce which is on p. 173.

salmon and spinach quiche

It may seem a little obvious to include a quiche recipe, but this is a good one for anybody who wants to follow a tried and tested one. Suitable substitutions can be trout for salmon, and 4 oz (110 g) mushrooms instead of the spinach. The quality of pastry and cheese are two factors which make a huge difference to the end-product—when using salmon as the main ingredient, it is worth the small effort of making pâte brisée.

If using left-over salmon, don't cook it again before adding to the other ingredients or it will turn out rather dry. A 14 oz (400 g) piece of middle-cut salmon will yield the 12 oz (340 g) required.

Serves 6–8

Pâte brisée
10 oz (280 g) flour
1 teasp salt
large pinch sugar
8 oz (225 g) butter
4 fl oz (110 ml) cold water

Filling
12 oz (340 g) salmon meat
1 large onion
1 oz (25 g) butter
2 oz (50 g) fresh leaf spinach
3 eggs
4 oz (110 g) sharp cheese
4 tablesp milk
4 tablesp cream
salt, pepper

Start by making the pâte brisée so that it can rest. Make sure everything is well-chilled, including your hands. Mix flour, salt and sugar together and quickly rub in the cold butter. Leave it fairly coarse at this stage. Dribble in the water, using the minimum possible to collect the dough into a barely cohesive lump. On a lightly floured board, smear pieces of this lump away from you with the floured heel of your hand. This process distributes the butter as much as is necessary. Scrape the pastry into a ball and leave to rest in a cold place for at least 1 hour.

Then roll it out and use to line two 9-inch (23 cm) round tins. Prick with a fork and bake blind for 10–12 minutes in a hot oven (Mk 6, 400°F, 200°C), removing beans or foil after 7 or 8 minutes to dry the base. This partially cooks the pastry.

For the filling, chop the onion and slowly soften it completely in the butter. Chop up the spinach and the salmon meat, not too fine. Draw the pan off the heat and stir in spinach and salmon to soften slightly.

Beat the eggs and add the grated cheese and milk. Add the spinach and salmon mixture and moisten with the cream. Season with a good pinch of salt and some pepper and turn into the prepared pastry cases.

Bake in a moderately hot oven (Mk 5, 375°F, 190°C) for 15–20 minutes. If you are leaving it to cool, this is enough. If you can serve it immediately, then another 10 minutes will make it more puffed and golden, but beware of drying it out.

seviche/marinated salmon

Seviche is a Mexican dish where slices of raw fish are steeped in lime juice. Citric acid quickly turns the fish opaque, giving it a cooked appearance, though it remains sharp and succulent.

If you like raw fish there are endless variations on this theme. Here are some suggestions which can be altered to taste. Perhaps you could serve a selection. In each case, take 6 oz (170 g) raw boned salmon and cut it into strips or slices. Steep them in one of the following mixtures for a few hours, then serve with a salad or brown bread and butter. These are merely methods of flavouring raw fish, not preserving it.

1. Mix together: 1 tablesp soy sauce, juice ½ lemon, 1 crushed clove garlic, small pinch salt, milled black pepper.

2. Mix together: juice ½ lemon, 2 tablesp red wine; pinch salt, black pepper.

3. Mix together: 2 tablesp tomato purée, 2 tablesp sweet white wine, a few drops anchovy essence.

4. Mix together: 1 tablesp soy sauce, juice ½ lemon, 1 teasp grated root ginger, pinch of sugar.

smoked salmon in olive oil

If you should be lucky enough to have more smoked salmon than you can cope with, then there are two options. Smoked salmon will deep-freeze perfectly successfully, but if it has already been frozen then you may not want to do this. So here, from Norway, is a particularly delicious and simple way of preserving smoked salmon indefinitely.

Slice the smoked salmon thickly and place in a glass jar. If desired, fresh dill or fennel leaves may be tucked in between the pieces. These herbs, however, should be blanched beforehand for a minute or so in boiling water to sterilise them, then thoroughly drained. Fill the jar completely with olive oil, so that none of the fish can surface, and close the lid tightly.

Serve with brown bread and butter, or use as Christmas presents for people who have everything except a jar of Norwegian preserved salmon.

smoked salmon and asparagus puffs

A truly luxurious dish this, keep it for your Best Beloved as a prelude to quails. It is only worth doing if you can get hold of really fresh asparagus—those aged yellowing stumps are to be avoided as they are bitter. Choose whippy bright green spears no more than ¼ inch thick. And before you buy the smoked salmon ask to try it and check that it really tastes of salmon, not just salt and spices.

Serves 4

6 oz (170 g) thin cut smoked
  salmon
8 oz (225 g) fresh asparagus
5 small eggs
2 oz (50 g) butter
half a juicy lemon
2 tablesp double cream
1 teasp finely chopped truffle
  (optional)

Puff shells
¼ pt (150 ml) water
1½ oz (40 g) butter
½ teasp each salt and nutmeg
2 oz (50 g) flour
2 size 4 eggs
black pepper

First make the puffs. Put the water, butter, salt, nutmeg and a little black pepper into a pan and bring to the boil. Remove from the heat and beat in the flour. It will look horribly lumpy, but return to a lower heat and keep beating. The lumps will disappear and soon a whitish film will appear on the bottom of the pan. Remove from the heat again and make a well in the paste. Beat the first egg in quickly and then the second gradually so that the mixture is capable of being formed into puff shapes. Butter and flour a baking sheet and, using an icing bag with a ½ inch (1 cm) nozzle, make 4 large puff shapes 3 inches (1 cm) in diameter. Any left-overs can be made into éclairs or profiteroles. Brush the tops only with any remaining beaten egg and bake in a hot oven (Mk 7, 425°F, 220°C) for about 20 minutes, when the puffs should be twice the size and golden brown. Then pierce each bun and return to the now turned-off oven for 10 minutes. This releases excess steam and stops the puffs collapsing.

Now for the fillings. Cut the most tender parts off the asparagus, steam them, and set aside. Steam the rest for a little longer and pound them to a lovely green mush. Make a hollandaise sauce (p. 167) with 3 egg yolks and 2 oz of the butter. Add the asparagus mush and season delicately with salt and a squeeze of lemon. Keep warm, but not hot in case it curdles. It will thicken as it waits.

Reserve the four best slices of smoked salmon and put the rest into a food processor with 2 whole eggs and the cream, and process to a fine paste. Add the truffle and a squeeze of lemon to taste, and stir in a bain-marie until it is nice and thick. Salt will probably not be necessary.

To assemble, slice the puffs in half and scrape out any gooey insides. Fill them with a quarter each of the two contrasting sauces, keeping back a tiny amount. On every plate beside the puff, put a little bundle of asparagus tips neatly wrapped in a slice of smoked salmon, and also a tiny blob of the coloured sauces for decoration. I am sure that with the right ambience, a great deal of symbolic significance can be construed.

salmon roe

Any time from September onwards, a hen salmon is liable to have a good quantity of ruby-red eggs inside her. Once you have lamented the loss of potential salmon, you then have to decide what to do with them. Whatever the decision it must be done quickly. You can freeze them, surprisingly, either raw or cooked. Raw frozen eggs are a good deal more fragile, so I would only freeze them as a desperate measure.

1. In Norway the roes, after having the membranes removed, are tossed in well-seasoned flour, then quickly fried in hot oil till golden brown and served with lemon juice and brown bread. They are slightly chewy—if you fry some parsley along with the roes, it makes a good accompaniment.

2. In Japan, salmon eggs are regarded as a great delicacy and are often served with a variety of other raw fish (sashimi) as tiny but tasty and colourful morsels. Sometimes they are absolutely plain, ready to be dipped into various condiments. Sometimes they are marinated in soy sauce and lemon juice with pepper sprinkled on top. However, since only half a dozen eggs are served to each person (they have an oily taste like this and a little goes a long way) this is not going to solve the problem.

3. You could make some salmon caviar. I first encountered this method in Julia Drysdale's excellent game book. You simply put the eggs into jars, sprinkling a generous amount of salt between each layer. Cover the jars tightly and refrigerate. They will keep for weeks and, like conventional caviar, can be served with toast, lemon and raw egg yolks, not to mention Schnapps.

If you use any of the above three methods, you must remove the eggs from their membraneous sac. This is no mean task, I may say, and if you baulk at the thought of it, try the fourth method which produces a somewhat coarse but very delicious kind of Taramasalata. This is the most suitable method for immature eggs which are too small to remove individually.

Here's how to remove the eggs. Hold the sac in one hand and with a fork, gently tease the eggs into a dish. The sac is slippery—dipping your fingers in salt gives a better grip. Put the eggs into a sieve and rinse them under cold water. Horrors! They go all white and lots of pieces of membrane appear as if from nowhere. When you have picked them all out, the eggs revert to their previous jewel-like appearance as if by magic. Once I have gone through this performance, I am thinking that bought caviar is quite cheap.

4. This is what I do when my patience is exhausted and at last I have a wee jar of caviar. Put the eggs, membranes and all, into a pan and cover with water and a good pinch of salt. If using the entire sac, break it up as much as possible. Bring to the boil and simmer and skim for about 15 minutes. Once most of the eggs are

pale pink and opaque, they can quite easily be shaken out of the sac whilst cooking, and the membranes discarded. A small amount won't do any harm. Then drain and leave to cool. They are very good eaten just like this with brown bread and butter, and lemon juice.

The 'taramasalata' can be made with a liquidiser or a pestle and mortar. The hand method produces a stiffer mixture (as with mayonnaise) which needs no breadcrumbs to stiffen it.

For every 12 oz (340 g) of cooked eggs you will need:
4 cloves garlic
4 tablesp good olive oil
salt, lemon juice and pepper
    (black or cayenne) to taste

If using the liquidiser:
up to 4 tablesp fine
    breadcrumbs

Crush the garlic and put it with the eggs into the pestle and mortar (or liquidiser) and pound to a paste. It will never be completely smooth. Dribble in the oil as you keep pounding, then add the breadcrumbs if used. Season with salt, pepper and lemon juice, and serve with brown bread or toast.

potted salmon

Here is another way to use up some cooked salmon. It is very rich. Even when sealed in clarified butter it doesn't keep indefinitely.

Serves 6

8 oz (225 g) cooked salmon
    meat
2 teasp white wine vinegar
1 egg yolk (optional)
⅛ teasp ground mace
⅛ teasp ground coriander
black pepper, pinch of salt
2 oz (50 g) butter
clarified butter (optional)

Remove any stray bones and put the salmon into a food processor with the plastic blade. Don't process yet. Add the wine vinegar, egg yolk, spices and seasoning. The egg yolk keeps the mixture moist, but if the salmon is very juicy already the yolk may be omitted.

Melt the butter in a little pan and pour it into the food processor, running the machine for only a few seconds. The salmon is best when not reduced to a complete paste, hence the plastic blade. Turn into little pots and either sprinkle black pepper and coriander on top, or cover with melted clarified butter.

To make it by hand, mix the vinegar, egg yolk, spices and seasoning and stir them into the flaked salmon. Pour on the butter and pound it until the desired consistency is reached. Remember that it will be slightly stiffer when cool.

salmon or trout mousse

This is my favourite mousse recipe. It is ideal for small dinners or enormous banquets. We made enough for 40 people once, and put it into our walk-in freezer to make sure it would set by the evening. We came across it the next morning, frozen hard into its ornamental glass bowl. Although I wouldn't recommend freezing, it was surprisingly unharmed.

Serves 8

6 oz (170 g) raw boned
  salmon or trout
a bunch of fresh herbs
¾ pt (425 ml) fish fumet (see
  p. 163)
8 oz (225 g) chopped
  mushroom heads
½ oz (15 g) gelatine
⅛ pt (75 ml) dry vermouth
small carton of whipping
  cream
salt, pepper
oil

Put the fish and herbs into the fumet and simmer gently for about 10 minutes so that the fish just breaks when you insert a knife. Discard the herbs, strain the fish and put it in a liquidiser. Poach the mushrooms in the stock for another 10–15 minutes, remove them from the stock and put them in a large bowl. Soften the gelatine in the vermouth and add it to the stock, stirring until it is quite dissolved. Pour this into the liquidiser with the fish and blend until nicely puréed.

Stir this purée into the mushrooms, season to taste, and chill until it is beginning to set. Then whip the cream lightly and fold it into the mixture. Turn this into an oiled mould and chill till set. Those delightfully elaborate Victorian moulds are superb if you feel confident enough to turn them out, but metal moulds are actually a lot easier to use. If you wobble at the thought of turning out a large mould, pour the mousse into small individual moulds or dishes.

rollmop trout

This traditional way of serving herring works extremely well with trout. Some argue that this is a Scandinavian dish, but up here we firmly believe it is Scottish.

Serves 4–6

4 × 8 oz (225 g) trout
salt, pepper
1 onion
1 bay leaf
1 dessertsp pickling spice
1 teasp peppercorns
½ pt (300 ml) distilled
  vinegar
8 fl oz (225 ml) water

Scrape the scales off the trout, cut off the heads and tails, and bone them to produce 8 fillets with the skin left on (see p. 8). Sprinkle the inside of each fillet with salt and black pepper. Cut the onion into eight long pieces.

Starting at the tail end, roll up each fillet around a piece of onion. You may like to secure them with cocktail sticks. Pack the rolls tightly into a deep dish and scatter the spices amongst them. The spices can be varied to taste, or even omitted. Mix the vinegar and water together and add enough to just cover the fish.

Cover the dish and bake in a slow oven (Mk 2, 300°F, 150°C) for 1 hour, then remove the lid and cook for a further 20 minutes. Then leave the whole dish to cool thoroughly before serving.

sweet pickled trout

This is the Scandinavian way of curing herrings, but it works extremely well with trout, farmed or otherwise. The quantities given here make the traditional sweet pickle, but the sugar can safely be cut down if wished. I have given a few variations to the basic recipe, but there are endless permutations.

Serves 4–6

1 × 2 lb (900 g) trout
5 tablesp sea salt
4 tablesp sugar
milled black pepper
4 shallots
1 small carrot
¼ pt (150 ml) distilled
    vinegar
8 fl oz (250 ml) water
3 oz (80 g) caster sugar
4 bay leaves
black peppercorns

Variation 1
tablesp wholegrain mustard

Variation 2
3 tablesp tomato purée
3 teasp anchovy essence

Variation 3
fresh grated ginger

Scrape all the scales off the trout with a flat knife, then lift off the two fillets (see p. 8). Mix the sea salt and sugar with a generous amount of milled black pepper. Scatter some on to a dish and lay on one fillet, skin side downward. Put most of the remaining mixture on top and lay the second fillet, skin side upwards, over it. Scatter on the rest of the mixture, cover, and leave for 12 hours in a cool place. Then take the fillets and run them quickly under a cold tap to remove excess salt. Take the skin off and cut the flesh into strips. The skin is rather tough, but comes off easily once a start has been made.

Slice the shallots and carrot thinly. Put them in a pan with the vinegar, water and sugar, and bring to the boil. Simmer briskly for 1 minute, then leave to cool. Strain the vinegar off the vegetables.

At this point any of the three suggested additional flavourings (1, 2, or 3) can be mixed into the vinegar, though the plain variety is also good. Then fill a glass jar loosely with the strips of fish, tucking in shallots, carrots, bay leaves and peppercorns as you go. Cover completely with the flavoured vinegar, cover tightly, and leave for at least 5 days before eating. Avoid metal containers or lids as they will corrode with the vinegar.

quicker scots method

If you can't wait 5 days, then here is a Scots way which is ready in a few hours (after the initial salting). It is considerably stronger if kept for very long.

Serves 4–6

2 × 1 lb (450 g) trout
½ lb (225 g) sea salt
3 onions, sliced
pepper, salt
1½ tablesp brown sugar
½ pt (300 ml) distilled
    vinegar

Prepare the salt trout as above, but omit the sugar this time and leave the skin on. Because they are smaller, 12 hours' salting will be enough. Rinse under the cold tap and cut into half-inch strips.

Put into a deep dish with the onions. Sprinkle with pepper, salt, and the brown sugar. Mix together, then pour on the vinegar. The fish should be covered, so weigh them down with a saucer if necessary. They will be ready to eat after 8 hours, but will keep up to 10 days in the fridge provided they are always submerged.

pâté of smoked trout

I'm pretty sure this is the Rev. John Eadie's recipe. I scribbled it down as he described it on the radio and it was not easy to decipher afterwards. If not, no matter as it tastes good.

Serves 8

1 lb (450 g) hot-smoked trout
  flesh
4 fl oz (125 ml) double cream
  or yoghourt
4 oz (110 g) cottage cheese
4 tablesp mayonnaise
salt, milled black pepper,
  lemon juice

Make sure there are no bones left in the smoked trout. Flake it roughly, then pound in the cream, cheese and mayonnaise and season to taste with salt, pepper and lemon juice. You can of course do it in a food processor, but turn it on for only a few seconds or it will become too smooth. 8 oz (225 g) of cream cheese may be used in lieu of the cream and cottage cheese. Chill before serving.

kedgeree of smoked trout

Kedgerees have been adapted to suit personal tastes ever since they were introduced from India in our colonial days. Salmon is used by many people, but I prefer the stronger taste of hot-smoked trout. You may add or subtract at will—the only two ingredients common to all 'kidgerees' as Eliza Acton calls them, are rice and fish, though eggs nearly always feature. Traditionally a breakfast dish, I have given quantities for 6, but they would only do 4 for lunch.

Serves 6

1 lb (450 g) smoked trout
6 oz (170 g) rice
4 eggs
3 oz (80 g) butter
1 onion
curry powder *or* cayenne
  pepper
4 firm tomatoes
milk *or* cream (optional)
salt, pepper

Wash, then boil the rice till just cooked—overdone rice will turn into a great soggy pudding. Rinse all excess starch out under plenty of cold water. Hardboil the eggs, crack the shells and cool in cold water before shelling. Remove skin and bones from the trout and coarsely flake the meat.

Melt the butter and soften the finely chopped onion. Add just a little curry powder or cayenne pepper—I use less than ¼ teaspoon, but tastes vary. Then add the rice and fish and gently warm them through. When half-warm, add the chopped tomatoes and hardboiled eggs. Season if necessary. If you like it less dry, moisten with a little milk or cream. The easiest way to warm the kedgeree without it sticking to the bottom of the pan is to heat it in a bain-marie.

Poaching and Steaming

POACHING

Poaching is a most sympathetic way to cook fish. It is gently cooked in a bath of warm liquid. Sometimes the liquid is discarded, sometimes it becomes the foundation for a sauce, sometimes it is the sauce itself. When fish is to be served cold, poaching is the ideal cooking method because the liquid keeps the fish moist and succulent as it cools.

the method explained

The most important feature of poaching is the slow cooking temperature which ensures successful results. The liquid should never even reach simmering point once the fish has gone in. Small bubbles appear on the base of the pan, but should barely disturb the surface of the water as they rise. Formerly it was believed that fish should be boiled, otherwise it would be indigestible. Today we know differently. The correct poaching temperature is around 150°F/75°C. This is well below the point at which albumen hardens, proteins break down, and fish loses both succulence and nutrition. It took me a remarkably long time to discover this simple fact on my own, but, like so many cooking processes, once the system was understood, everything became delightfully easy.

For a simple example, try poaching an egg. In one pan have the water simmering merrily, in the other let it barely move about as directed above. Now break an egg into each pan and observe. In the first pan the egg white disintegrates into flakes which quickly become hard and rubbery. What a disaster, but then it wasn't poached, was it? In the second pan the white and the yolk stay together and gently cook through. The result is a light curdy white and a perfectly cooked yolk. That is poaching, and the principle applies to meat, poultry and quenelles alike.

cooking vessels

The vessel used depends on the size of fish. A fish kettle is great, but we don't all possess one so an alternative must be found. A large pan or enamelled casserole will accommodate hefty chunks, and the biggest roasting tin can be used to poach longer pieces (avoid rusty tins—they give a nasty metallic taste). A long fish can be cut in two and joined together afterwards, though, if looks are important, it will need to be disguised in some way (mayonnaise or cucumber if cold, a thick sauce when hot). Or you can bend the fish into a lively S-shape so that it appears to be swimming along, but don't attempt to bone it afterwards!

A huge fish too long to fit into a tray may have to be cooked in the oven. Wrap it in several layers of foil and draw up the poaching liquid around it. See 'Baking' p. 44, for cooking times. Big fish can even be cooked in the dishwasher (sans soap), again thoroughly wrapped in foil to protect them from rinse-aid. I haven't tried this, but Pru Leith recommends 1–2 complete cycles depending on the size of fish. But with both these methods fish can be tricky to handle when cooked.

preparation

Even if salmon is going to be skinned, it is better to remove the scales before cooking because they go all over the place. It doesn't take long and is a rather satisfying job. Just scrape them off with a flat-bladed knife.

If you forgot to ask the fishmonger to remove the gills, then cut them out. The larger the fish, the more important it is, as the longer cooking time draws a bitterness out of the gills.

Prepare the cooking liquid. A court bouillon (p. 162) is most commonly used. The more flavoursome fumet or fish stock (p. 163) is employed when some liquid is needed afterwards to flavour a sauce, such as hollandaise with fish glaze, or a salmon mousse.

When ready to go, place the fish on large strips of folded foil or cloth, leaving the ends long enough to grasp so that you can lift up the fish after cooking. Then immerse it in the hot liquid.

cooking times

Cooking times are determined more by the thickness of fish than the total weight, and also by whether the fish is to be eaten hot or left to cool. In either case, the court bouillon is brought to poaching temperature (150°F/75°C), the fish is put in, and the liquid brought back up to temperature. Then start timing. As a rough guide, to serve fish hot, allow 9–10 minutes per pound (19–22 m/kg) for thick fish and 7 or 8 (15–17 m/kg) for thin. To serve cold, allow barely 6–7 minutes per pound (13–15 m/kg) for thick and 3–4 (7–9 m/kg) for thin. Then leave to cool in the liquid. This completes its cooking.

Rough guides can be deceptive. Obviously a tiny little trout poached in a great vat of liquid will take ages to cool and can be overcooked. Conversely a medium-sized fish poached in foil with a small amount of liquid will cool proportionately quicker. Here are some examples for cooking fish to serve hot:

One 1 lb (450 g) trout will need about nine minutes poaching after being brought back to temperature. Four 1 lb (450 g) trout will also only need nine minutes poaching, but the total cooking time will be longer because of the extra time taken to regain poaching temperature after the fish went in. A 4 lb (1.8 kg) piece of middle-cut from a chunky fish will need 35 minutes poaching because of its thickness. Going to the other extreme, a huge 20 lb (9 kg) salmon will be amply cooked in 1½ hours. That is only 4½ minutes/lb (9 m/kg) but once again it will take a while to regain poaching temperature before being timed.

For notes on microwaving, see p. 44.

If you now feel thoroughly daunted—don't despair! Remember that you can always take a sly peep to reassure yourself that all is well. Insert a knife along the thickest part of the back and gently lift so that you can see the meat around the backbone. The aim is to produce a fish that is just cooked and no more. The flesh will only just flake away from the centre bone and will have barely lost its translucence, remaining moist and slightly yielding when pressed with a finger. There may be some creamy-looking curds between the flakes. They should be soft—this is albumen which curdles completely when over-heated, leaving behind dry flesh with a watery liquid fast draining out of it. Remember the poached egg.

serving

To serve the fish hot, carefully lift it out and skin it if you like. Then serve as soon as possible. If it has to wait about, don't skin it, just keep it warm. If you know in advance that it will have to wait, slightly undercook so that it is *à point* after its period of keeping warm.

To serve cold, lift out the fish and skin the top side, leaving the head and tail. It is worth boning the fish for a buffet as people usually can't be bothered to do it themselves. Pull out the fins with their little bones. Then with a large palette knife or two fish slices, carefully remove the top two fillets. Snip the backbone at head and tail and ease it off. Then replace the fillets. You may now decorate as the fancy takes you, with mayonnaise, cucumber, aspic or all three.

STEAMING

Sometimes when a fish is wrapped in foil with only a small quantity of liquid it is virtually steamed—another excellent way of cooking fish. Steaming preserves the flavour in all its purity and is ideal for the health-conscious. It is most successful with small fish or thin pieces so that the process is carried out quickly, losing none of the nutrients or flavour. Steamed fish require the most delicate sauces of all. But because there are usually some trimmings left, a little excellent stock can be made to enhance a sauce. If you don't have a steamer, use a colander or sieve and cover with a lid. Avoid rusty metal utensils or your efforts will be wasted. Small pieces will only need a few minutes to steam. They can be left plain, lightly salted or steamed with a few aromatic herbs.

Smelt

roulade of salmon

This is an excellent way of using up some left-over poached salmon and mayonnaise, but it is good enough to justify cooking a little piece specially. The roulade mixture is not unlike that of a soufflé omelette, so there is no reason why you couldn't serve it as a filled omelette if you think a roulade sounds too fancy. It is, however, extremely quick and simple to do.

I shall assume you are starting from scratch. Keep back some of the vegetables used for poaching the fish. They have just the right crunchy consistency and slightly sharp taste. A few pickled capers could be used as a substitute, especially if using trout instead of salmon.

Serves 6

8 oz (225 g) piece of salmon
½ pt (300 ml) dry white wine
1 carrot
1 onion
1 bay leaf
6 peppercorns
salt

Roulade
4 oz (110 g) flaked almonds
½ oz (15 g) butter
4 eggs
3 oz (80 g) Gruyère cheese
¼ pt (150 ml) double cream
pepper

Filling
3 tablesp poached vegetables
2 heaped tablesp mayonnaise
dillweed *or* chives (optional)

Put the salmon in a small pan with the wine, sliced carrot and onion, bay leaf, peppercorns and a small pinch of salt. Bring gently to the boil and simmer for 5–10 minutes depending on the thickness of the piece. Allow it to cool in the liquid, then remove skin and bones.

While it simmers, chop the flaked almonds till pretty small, then crisp them in the butter with a tiny pinch of salt. Thoroughly butter a Swiss roll tin about 9 × 14 inches (23 × 36 cm), and scatter the almonds over the base, reserving a tablespoon for later.

Separate the eggs. Grate the cheese very fine and mix it with the yolks and cream and a little pepper. Beat up the egg whites with a pinch of salt and fold them into the cheese mixture, once again reserving a tiny bit. Turn the mixture into the Swiss roll tin (it looks pretty bulky but contracts after cooking), and bake in a moderately hot oven (Mk 5, 375°F, 190°C) for about 10 minutes. The top should be golden-brown and just firm to the touch. Turn it out carefully on to a tea towel.

Prepare the filling while the roulade cooks. Chop the poached carrot and onion finely and stir them into the mayonnaise. Flake the salmon and mix it in. Add a sprinkling of dill weed, or chives if wished. Spread this on to the turned-out roulade and roll it up just like a Swiss roll with the end underneath. Brush the top with the reserved egg white and gently press the remaining almonds lightly on top. You may want to slice off the two ends to give a neater appearance. Use a very sharp knife. Serve with a salad or perhaps one of the Green Mayonnaise Sauces on pp. 171/172.

salmon and prawns with spaghetti

Too many of us consider spaghetti dishes as second-class affairs to be produced when we are feeling lazy or in a hurry. It is surprising, therefore, that nearly everyone in this country ruins it by overcooking. British-made spaghetti, although made from durum wheat, has a tendency to degenerate into a glutinous mush very quickly. This is quite different from Italian spaghetti, which takes a minute or two longer to cook but retains its firm character.

After a little lecture on these important points, Michele Viliani cooked this simple dish for us just to prove his point. The quantities are for small to medium-sized portions and would precede a not-too-filling main course admirably.

Serves 6

6 oz (170 g) raw salmon meat
6 oz (170 g) cooked shelled
    prawns
2 tablesp olive oil
4 cloves garlic
4 tablesp dry white wine
salt, pepper, parsley
1¼ lb (550 g) good spaghetti
boiling water

Start by putting on a huge pan of salted water to boil for the spaghetti. Cut the salmon into little pieces the same size as the prawns. Heat the oil in a large pan and gently cook the garlic, chopped finely. Add the salmon, prawns and wine and cook gently for a minute or two. Season with salt, pepper, and a generous amount of chopped parsley, then draw the pan off the heat.

When the water is boiling, feed in the spaghetti. Proper Italian spaghetti will take 7 minutes to cook, British-made will only need 5. Drain thoroughly, then add it to the pan of fish. Over a very low heat, toss the spaghetti around for another couple of minutes to finish the cooking, then serve immediately so that the spaghetti is still properly *al dente*.

salmon or trout quenelles

Are made in exactly the same way as the pheasant quenelles on p. 84. Because fish has a more delicate flavour, use 1 lb (450 g) of skinned and boned flesh. Then adapt as follows:

For salmon, replace the juniper berries with ½ teaspoonful of crushed fennel seeds and add a few finely chopped chives. Some people like to add a tablespoon of tomato purée to improve the colour, but I don't. White Butter Sauce (p. 177), Warm Green Sauce (p. 172), the Buttery Tomato Sauce (p. 174), or Sauce Mousseline (p. 168) would all be fitting accompaniments.

For trout, omit the juniper berries and add some finely chopped chives or thyme, and beat in 2 tablespoons of very finely grated Gruyère cheese. Suitable sauces are the Buttery Tomato Sauce (p. 174), or the Mushroom Purée (p. 178), thoroughly blended and let down with a few tablespoons of cream.

savoury cakes with a salmon filling

Despite its rather clumsy title, this is a truly exquisite dish. The 'cake' layers are light and slightly moist inside—a cross between an omelette and a soufflé, I suppose. The salmon is briefly cooked with the sauce so that it remains succulent and creamy.

Although it may look a complicated recipe it is in fact remarkably quick and simple. It's just that in order to have everything *à point* at the right moment, a little chopping and changing is necessary. The only 'don't' about it is: don't try to make this in advance or the cakes will be flattened and soggy and, if overcooked, the fish will completely lose its succulence. So read through the recipe first to make sure you know what to do.

The quantities given are right for 4 people as a starter. Depending on appetite, they will do 2–3 people for a main course.

Serves 4

8 oz (225 g) raw salmon flesh
1 egg
4 tablesp double cream
zest and juice ¼ lemon
pinch of salt
2 tablesp dry white wine
a few herbs to decorate

The cakes
butter, flour
2 eggs
1½ oz (40 g) Edam *or*
    Gruyère cheese
2 oz (50 g) petit-suisse
1 tablesp double cream
zest of ¼ lemon
chives
pinch salt, pepper
melissa *or* pretty herb leaves
    (optional)

The best approach is to get everything ready to cook the sauce and salmon, then to break off and prepare the 'cakes'. While they bake, you then finish off the quick cooking of the salmon. The little cakes will collapse a little when they come out of the oven, but although they are still delicious even when a little deflated, they are obviously best served as soon as possible.

To make the sauce, beat the egg until smooth, then beat in the cream, lemon juice and zest, and the salt. Chop or flake the salmon into small scraps and stir them in. Pour all this into a heavy bottomed saucepan but do not start to cook yet.

To make the 'cakes', butter two 7-inch cake tins and dust them thoroughly with flour. Separate the eggs and grate the hard cheese very finely. Beat together the egg yolks and petit-suisse until smooth. Then beat in the double cream and grated cheese, the finely grated lemon zest and a few chopped chives. Add a pinch of salt and a little pepper. Whip up the egg whites till stiff and incorporate a generous tablespoon into the cheese mixture to slacken it a little. Then fold in the rest of the egg whites thoroughly but gently. Divide this mixture evenly between the two cake tins, gently smoothing it right up to the edges. Bake in the centre of a moderate oven (Mk 4, 350°F, 180°C) for 10–12 minutes. Check them after 10 minutes and turn the tins round if necessary. When done, they will have risen slightly and have a golden glazed-looking crust which is beginning to crack apart.

While the little cakes are baking, cook the salmon. Over a moderate heat, stir the sauce and salmon together, being careful not to let it reach simmering point. It will begin to thicken—add the wine and continue to stir.

This process will take 6 or 7 minutes, by which time the tiny pieces of salmon will be amply cooked. Remove the salmon with a slotted spoon and keep it warm. This is the filling, so it should be nicely moistened with sauce. Keep stirring the sauce until it has thickened to a good coating consistency.

When the cakes are done, turn them carefully out of their tins —one on to a warmed serving dish and the other on to a cooling rack. Make a layer of all the moist salmon on the first cake and invert the other one on top so that the appetising looking crust is uppermost.

Decorate simply with a few herbs (melissa or any pretty herb leaves are appropriate), and serve immediately, handing the sauce round separately.

fillets of trout poached in celery

Celery and trout complement each other in flavour, texture and colour, making this recipe light and summery. Use the more tender centre parts of the celery and choose a fresh green bunch which will contrast prettily with the trout especially if it is a pink one.

Serves 4

2 × 1¼ lb (550 g) rainbow trout *or* 4 × 6 oz (170 g) fillets
10 oz (280 g) celery
1½ oz (40 g) butter
small wineglass dry *or* medium white wine

Slice the celery thinly on the slant so that you get slivers rather than tiny pieces. Reserve 1 tablespoon of the fresh green tops for garnish. Soften the rest over a low heat with the butter, shaking the pan occasionally so that it does not burn (burnt celery is bitter).

In the meantime, bone and fillet your fish (see p. 8). Trim the fillets into nicely shaped pieces. You can leave them whole, but they are rather fragile to serve.

Once the celery is beginning to look translucent, pour on the wine. Either dry or medium can be used. They are both good; just different. Bring up the heat a little so that the wine, butter and juices amalgamate. Season delicately.

Arrange the pieces of fish on top of the celery, press them in slightly so that they are half-submerged, and strew or arrange the green celery tops round about. Then simmer very slowly until the fillets are just losing their translucent look. This only takes 2–3 minutes, so keep an eye on them lest they overcook and harden.

I usually serve this straight from the pan, but if preferred the final cooking of the fish could be done in the oven or even under a low grill, arranged in a warm serving dish.

marinated trout (cooked)

Here are two recipes for trout, both of which are steeped in a marinade as they cool. I would tend to use rainbow trout for the first slightly more robust recipe of Alexis Soyer's and brown trout for the second.

Recipe 1

Serves 4

4 × 8 oz (225 g) trout

Marinade
1 onion
1 carrot
2 sticks celery
handful parsley
1 oz (25 g) butter, *or* oil
1 bay leaf, 1 blade mace
4 black peppercorns
½ pt (300 ml) red wine
    vinegar
1½ pt (850 ml) water

In order to cook the fish evenly, you need to find a pan large enough for the four trout to lie side by side on the base. If this is not possible, it will probably be necessary to increase the other quantities so that the marinade covers the trout. Avoid curling the fish in the pan or they will surely break when you remove them. Also, avoid cast-iron or chipped enamel as it will flavour the marinade.

Slice the onions, carrots, celery and parsley (the more roots and stalks the better). Melt the butter or oil and cook the vegetables briskly for 5–10 minutes, stirring them to stop any burning. Then draw the pan off the heat and add the bay leaf, mace and peppercorns. Pour in the wine vinegar and return to the heat till simmering, then add the water.

Lay the trout in the pan and simmer for 20–30 minutes, then allow the fish to cool in the marinade. When completely cold, gently lift out the fish. I prefer to skin them, leaving the head and tail on. Serve with Cold Green Sauce (p. 171).

Recipe 2

Serves 4

4 × 8 oz (225 g) trout

Marinade
1 small onion
bay leaf
peppercorns
thyme, 1 clove
½ pt (300 ml) dry white wine
1 dessertsp white wine
    vinegar
¼ pt (150 ml) fish stock
6 tablesp good oil
1 large juicy lemon
bunch fresh herbs: parsley,
    thyme, chives
chives *or* shallot for serving

Slice the onion. Make a bouquet of a bay leaf, a clove, some thyme and 6 peppercorns tied into a cloth. Put them in a pan with the wine, wine vinegar, fish stock and oil and bring to the boil. Simmer gently for half an hour. When nearly ready to pour over the fish, bring it to a rolling boil for 5 minutes to reduce it a little. If the fish stock was unsalted, add a pinch of salt.

While the stock simmers, pare the rind thinly off the lemon, leaving all the pith behind. Put some peel and fresh herbs into the cavity of each trout. Wrap them in well-oiled foil and bake in a moderate oven (Mk 4, 350°F, 180°C) for 20 minutes. As soon as you can, skin the fish and lay them in a deep dish.

Gently strain the boiling marinade over the warm trout and leave to cool. Lift the fish on to a serving dish. If the heads and tails annoy you, then lift the fillets carefully off the bone, keeping them intact. Serve chilled, with the finely chopped chives or shallot, and the juice from the lemon sprinkled on top.

mignonnes of rainbow trout with leeks and almonds

For a fish dish, this is a rich one with a robust flavour. Just the thing, as foreign friends have ruefully pointed out, for those cold summer evenings spent in front of the roaring log fire.

The browned butter in the sauce marries together the sharpness of the leeks and the blandness of the almonds. It is most attractive—pretty pink rounds of trout on top of the bright green sauce.

Serves 6

3 lb (1½ kg) rainbow trout
2 oz (50 g) butter
stock
8 oz (225 g) leek greens*
4 oz (110 g) butter
6 oz (170 g flaked almonds
white wine, thin cream
    (optional)
salt, pepper

Stock
bones and scraps of the 3
    trout
4 oz (110 g) filleted white fish
bunch of parsley stalks
1 small onion, sliced
1 large clove garlic
¾ pt (425 ml) water
¾ pt (425 ml) dry white wine

*By leek greens I mean the middle third of a leek, i.e., the fresh green part, not the ropey old top bits.

Remove the bones, head, tail and fins from the trout, without splitting down the backbone (see p. 10). Slice the fish into tiny round steaks (mignonnes), all a uniform 1 inch (250 mm) thick. Leave the skin on at this stage, as it keeps the edges of the fish moist, and arrange the mignonnes in a shallow-sided dish so that they fit snugly.

Make the stock by putting the trout bones and scraps (but not the heads) into a large pan with the rest of the stock ingredients. Bring to the boil, skim, and simmer for 1 hour. Skim again and strain off the stock. You should have about 1 pint (570 ml).

Divide the first 2 oz (50 g) of butter into pieces and put one on each mignonne. Fill the dish with enough stock (¾–1 pt, 425–570 ml) to come halfway up the fish. Don't knock the butter off!

Next, start the sauce. Sweat the leek greens in 2 oz (50 g) butter until quite soft but not at all brown. Purée them until completely smooth and keep the purée warm in a bain-marie.

Bake the fish in a moderate oven (Mk 4, 350°F, 180°C) for barely 10 minutes. They are done the minute they lose their transparency. While they cook, complete the sauce. Brown the almonds in the remaining butter and a pinch of salt, then strain this butter into the leek purée. Beat hard. Thin the purée with white wine, thin cream, or best of all, some of the stock the fish was cooked in. The sauce should nicely coat the back of a spoon. Adjust the seasoning to taste.

Spoon the sauce into a large flat dish or individual plates, arrange the pretty pink pieces of trout on top, and either strew the almonds over them, or serve separately in a hot dish.

Most of this can be prepared in advance, leaving just the cooking of the fish etc. to the last minute, but bear in mind that the fish will take a little longer to cook if the stock is cold. If you are feeling kind, you can whip the skins off the mignonnes before serving.

fillets of trout in a creamy celery sauce

This is a very quick meal to produce. It takes about half an hour, including filleting the fish. Serve immediately, though, so that the fish is moist and succulent, the whole point being the fresh simple contrast of taste and colour. Strips of salmon can be treated in the same way.

Serves 4

2 × 1¼ lb (550 g) rainbow trout *or*
4 × 6 oz (170 g) fillets
12 oz (340 g) celery (the centre part including a little greenery)
2 oz (50 g) butter
4 fl oz (110 ml) double cream
salt, pepper

Chop the celery finely and stew it gently in the butter until just soft. Keep a lid on the pan and stir occasionally to prevent browning. This process will take about 15 minutes.

Meanwhile fillet and skin the fish (see p. 8). Cut each of the four fillets in two lengthways and roll up each piece into a curl, securing with a cocktail stick. Purée the celery in a blender and return to the pan. I do not rub this purée through a sieve, as I rather like the texture of the celery, but if you prefer a smoother sauce, use a Mouli-légumes to remove the fibres. Add the cream and gentle seasoning and stir over a low heat for a moment until blended together.

Pour into an ovenproof serving dish and arrange the curls of trout in the sauce. Cover the dish and bake in a moderate oven (Mk 5, 375°F, 190°C) for 5–10 minutes. The fish is done when it is just losing its transparency.

Perfectly satisfactory results can be had by barely simmering the fish in the celery over a low heat for 3–4 minutes but in this case I would not roll up the fillets as they will not cook evenly, and there is a danger of the sauce turning oily.

fillets of trout in a mushroom cream sauce

Follow the above recipe, replacing the celery with 4 oz (110 g) of button mushrooms, chopped very fine. If you like almonds, crisp some in butter and thyme and strew them over the trout.

trout fillets in red pepper sauce

A beautiful deep peach-coloured sauce surrounds lightly poached trout fillets. Salmon cutlets can also be used successfully here, but they should be skinned before serving. If you simply can't be bothered to skin and fillet the trout, then there is no reason why you shouldn't poach the fish whole, and serve the sauce separately. It won't look so nice and is more hassle to serve, but it will taste just as good. You will need a little extra wine for poaching, so take that into account afterwards.

Serves 4

1½ lb (675 g) skinned trout fillets
1 huge sweet red pepper
8 fl oz (225 ml) dry white wine
½ pt (300 ml) double cream
salt, black pepper

The trout fillets may be poached flat or else rolled up loosely. If poaching them flat I would cut them into manageable pieces so they don't fall to bits. I use a big frying-pan for this dish because the sauce is reduced quickly, therefore the fish doesn't have time to dry up.

Cut the red pepper into small pieces, discarding the core and seeds. Cut a few pieces into minute dice and reserve these for decoration.

Very gently poach the fillets in the wine. Flat pieces will only need a minute, the little rolls and salmon cutlets will take longer and should be gently turned so that they cook evenly. They want to be only half-cooked as they will now have to wait a little. Remove them from the pan and keep them just warm and no more.

Add the chopped pepper to the pan and simmer until there is practically no liquid left. Then add the cream. Turn up the heat slightly and boil gently, stirring all the while until it is reduced and thick. Then tip it into a blender and purée. It will probably not come out absolutely smooth, so press it through a sieve to remove any small pieces of pepper skin.

Season with salt then pour it on to four warm plates either around or over the pieces of fish. They should have just lost their transparent look by now. Give each fish a couple of turns of black pepper and sprinkle with the tiny pieces of red pepper.

salmon or trout soufflé

Once again, follow the directions for Pheasant Soufflé on p. 85, with the same modifications given at the foot of p. 33 in the recipe for Salmon or Trout Quenelles. I would, however, use 3 instead of 2 tablespoons of cream.

little cakes of salmon in a fresh tomato sauce

We are lucky enough to live quite close to the Peat Inn Restaurant, where David and Patricia Wilson enthusiastically serve the most exquisite meals. Fish and seafood are David's speciality, though I may say he also cooks venison and pigeons to perfection. He kindly gave me this recipe for a first course which, unlike much restaurant cooking, is straightforward enough to do at home.

Serves 8

11 oz (300 g) raw salmon
    meat
1 whole egg
1 egg white
½ pt (300 ml) double cream
salt, pepper

sauce
1 tablesp finely chopped
    carrot
1 tablesp finely chopped
    onion
½ clove finely chopped garlic
a little lemon peel, finely
    chopped
1 dessertsp olive oil
¼ pt (150 ml) dry white wine
¼ pt (150 ml) fish stock
4 ripe tomatoes
pinch tarragon and basil
salt, pepper

Garnish
fresh herbs

Cut up the salmon meat roughly and liquidise until it is an almost smooth paste. Add the egg and egg white and liquidize again to mix thoroughly. Remove to a bowl, cover with cling film, and chill along with the cream. This helps the cream to be more completely absorbed into the salmon mixture. When you are ready to cook the salmon cakes, work in the cream thoroughly by hand and season with salt and pepper. However, I would advise making the sauce before cooking the cakes.

So, to make the sauce, put the first six ingredients into a saucepan, bring to the boil and reduce by two-thirds. Add the fish stock, bring back to the boil and simmer until it is of a good consistency. Peel the tomatoes by plunging them first into boiling water for a few seconds, then chop them to a pulp. Add this pulp to the sauce with the tarragon and basil and season to taste.

To cook the cakes, take 8 ring moulds (egg rings or even pastry-cutters placed cutting side uppermost will do), and stand each one on a piece of aluminium foil. Bend the foil up round the outside of the ring so that it is sealed. This also gives you something to take hold of when removing the rings after poaching. Brush the sides and base lightly with melted butter or oil. This is particularly important if using fluted pastry-cutters.

Fill the rings to the top with the salmon mixture and decorate the top with little strips of vegetable or herbs. Place the rings in a fish kettle or other wide container and pour a little hot stock or water to come about halfway up the rings. Steam gently until the cakes are just firm to the touch (about 10 minutes).

To serve, remove the rings carefully from the fish kettle and place them on warm serving plates. Fold down the foil and slide the ring mould off on to the centre of the plate. Run a sharp knife round the inside of the ring mould and lift it off. Surround each cake with the sauce, and if desired, decorate with a sprig of fresh herb.

Grilling and Sautéing

These can be quite vicious ways to cook fish, and are more appropriate to small fish or pieces—steaks, fillets etc, since they are cooked quickly. The aim is usually to produce a crisp outside which contrasts with a succulent interior. In order to achieve this, the general rules are: grill thick pieces (whole trout, large fillets or thick steaks), and sauté thin ones so that the fish has not dried out by the time the surface is crisp.

Grilling is most successful when the fish has some sort of protection. It could just be the skin which is peeled off afterwards, or perhaps a coating of thick sauce, mustard, coarse salt and so on. Only a few minutes hot grilling is necessary, lowering the heat to cook very thick pieces, and turning them once.

Sautéing (OK frying!) should be carried out in the largest possible pan, particularly when many pieces are to be cooked. If you don't have a big pan, sauté in batches, otherwise the temperature is reduced so much that the fish stews rather than browns, and won't become crisp until the fish is desperately overdone. The surface of the fish should be dry, again to ensure rapid browning. Heat the butter, oil, or a mixture of both, until smoking hot (but not burnt) and flash in the fish for just long enough to crisp the exterior and no longer. Serve sautéed fish immediately so that the outside doesn't become soggy.

Another form of pan-cooking is when, for example, fillets are cooked over a gentle heat in either a sauce, or some melted butter, perhaps with a splash of wine. This is completely different from sautéing, though no less delicious; here the fish is really being poached or stewed and those are the principles to apply.

Charcoal grilling is halfway between grilling and baking. The skin frequently sticks and breaks, but who cares, it tastes so good. Wrapping the fish in buttered foil will prevent untidy fish, and then various herbs or liquids can be added, but this is more akin to baking, and the wonderful carcinogenic flavour of charcoal-grilling is lost.

trout with garlic and mushrooms

A quick and simple meal with a cheerful bistro flavour, and a fine way to cook rainbow trout.

Serves 4

1 lb (450 g) trout fillets
2 oz (50 g) butter
4 oz (110 g) fresh brown
    breadcrumbs
3 large cloves garlic
12 oz (340 g) mushrooms
1½ oz (40 g) butter
bunch fresh thyme

Skin the trout fillets and cut them into strips. Keep them aside. Melt the 2 oz (50 g) of butter in a pan and add the breadcrumbs and garlic (crushed). Stir them around until they are crisp and golden. Remove to a serving dish to keep warm.

Slice the mushrooms thinly and gently toss them in the remaining butter until soft. Add the thyme leaves and strips of trout, tossing them gently with the mushrooms until just cooked but still succulent. At the last moment, stir in the breadcrumbs and serve immediately while they are still crisp.

truite meunière

You could do a lot worse than stay with this traditional recipe, though some people deprecate serving almonds with trout. They could substitute fresh parsley for the almonds, and very good it will be. The rest of us can content ourselves with the Roman belief that eating a few almonds enables us to 'acquire the ability of drinking astonishingly'.

Serves 4

4 small cleaned trout
seasoned flour
4 oz (110 g) sweet almonds
4 tablesp oil
2 oz (50 g) butter
salt
juice 1 lemon

These trout are cooked whole, but cut off the heads and tails if you wish. Roll them in well-seasoned flour. Prepare the almonds by slicing into flakes. If you want them peeled, plunge them into boiling water and the skins will rub off.

Heat the oil until just beginning to smoke. Put in the trout and cook for 3–4 minutes per side, depending on thickness, then remove to a warm serving dish.

Pour off most of the oil and make sure there are no burnt specks left in the pan. Then add the butter and throw in the almonds. Stir until golden brown. Almonds can burn very quickly, so whip them off the heat as soon as they are done. Season with salt and lemon juice and pour the sizzling almonds over the trout. Serve at once.

trout fried in oatmeal

By the time a whole fish has cooked through, the oatmeal has burnt, so fillets are best for this dish. It is becoming very popular on Scottish hotel breakfast menus.

Serves 4

1½ lb (675 g) trout fillets
milk *or* beaten egg
4 oz (110 g) oatmeal
4 oz (110 g) fatty bacon
1 large lemon

I use medium oatmeal here, but some prefer pinhead (coarse). The latter is altogether too toothcracking for me, but you could use a mixture.

Moisten the fillets with milk or a little beaten egg and press them into oatmeal till well covered. Chop the bacon into little pieces and fry gently until it has exuded plenty of well-flavoured fat. Add a little extra if there is not enough. Remove the bacon and fry the fillets quickly on both sides so that the oatmeal is crisp and the fish is moist. If the fat is not smoking hot, the oatmeal will soak it up and become greasy. Serve immediately with lemon.

grilled trout with mustard and oats

Rolled oats are not so crunchy as oatmeal but, used this way, they make a good foil to grilled trout.

Serves 4

1½ lb (675 g) skinned trout fillets
6 tablesp rolled oats
3 oz (80 g) butter
mustard

Melt the butter and stir in the rolled oats. Brush the fillets on one side with mustard. English mustard is potent when not cooked for long, so use it sparingly. My preference is for a wholegrain mustard such as Meaux, especially when children are being fed. This can be spread thicker.

Coat the mustard side with oats and cook under a hot grill until crisp. Then turn the fillets over and repeat. If the fillets are thin, grill them on one side only, as by the time the second lot of oats had cooked, the fish would be as dry as a bone.

salt-crust salmon steaks with spicy butter

This hardly sounds a healthy way of eating, but it is in fact a very good method of keeping salmon steaks moist, and you can always substitute a less fattening accompaniment, such as the first recipe for Tomato Sauce, p. 174.

Serves 4

4 salmon steaks
12 oz (340 g) coarse salt

Spicy butter
sprig parsley and chives
1 teasp Worcestershire sauce
1 crushed clove garlic
1 medium gherkin
1 anchovy fillet
2 spring onions
8 turns ground black pepper
3 oz (80 g) softened butter

First make the butter. It is worth making extra and keeping some in the freezer. Put all the ingredients except the butter into a liquidiser and blend until finely chopped, then beat them into the softened butter. Allow it to chill slightly (or you will make no end of a mess), then roll into little balls with Scotch hands (butter pats), or else into a cylinder which you can slice into neat rounds when further chilled. Use a slightly warmed knife for this job.

Now for the steaks. Make a thick paste from the coarse salt and water and thickly coat each steak on one side and round the edges. (If you do this with the steaks already on the grill pan it will prevent the salt slithering off when you transfer them). Grill at full heat for a few minutes until the salt is dry and hard and then very carefully turn the steaks over, being careful not to break the crust. Repeat the process with the other side, then turn down the heat to allow the fish to cook through.

Crack off the salt crusts and serve the steaks with a knob of spicy butter on top.

Baking

Baking fish encompasses several different techniques. Some tiny trout might be quickly baked in a hot oven with some butter and fresh herbs. Salmon steaks can be wrapped in foil with vegetables and a little liquid. A huge fish, too large to fit into any poaching vessel might be wrapped in buttered foil with or without some liquid and baked in a slow oven. The general rule is that small fish can be open-baked and should be done quickly if a crisp skin is wanted, whereas large fish or chunks should be covered and baked slowly so that the outside has not overcooked by the time the centre is done.

The preparation is the same as for poaching (see p. 29). Sometimes it is worth protecting the head and tail of a large fish with buttered paper before wrapping in foil.

Small fish will only need 5–10 minutes in a hot oven (Mk 7, 425°F, 220°C). Large fish cooked in a slow oven (Mk 3, 325°F, 170°C) will need about 25 minutes per pound (35 m/kg). You can check progress by sliding a knife into the centre of the back, inserting it into the thickest part, and seeing that it is not still raw. The minute it starts to become opaque it is done. To serve cold, reduce the cooking times by 5 minutes per pound (8 m/kg) and leave to cool. If baked in a china rather than metal dish, it will take a few minutes longer.

The largest fish I ever cooked was a 22 lb salmon. It was far too long to fit into a fish kettle or the oven so we cooked it over a brazier. It was wrapped in many layers of foil to give a measure of rigidity, with butter, dry white wine and herbs tucked around it. The braziers (two oil drums) were lit well in advance and the fire kept about two feet away from the fish. We cooked it for about an hour and a half, carefully turning it from time to time, and then left it to cool. It was perfect. This is considerably less than the times given above because it is the thickness of the fish, rather than its weight alone, which is the relevant factor. So bear this in mind should you also be so lucky.

MICROWAVING

I should need another 2 years testing and another book to boot, before I could blast you with the full radiance of microwave cookery. It is, I suppose, a form of baking, and is an excellent way of cooking fish as it retains moisture and freshness and can be done with little or no added moisture or fat.

The head and tail should be protected with foil so that they don't overcook. If applicable, place the thinner tail ends to the centre of the dish. Plump fish (particularly if stuffed) will cook more evenly if slashed once or twice in the thickest part. The fish can be cooked plain or rubbed with any preparation that takes your fancy—garlic, wine, mustard, finely chopped vegetables, butter, etc. Then cover them with cling film, pierced so that it doesn't burst.

Cooking times will vary according to the power of your microwave, so it is best to refer to your handbook, if necessary using cooking times recommended for similarly shaped fish. As microwaving is so quick, it is always better to err on the undercooked side, since the fish can either go back for another minute or be left to rest. Since microwaves only penetrate about 2 inches (5 cm), thick pieces may need turning. Alternatively they can be slightly undercooked and then left, covered, to rest and let the heat work its way to the centre. When fish have large amounts of bone, as for example the tail-piece of salmon, they will cook very much quicker as microwaves are attracted to bones.

salmon pieces en croûte with a green herb sauce

The quantities given are for a first course, but if used as a main course they will do 2–3 people. In this case I would make them in larger portions rather than tiny cases, and you will need less pastry. It is a good way to use small scraps of salmon meat from around the head or tail-piece.

Serves 8

6 oz (170 g) raw salmon meat
1 egg
½ oz (12 g) Edam *or* Gruyère
  cheese
lemon zest, salt, pepper
¼ pt (150 ml) double cream
1 lb (450 g) puff pastry
milk *or* egg yolk

Sauce
8 fl oz (225 ml) single cream
spinach *or* chard leaves
parsley, chives, thyme,
  melissa
2 tablesp dry white vermouth
salt, pepper

Start by making the sauce so that it is ready when the puffs are cooked. Take a handful of fresh spinach or chard leaves, a sprig of parsley, a small bunch of chives and a little bunch of thyme and melissa. Discard any tough stalks and simmer the rest in the cream for a few minutes till soft. Then tip into a liquidiser and blend until smooth and green. Sieve this into the rinsed-out pan, add the vermouth and season to taste. If the sauce is a little thin, reduce slightly. Keep warm.

Beat the egg and put it in a blender with the salmon. Skin and bones should of course have been removed. Blend for a few seconds—the salmon should not be reduced completely to a paste as a little texture here is good.

Turn into a bowl and beat in the very finely grated cheese, a pinch of salt, a little pepper, and the finely grated lemon peel. The zest of half a small lemon will be quite sufficient—you don't want to drown the taste of the salmon. Then pour the cream over the top and chill. Chilling helps the cream to become incorporated into the fish mixture more effectively.

While the cream chills, roll out the pastry extremely thin until it measures 12″ × 24″. These little puffs should be very light and you don't want a great wodge of pastry drowning the salmon filling. Cut out 32 rounds with a biscuit cutter and line 16 little tins, reserving the other 16 for the tops.

Once the fish and cream are thoroughly chilled, beat them well together and fill the little cases with the mixture. Moisten the edges of the remaining circles with milk or egg yolk and cover the filled cases, making a tiny hole in the top of each.

Brush with egg yolk and bake for 10–15 minutes in a moderate oven (Mk 4, 350°F, 180°C) until the pastry is puffed and golden. Serve whilst still warm, on top of the bright green sauce.

salmon in foil with vegetables

Like most of the best ways of cooking salmon, this is very simple and can be prepared in advance up to the final cooking which must be brief so that the salmon doesn't dry out.

Serves 4

1½ lb (650 g) salmon,
    skinned and boned
4 oz (110 g) each of carrots,
    onions and mushrooms
4½ oz (120 g) butter
salt, white pepper
1 teasp fresh tarragon
1 shallot
big glass dry white wine
small glass good stock (made
    from trimmings)

Dice the vegetables (or, to be more refined, cut them into thin strips). Soften the carrot and onion in one-third of the butter, adding the mushrooms after 5 minutes. Do not let them brown. Season with just a little salt and white pepper and remove from the heat, adding the tarragon at this point. If you use dried tarragon, halve the quantity.

Cut the salmon into even slices about ⅓ inch (1 cm) thick, and season with a little salt, pepper and the very finely chopped shallot. Cut four large rounds of foil, bend up the edges and divide the vegetables between them. Lay 2 slices of salmon on each pile and add a knob of butter and a quarter each of the wine and stock. Then crimp the foil together to seal the little parcels.

Put them into a lightly oiled and pre-heated dish, nicely spaced out, and bake in a hot oven (Mk 9, 475°F, 240°C) for 5 minutes. If you have prepared this in advance, allow another couple of minutes since the vegetables will be cold.

salmon baked in a salt paste

You can bake fish in nothing but coarse salt, but you need an awful lot and it is sometimes fiddly to get it all off; so I make a salt paste instead. It is ideal for a cut of salmon and keeps it beautifully moist. A fine salty tang remains, not overpowering but reminiscent of the sea.

Serves 4

1¼ lb (560 g) middle-cut
    salmon
butter, herbs (optional)
7 oz (200 g) flour
4 oz (110 g) coarse *or* sea salt
water
1 small egg

There is no need to de-scale the fish because the skin lifts off with the crust. If you want to, stuff the cavity with butter and fresh herbs, but the salmon will be very delicious on its own.

Mix the flour and salt together, then add enough water to make a very stiff paste. Separate the egg and whisk the white. Add just a little to the paste and knead it in. Refrigerate for 1 hour. The paste becomes slacker as some of the salt is dissolved.

Roll it out and completely envelop the salmon. Place it on a greased baking sheet with the ends tucked underneath. Brush the top with egg yolk and decorate with thin pastry scraps if you like. Once the paste is on, the fish must be baked at once or the paste may disintegrate.

Bake in a moderate oven (Mk 4, 350°F, 180°C) for 30–40 minutes depending on thickness. This extra cooking time is needed because of the paste.

The crust is *not* to be eaten—crack it off and the skin will come away as well, leaving the fish very succulent. The recipe for fennel (see p. 182) goes extremely well with this.

trout or salmon baked in limes

The wine may be dry or medium, depending on your taste. I would tend to use dry wine for salmon, but a sweeter wine goes rather well with trout. If you use lemons instead of limes, use slightly less juice as lemons are more acidic.

Serves 3

1 lb (450 g) fish
butter *or* oil
1 large glass white wine
juice 2 limes
thinly sliced shallot
salt, pepper
chives, melissa, etc

Line a dish with aluminium foil and lightly brush it with a very little butter or oil to stop the fish sticking. Place the fish in the foil and pour the wine and lime juice over it. Tuck the herbs and shallot in and around the fish, and add a pinch of salt and a little pepper. Fold up the foil loosely and envelop the fish, if possible making sure the foil does not touch the skin lest it should stick.

Bake in a fairly hot oven (Mk 6, 400°F, 200°C) till the fish is cooked. This will obviously depend on the form of the fish. A whole 1 lb trout will take about 15 minutes, whereas a chunk of salmon would take more like 20–25 minutes. Trout fillets will take hardly any time at all. Once the foil and ingredients have heated two or three minutes are all that is necessary. Even a frozen 1 lb trout was cooked to perfection in half an hour.

Trutta Salmonata

47

trout baked in vermouth and cream

Vermouth and cream are such a classic combination that it is difficult not to be seduced into using them all the time. But once again I am seduced and a simple but delicious dish emerges.

Serves 4

1 × 1½ lb (675 g) trout
good bunch mixed fresh
　herbs
3 cloves garlic
salt, pepper
¼ pt (150 ml) dry white
　vermouth
¼ pt (150 ml) whipping
　cream

Prepare the trout and, if wished, remove the backbone (see p. 10). Place it on a piece of foil large enough to encase the fish, in a baking dish. Tuck the herbs in and around the fish. Appropriate herbs are chives (chopped), thyme, melissa (lemon balm), mint, mace, fennel etc—not all of these at once or there may be a confusion of tastes. Add the garlic (chopped), 2 pinches of salt and a little pepper. Then pour the vermouth and cream over the top and seal the foil. Give it plenty of room to steam and make sure the foil does not touch the top of the fish lest it stick to the skin.

Bake in a moderately hot oven (Mk 5, 375°F, 190°C) for about 20 minutes. The fish should not be overcooked. Then carefully remove the trout to a serving dish and keep warm. Strain and press the sauce through a sieve or Mouli into a small pan, crushing the herbs and garlic through to emerge as a fine speckle in the sauce. Reduce a little, then pour it around the trout and serve immediately.

trout fillets with non-lemon sauce

When I serve this up, nobody believes that there isn't any lemon in it. Sorrel provides the delicate lemon taste, and it also slightly curdles the cream into a soft curd. Sorrel is extremely easy to grow so try to get hold of a cutting. The only difficult part is preventing helpful visitors from digging up the young plants, as they look so similar to dockens!

Serves 4

4 × 6 oz (170 g) trout
　(filleted, see p. 8)
2 oz (50 g) butter
12 large sorrel leaves, sliced
¾ pt (425 ml) thin cream
salt, pepper, nutmeg
flaked almonds and butter
　(optional)

Butter a shallow dish and lay the sorrel strips on the bottom. Arrange the trout fillets on top, pour the cream over them, and sprinkle with a little salt, pepper and nutmeg. Put into a hot oven (Mk 6, 400°F, 200°C) for about 10 minutes by which time the fish will have only just lost its translucent look, and the cream will have slightly curdled.

If you overcook the fish it will go hard and dry. I am a sucker for flaked almonds fried in salty butter and find them hard to resist with trout, but they aren't actually necessary to this simple dish.

trout in cheese and mustard sauce

In the good old days, the herring boats at Mallaig used to unload their catch from wicker creels, which would conveniently spill a generous amount on to the quayside where we would scoop up a great bagful. Nowadays the herrings are packed into non-spill boxes and are a comparative luxury, so I use trout instead for this good homely dish.

Serves 4

1¾ lb (800 g) cleaned trout,
  or 1 lb (450 g) skinned
  fillets
2 oz (50 g) butter
2 rounded tablesp flour
1 pt (570 ml) milk
8 oz (225 g) cheese
2 dessertsp mustard

If using a whole trout, remove the fillets and skin them. It is the work of minutes—see p. 8.

Make a white sauce from the butter, flour and milk. Add the cheese, reserving 2 tablespoons, and cook slowly for 5 minutes. Then add the mustard. Using Dijon mustard, this quantity is not too overwhelming, but it is very much a question of taste. English mustard is stronger, so start with less—you don't want to drown the taste of the trout. Cook for another few minutes.

Pour a third of the sauce into a wide serving dish, lay the trout fillets on top, and cover with the rest. Sprinkle the remaining cheese on top. If you prefer a crisp topping, mix a handful of breadcrumbs or medium oatmeal with the cheese.

Bake in a very hot oven (Mk 8, 450°F, 230°C) for 10 minutes. The cheese is beginning to brown and the trout is succulent. If you want a browner top, take it out 2 minutes early and finish under a hot grill. Obviously if baked in a smaller deep dish, the fish will need a little extra cooking.

brown trout with almond biscuits

Anyone who has spent a midgy summer's day beside an overstocked hill loch may wonder what to do with a bagful of tiny speckled trout, none of which is more than 5 inches long and all of which taste divine.

Serves 4

8 tiny trout
herbs
butter

Cook the fish simply: cover with fresh herbs and a buttered paper and cook in a buttered dish for 8–10 minutes in a hot oven—no more or they will dry up. But because they are so especially beautiful, honour them by serving a simple green salad (no peppers, but maybe a few dandelion leaves or wood sorrel wouldn't go amiss), White Butter Sauce (see p. 177), and this little savoury biscuit.

For 8 biscuits
3 oz (80 g) ground almonds
¾ oz (20 g) softened butter
pinch of salt
1 small egg white, lightly beaten
flour

Rub the butter and salt into the ground almonds and amalgamate with the egg white into a soft dough. Roll out on a lightly floured board and cut into shapes (make them fish if you like). Bake them on a flat sheet which has been buttered and floured, in a moderate oven for only a few minutes until golden brown. Do not take your eyes off them for a minute as they burn very suddenly! They are a little fragile, but I have resisted the temptation to add flour which would make them stronger but not so good.

trout and the times

Major Stewart insists this is the best possible way to eat trout. Depending on how optimistic a fisherman you are, you either light your fire first, or start casting. In any case, first catch your trout.

As soon as you have landed your catch, gut it and open out your copy of *The Times*. If not too ravenous, scout about for a few wild herbs, but these are not essential. Lay the fish and herbs on to the newspaper and wrap them up, folding in the ends. Put the parcel to the fire, and when the paper is charred the trout will be cooked to perfection.

After trying this curious recipe washed down with a little something from a hip flask, it was suggested that perhaps the *Financial Times* would imbue the fish with pink colouring, turning it into a seatrout. Try it with a farmed rainbow trout and you will be amazed. After further discussion we came up with:

lord gnome's trout

This tastes and smells just as you would expect it to—like fish and chips with salt 'n' sauce. Why not, you may say, cook the trout in batter and have the sauce on the chips? Why not indeed. It would probably be better.

Serves 2

2 × 8 oz (225 g) trout
1 copy *Private Eye*
HP sauce
2 portions very crispy chips

(That's enough newspapers—Ed.)

Open out your copy of *Private Eye* and remove the staples. Lay each fish on to half of the paper. Shake HP sauce cautiously (unless you are really addicted) over the fish and into the cavities. Roll up the paper into neat parcels and either barbecue them as before or bake in a hot oven (Mk 6, 400°F, 200°C) for 20 minutes. Serve with chips.

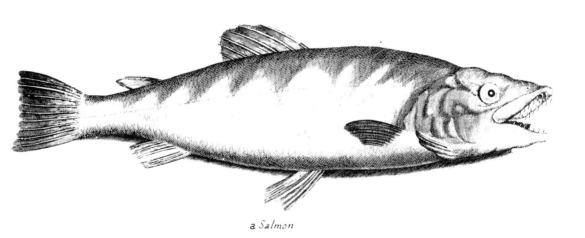

a Salmon

From a border round an
illuminated manuscript
ca 1400. by John Siferwas
who was particularly
good at birds.

Pheasant
Eye
(narcissus
poeticus)

Summer Pheasant's
Eye

Detail of pheasant
on 6th - 7th C.
Persian
rug —

3
Pheasant and Guinea Fowl

Ben Jonson's 'purpl'd pheasant with the speckled side' and the attractively mottled guinea fowl have provided us for centuries with some of our most recherché dishes.

The pheasant came to us from Asia and the Far East, whereas the guinea fowl is a native of North Africa. Both species filtered into northern Europe via the Greeks, followed by the Romans who avidly embellished Greek culinary practices and then marched their pheasants (along with fallow deer and rabbits) northwards, eventually introducing them to Britain.

Pheasants

In early Roman Italy, pheasants were a rarity. But once they became sufficiently numerous the Romans gleefully partook of them. They were not game in those times but kept as farmyard fowl like peacocks. Eventually we hear that Heliogabalus would only eat pheasant three times a week, even though Galen, a renowned physician, recommended their light flesh as being a most healthy meat.

Pheasants were first mentioned in Britain before the Norman conquest, appearing in King Harold's records as a royal bird. But they, like their Roman counterparts were raised for the table. Henry VIII reared pheasants for his banquets, employing a French priest to supervise their fattening. It took until the sixteenth century for pheasants to start establishing themselves in the wild, and until the late eighteenth century before they were endemic throughout Britain.

By that time, of course, pheasant shooting had emerged as a sport, and by the nineteenth century, many farmers and estate owners discovered that, due to the current agricultural depression, they could earn more by rearing pheasants than by conventional farming.

This was somewhat of a mixed blessing to the community. Whilst the countryside has undoubtedly benefited from the woods and coppices planted as cover, the less wealthy folk of the time must have found it galling to see such wealth expended on what was merely a rich man's pastime instead of producing much-needed corn.

However, the luckier and more enterprising ones managed to eke out their family's diet with pheasant, using such time-honoured methods as the rum-soaked raisin, the horse's hair and the paper hat (I'd better not go into this in great detail!).

Pheasant shoots reached their zenith in the first part of this century. Edward VII was particularly partial to his shooting, though some people discreetly disapproved of his behaviour. Once upper-class Britain had recovered from the rigours of the First World War, pheasant shoots yielded scarcely credible numbers, but eventually they declined, reflecting contemporary economic depression.

Nowadays pheasants are staging a considerable come-back (as opposed to grouse's go-back), affording a welcome change of air to city-dwellers and a useful number of jobs in the countryside. I for one would be delighted to see pheasants being reared exclusively for the table again. I suppose we'd have to forgo the French priests, but something along the lines of free range hens might work very satisfactorily. Could that possibly be the next project?

Guinea Fowl

Compared to the pheasant's illustrious history, the guinea fowl has much less noble associations. The Greeks and Romans certainly paid large sums for the rare 'hens of Numidia' as they were called, but it seems that their appearance at great banquets was a display of opulence as much as anything else.

Both Pliny the naturalist, and Martial 'raised great objections against this ostentatious and useless rarity'. And in a hunting poem written in A.D. 283, Nemesian scornfully dismisses them as 'the most stupid of birds', who fall over their own feet when pursued.

It seems to be the French who appreciate guinea fowl more than any other nation. Since they first appeared there in the fifteenth century, they have been reared in vast numbers, both for their flesh, which is not unlike pheasant, and for their eggs, which are apparently excellent, even if the thick shells do require a little exertion to open.

Perhaps the Romans would have loved their hens of Numidia a little more if they had used them as guards, like their revered geese. In Victorian times, guinea fowls were sometimes used to guard pheasant coverts—anyone who has heard guinea fowl in a farmyard will appreciate that they make very good watchdogs.

Cooking and Ageing

Many of the recipes in this section can be interchanged because both birds have a similar type of flavour. The colour and taste of guinea fowl is halfway between that of pheasant and chicken. Because of the tenderness factor, I advise using your pheasants for the guinea fowl dishes. Grouse and partridge may also be cooked using these recipes. Bear in mind that a grouse or partridge will only feed two people, so adjust the ingredients accordingly. And being smaller, they will roast more quickly—take 5 minutes off all the roasting times given for pheasant and guinea fowl.

These birds are light-boned, so what may appear to be a small bird will yield plenty of good eating. A great advantage of guinea fowl is that the drumsticks are not sinewy like pheasants' and they tend to be leaner. Most guinea fowl sold in this country are reared in Belgium. Unlike pheasants, they are not subject to close seasons and can be bought from the more enterprising supermarkets and butchers. If you have difficulty finding them, try wholesale game-dealers. They are usually happy to sell any quantity.

The fat on a plump pheasant is often very yellow. I like to think this is due to the pheasant's predilection for buttercup tubers, but John says it is much more likely to be a diet of maize!

Once trussed, a pheasant is impossible to age. The only assumption you can make, and this is by no means infallible, is that small birds are more likely to be young. In full feather, there are two points which will help to age a pheasant, but having gone through racks of them with Ian Thomson, I realise that it is not easy to age pheasants reliably. For instance, an old cock pheasant is conspicuous by his magnificent fighting spurs, whereas a very young one's will be short and blunt. But, under good conditions, ferocious specimens can be seen on birds of less than a year. Older birds of both sexes grow a second nail on their claws, which may be harder and scalier and, if you press the breastbone, it will be softer on a young bird than an old one. The only definitive test of youth is to examine the bursa. This is a small opening in the vent which in young birds will be about an inch deep. Later on the bursa closes up, sometimes leaving a slight lump.

Having said all this, I would echo Ian's comment that your chances of having a young bird are pretty favourable. He reckons that a good 80 per cent of his pheasants are birds of that year. Once the age is ascertained, you may hang from the neck and/or marinade the pheasant as you wish. Both subjects are covered in detail elsewhere.

Old pheasants which are liable to be tough must either be cooked very quickly so that the meat is still pink and moist, or else gently simmered for a long period to make them tender. There is no successful halfway measure. Young birds are a little more versatile.

Bear in mind that recipes using powerful flavours are all the better for using a well-hung bird. Subtle accompaniments are often inappropriate with a really gamy pheasant and, equally, a powerful sauce will completely drown the delicate flavour of a young bird. Both are excellent in their own special way, so try to introduce greater variety in both hanging and cooking methods.

This is my answer to all the people who have asked me to make their pheasants more interesting. I hope those people will remember how lucky they are and never again groan at the sight of a colourful profusion of pheasants. If they do, send 'em to me!

Roasting

There are lots of clever things you can do with pheasants, but the traditional roast pheasant with all the trimmings is not to be spurned. As a general rule, make twice as many breadcrumbs as you think you will need, and half as much bread sauce, unless my husband John is coming to dinner.

In theory, if you have two pheasants of the same age and sex, shot on the same day, from the same area and hung under the same conditions, they will cook to equal perfection. In practice, it doesn't usually work out so neatly because it is usual to be presented with a brace of pheasant, i.e., a cock and a hen. A disgruntled friend of mine growled back at his game-dealer that he wanted to eat the pheasants, not breed from them. Whatever the slight difference in flavour may be, the size factor is bound to make them cook unevenly, so at least try to get two of the same size.

Unless you like rare or at least pretty pink meat, avoid cooking an old pheasant with a young one. But, contrary to what many people imagine, old pheasants are very good when roasted briefly, as the meat has no chance to toughen up. Carving paper-thin slices helps a great deal, as does resting the meat before serving.

There are lots of 'best ways' of roasting pheasant, but most are agreed that the most satisfactory is to cook the pheasant upside down on or its side, turning it around so that the breast meat doesn't dry out. Being thinner, the breast cooks much quicker than the thighs. One way to counteract this effect is to stuff something underneath the skin of the breast: bacon, cream cheese, fruit or conventional stuffing. All these help to keep the meat moist and increase bulk so that it cooks more evenly. Bacon goes well with roast pheasant, but don't cover the breast with rashers because they fall off when you turn the pheasant. Instead, cook bacon rolls beside the bird and baste with the flavoured fat.

This is how I recommend roasting pheasants: first brown them quickly all over in hot bacon fat, butter or oil. This in itself takes five or ten minutes and starts heating the meat. Then put the pheasants on their side in a roasting tin with plenty of hot fat poured over them. Roast in a hot oven (Mk 7, 425°F, 220°C) and keep basting and turning them so that a thigh is uppermost. Small pheasants weighing 1¼ lb (550 g) will need 20–25 minutes, depending on how pink you like the meat. Larger ones will need up to 15 minutes more. You can roast them less if you want, but no more. Remember to include any stuffing in their weight.

At this stage the pheasant is nearly cooked to your liking, but not quite, so rest it in a cool oven or turn the oven off and open the door. Rest the pheasant for 10 minutes at least, longer if you don't like any pink. During this period the heat still travels inwards, but the slightly too pink juices in the middle are drawn back towards the edge, leaving the meat relaxed and succulent. At the same time drain off all that well-flavoured fat and use it to fry the breadcrumbs.

If you roast pheasants any longer than this, they will surely dry up. Some folk hanker after roast pheasant which is so well done that the legs practically fall off. They should never dry-roast pheasants. They should *braise* them instead, thus: brown the pheasant thoroughly all over, then put it into a deep dish with plenty of fat and a little drop of liquid. Cover tightly and cook in a slow oven (Mk 3, 325°F, 170°C) for 2–3 hours, turning and basting frequently as before. Unless the breasts are well larded, they are inclined to be dry, but the legs are undoubtedly improved.

Phasianus mas
A Cock Pheasant.

pheasant with leek purée and soy sauce

Here is my favourite way of roasting a pheasant. The leek sauce has a pleasant nutty flavour and the cheese under the skin keeps the bird moist as well as looking attractive. Because both pheasant and sauce are rich, keep other accompaniments simple.

Serves 4–8

2 pheasants
6 oz (170 g) cream cheese
chopped parsley *or* chives
    (optional)
3 tablesp soy sauce
1½ lb (675 g) leeks
6 oz (170 g) butter
2 tablesp double cream
a little cornflour
white wine and/*or* stock
pepper, salt

Remember to remove the sinews from the legs before you start. Mash the cream cheese with some salt and black pepper. If you like you can also add some chopped parsley or chives. Starting at the wishbone end of the bird, gently start to ease the skin away from the flesh with your fingers, taking care not to tear it. Using a teaspoon, ease in the cream cheese, pushing it back as far under the skin as it will go, making an even layer.

Pop a knob of butter into each bird and secure the skin at the opening by 'sewing' it with cocktail sticks. This will stop any shrinking. Tie the legs so that they lie snugly against the carcase.

Butter a shallow dish and lay in the birds. Sprinkle the soy sauce over them and cover with a greased paper. If you don't grease the paper it will stick to the skin.

Cook in a hot oven (Mk 8, 450°F, 250°C) for 25 mins reducing to very moderate (Mk 3, 325°F, 170°C) for another 25 mins. It is most important that the birds are basted frequently, so that the soy sauce gradually coats the birds with a lovely dark glaze. Then put them on their dish, still covered, to rest for 10–15 minutes.

While the pheasants are cooking, prepare the leek sauce. Trim the leeks so that you are left with 1 lb which should include a fair bit of the green part as this gives the sauce its lovely colour. Chop them and put in a pan with 2 oz softened butter. Cover the pan and cook over a low heat, shaking the pan or stirring, until the leeks are soft but not browned. Then liquidise to a smooth paste.

In a thick-bottomed pan, heat 1 oz butter until all the moisture has gone out of it and it is well browned (not burnt!). Take off the heat immediately to prevent further cooking, and stir in the leek purée. Dilute the sauce with the cream, and a little water if necessary, and season to taste. Keep the sauce warm over a pan of hot water to prevent the cream from turning oily.

With the pan juices make some thin gravy by skimming off most of the fat, using only a little cornflour to soak up the excess, and thinning it with a mixture of white wine and chicken stock.

Pour the sauce around the pheasants so that the dark brown birds contrast with the green sauce, and serve the gravy separately.

pheasant with walnuts

This is more or less Escoffier's recipe for Pheasant à la Géorgienne, and has a suitably autumnal taste. The green tea and walnuts give a faintly bitter tang which I find rather pleasant. You can reduce it, though, by omitting the tea and removing the walnut skins. A young pheasant is recommended here, but an older one may be used as long as it is not overcooked. In either case, slice the meat as thinly as possible.

Serves 4

1 pheasant
2 oz (50 g) butter
6 oz (170 g) shelled walnuts
¾ pt (450 m) grape juice
juice 4 small oranges
2 fl oz (60 ml) Malmsey *or* sherry
2 fl oz (60 ml) strong green tea
1 oz (25 g) flour
1 oz (25 g) butter
salt, pepper

If you want to peel the walnuts, do this first. Blanch the nuts in boiling water, and the skins will rub off (eventually!). Brown the pheasant quickly but thoroughly all over in the butter. Then put it in a casserole with the walnuts, the grape and orange juice, sherry and green tea.

Season, then put the lid on and cook in a moderate oven (Mk 4, 350°F, 180°C) for 40 minutes. During this time, turn the pheasant over in the juices so that it stays moist. Then turn the pheasant and walnuts out on to a serving dish and keep them in a warm oven to rest for 10 minutes.

Reduce the cooking liquids to just over ½ pint (300 ml), and check the seasoning. Then mash the flour and butter to a paste and whisk it into the sauce till thickened. Pour it over the pheasant and serve at once, carving very thin slices.

pheasant pastries with pear and spinach

You are well advised to have everything to hand before starting this recipe. It should be done quickly so that everything stays warm. If using yoghourt instead of cream, reduce the quantity slightly, and do not boil in case it curdles.

Serves 4

1 large pheasant
2 oz (50 g) butter
1 lb (450 g) puff pastry
egg yolk *or* milk
3 oz (80 g) spinach leaves
1 large ripe pear
1 tablesp brandy
6 fl oz (180 ml) cream *or* yoghourt
2 tablesp sherry
salt, pepper

Roll the pastry into four rectangles ¼ inch (5 mm) thick. Place on a baking sheet and brush with egg yolk or milk. With the tip of a sharp knife score a line round the top, ½ inch (10 mm) from the edge. Bake in a hot oven (Mk 8, 450°F, 230°C) for 10–15 minutes till risen and golden. Lift off the lids and scrape out any soggy interior. Keep pastries and lids warm.

Spread half the butter over the pheasant, season, and roast in a hot oven (Mk 8, 450°F, 230°C) for 20 minutes, turning once. Then leave to rest for 5–10 minutes—the meat should be nicely rosy.

Meanwhile blanch the spinach leaves, drain, and refresh them in cold water. Drain and chop. Peel and core the pear and chop finely. Melt the remaining butter and add the pear and brandy. Bring to the boil, then add the spinach and 4 tablespoons of the cream. Let everything cook and reduce a little and keep warm.

When the pheasant is cooked, remove to a board and quickly carve as many slices of thin meat as you can. Drain the butter out of the dish and deglaze with the sherry. Add the remaining cream and let it reduce and thicken quickly.

Into each pastry case, put a layer of pear and spinach and a layer of pheasant meat. Spoon the sauce over the top and replace the lids. Serve at once.

pheasant with mustard cheese sauce

This is the way that John likes to cook pheasant and guinea fowl. The basis is one of his beloved Elizabeth David's recipes for chicken, to which he adds his own touches.

Serves 4

2 small pheasants
2 oz (50 g) pheasant *or* chicken livers
onions, carrots, herbs
1 glass white wine
4½ oz (125 g) butter
2 tablesp flour
¼ pt (150 ml) double cream
dessertsp whole grain mustard
2 tablesp sharp cooking cheese
salt, pepper, tarragon *or* chervil

Cut the pheasants into joints, trimming off the wings. Put the wings, giblets and livers into a pan with some chopped onion and carrot and a few herbs. Add ½ pt (300 ml) water and the white wine and simmer for ½–¾ hour to make ¼ pt (150 ml) stock. Strain, but reserve the livers.

Brown the pheasant pieces all over in 3 oz (80 g) of the butter and remove to a roasting tin, pouring all the butter over them with 1–2 tablespoons of water. Roast in a medium oven (Mk 4, 350°F, 180°C) for 1–1½ hours, turning them over and basting from time to time.

Melt the remaining 1½ oz (40 g) butter, stir in the flour and cook for a moment. A little at a time, beat in the strained stock until smooth. Stir in the cream gradually and cook over a very low heat for 5 minutes.

Then stir in the mustard and grated cheese, and season with salt, pepper and a good pinch of tarragon or chervil. Pound the livers to a paste, discarding any gristle, and stir in to the sauce. Continue cooking very slowly for another 10 minutes.

When the pheasant has cooked, put the pieces in a serving dish. Skim off all the fat from the roasting dish and scrape any pan juices into the sauce. Pour the sauce over the pheasant and brown the top in a very hot oven or under the grill.

faisan normande (three recipes)

Here is a review rather than an ultimate recipe, since there are endless good versions of this culinary ode to autumn. You might argue that we should call it Devonshire pheasant, since that county produces apples and cream every bit as delicious as those in Normandy, but it just so happens that the French thought of it first. The combination of apples, cream and pheasant (or partridge) is particularly good, though one version does without cream. If the amount of cream makes you gasp, then the first version can be made with yoghourt instead. It will not then be Faisan Normande of course, but it will be a good dish. Cox's orange pippins make a good substitute for the reinette apples recommended in France.

Recipe 1

Serves 4

1 young pheasant
4 sweet apples
salt
4 oz (110 g) butter
6 tablesp double cream

This is the most common version with an uncomplicated country approach. Peel, core and slice the apples. Sauté them quickly in 2 oz (50 g) of the butter. They should only brown, not cook. Sprinkle with salt and remove to a plate. Melt the remaining butter and brown the pheasant really thoroughly all over. Put a layer of apples on the base of a casserole, place the pheasant on top and arrange the rest round the edge. Pour on the cream and cook, uncovered, in a moderate oven (Mk 4, 350°F, 180°C) for 20–25 minutes, and serve from the dish. The cream turns to a light curd in the buttery apple juices.

Recipe 2

Serves 4

1 young pheasant
4 sweet apples
4 oz (110 g) butter
small glass brandy *or*
    Calvados
⅓ pt (200 ml) double cream

This version has a smoother sauce, and more of it. Sauté the apples and pheasant as before, but sprinkle only 3 tablespoons of cream over the apples. Season and cook as above for 20 minutes. Then lift out the pheasant to a warm serving dish. Remove the apples with a slotted spoon and arrange round the pheasant. Keep them warm while you make the sauce.

Pour all the juices into a small pan and bring to the boil. Add the Calvados and ignite. You can use most spirits with equal effect. Calvados is the most authentic, but brandy, gin, or whisky will do just as well since the juices are already apple-flavoured. When the flames stop, add the remaining cream and simmer until the sauce has thickened a little. Pour it over the pheasant and apples. Elizabeth David's version (Faisan à la Cauchoise) is virtually the same except that the apples are not cooked alongside the bird, but sautéed and served as a side dish. She uses only two apples but more cream, nearly ½ pt (300 ml).

Recipe 3

Serves 4

1 pheasant
4 sweet apples
3 oz (80 g) butter
large glass dry cider
pinch cinnamon
salt, pepper

The amounts of cream in the previous recipes have been relentlessly increasing—here is the version without any. Like the first it has honest country appeal. Prepare and sauté the pheasant and apples as before. Pour the cider over the apples and season with salt and pepper. The merest suspicion of cinnamon is good too, but don't overdo it. Cook as before, for 25 minutes, then leave to rest for 5 minutes before serving straight from the dish.

quickly cooked pheasant in a wine and blackcurrant sauce

I used this recipe to show a friend that pheasant need not be cooked for hours to be tender. The only part that must not be hurried is the stock and sauce.

Serves 4–6

2 pheasants
2 oz (50 g) butter
2 rashers bacon
6 oz (170 g) mixed vegetables for stock
½ pt (300 ml) red wine
3 tablesp blackcurrants
½ teasp cornflour (optional)

Put the pheasants, upside down, in a small dish, spread with the butter and bake in a hot oven (Mk 6, 400°F, 200°C) for 20–25 minutes—no more. This will brown the backs of the birds nicely, and leave the breasts moist. As soon as you can handle them, remove the four fillets from the breast. They will be quite pink, but this is as it should be. If you want to make your two pheasants stretch for six people, then you must remove the thighs also and take out the bone. The thighs won't, I'm afraid, slice neatly, but they will taste fine. Leave the meat aside, unsliced for the time being.

Put the remaining meat and broken up carcases into a large pan. Brown the bacon and mixed vegetables in the butter left from cooking the pheasant and add all of this to the pan along with any juices. Cover with water and add the red wine and blackcurrants. Bring slowly to the boil and simmer for 1–2 hours. Then strain off the liquid and reduce to just over ¼ pint (150 ml). Skim if necessary. By this time it should be thickened and a good dark brown. Season to taste. If you feel that the sauce needs thickening at all, then add just a tiny amount of cornflour dissolved in water.

Cut the pheasant meat on the slant to make neat slices and gently warm them through with a tablespoon or two of the sauce without actually cooking them any more. Place a tablespoon of sauce on each plate and arrange the slices on top to serve. The Carrot and Spinach Parcels (p. 182) go very well with this dish.

pheasant in a gin sauce

Escoffier has a recipe for roe venison cutlets in a gin sauce. It is very good, and I thought it would work well with pheasant. It does.

Serves 4

1 pheasant
4 juniper berries
3 oz (80 g) butter
2 tablesp gin
3 fl oz (75 ml) double cream
4 tablesp concentrated stock
   or consommé
1 lb (450 g) eating apples
water
1 oz (25 g) butter
sugar, lemon juice (optional)
pinch of salt

Grind the juniper berries really fine with a pinch of salt and rub this all over the pheasant. In a fireproof casserole, quickly brown the pheasant all over in the butter, then roast in a fairly hot oven (Mk 6, 400°F, 200°C) for 30 minutes. Turn it frequently during the cooking, and baste. Remove to a serving dish and keep warm.

While the pheasant cooks, make the apple sauce. Peel, core and chop the apples. Melt the butter in a small pan and add the apples. Put the lid on and, over a low heat, keep shaking the pan until the apples are soft. Beat to a pulp, and moisten with a little water or apple juice if necessary. A little sugar, or lemon, or both, may need to be added, but the sauce should only be lightly sweetened.

Skim off most of the butter from the pheasant's casserole. Add the gin and set fire to it, shaking the casserole. Then add the cream and dissolve all the pan juices. Stir in the stock or consommé and season to taste. Serve with the pheasant and apple sauce.

pheasant with stilton or roquefort

Elga Giudici told me that I must include Pheasant with Roquefort in this book. This is a pretty robust dish and suits a well-hung bird admirably.

Serves 4

1 pheasant
6 oz (170 g) Stilton *or*
   Roquefort
8 oz (225 g) leeks
2½ oz (65 g) butter
salt, pepper
rounded tablesp flour
½ pt (300 ml) milk
a little stock for gravy

Take the pheasant and separate the skin of the breast from the meat with your fingers. Normally the skin is quite tough, but with a very high bird you may need to take extra care. Crumble a quarter of the cheese (the whiter part) and distribute it under the skin, reaching as far as possible over the thighs and legs as well.

Wash the leeks and discard any limp leaves. Then cut off most of the green tops, leaving behind about 6 oz (170 g). Stuff the tops inside the bird with ½ oz (15 g) of the butter. These are not for eating, but merely to impart aroma and keep the bird moist. Season with salt and pepper.

Melt 1 oz (25 g) butter in a small dish that will contain the pheasant snugly and place the bird upside down in the dish. Roast in a moderate oven (Mk 4, 350°F, 180°C) for 30–40 minutes. During the cooking turn the bird on to each of its sides, basting frequently. Then turn it the right way up, baste again, and keep in a very cool oven for 15–20 minutes while the sauce is prepared.

Slice the remaining leeks finely and soften them in the rest of the butter in a pan with the lid on. Do not let them brown. Scatter the flour on top to absorb the butter and beat to remove any lumps. Then stir in the milk, bit by bit, as you would for a white sauce. Stir and simmer gently for 10–15 minutes, then purée the sauce.

Return it to the pan and crumble in the cheese, stirring until it has melted in. Season to taste with salt and plenty of pepper and serve with the pheasant. A very little thin gravy may be made from the pheasant's roasting dish. Skim off any fat and deglaze the dish with a little stock and water, seasoning if necessary.

salmis of pheasant

A salmis is made from any kind of game that has been quickly roasted so that it is still rare. A wine sauce is then made from the bones and trimmings. Often this is a clear sauce, but it may be lightly thickened, either by using sauce ragoût (p. 166) in lieu of stock, or beurre manié (p. 15).

Serves 4

2 small pheasants
4 oz (110 g) butter
glass sherry
1 onion
1 carrot
2 sticks celery
bouquet garni of thyme, parsley, bay leaf, clove and mace
½ pt (300 ml) red wine
¾ pt (425 ml) game stock
salt, pepper
4 oz (110 g) mushrooms

Cook the pheasants on their sides in the butter in a hot oven (Mk 8, 450°F, 230°C) for 30 minutes, turning them over once. They should be quite rare. As soon as they are cool enough to handle, cut off the wings, drumsticks, the four breasts and thighs. Put them between two plates to weight lightly as they cool.

Break up the carcases and put them into a large pan. Dissolve the juices from the roasting tin with the sherry and add them to the pan. Chop the vegetables and add those, with the bouquet garni, to the pan. No salt or pepper yet. Add the game stock and wine, bring to the boil and simmer for 1 hour. Then strain this enriched stock and boil rapidly till it has reduced to just over ½ pint (300 ml). Now season to taste.

Slice the mushrooms thinly and simmer them briefly in the stock till softened. At this stage a small amount (½ oz/15 g butter to ½ oz/15 g flour) of beurre manié may be whisked in.

The pheasant may be presented in joints or else sliced thinly. I think the latter is preferable, though bear in mind that it will then warm through very quickly. Just before serving, add the pheasant to the sauce salmis and very gently warm it thoroughly. The sauce should barely simmer as the meat will toughen quickly.

sweet and sour pheasant

Whereas I wouldn't consider this recipe to be the ultimate way in which to enjoy a pheasant, nonetheless if you have a glut of them and long for a change, then you might like to try this one. It is a good recipe for a well-hung pheasant since its flavour can cope with the powerful sauce.

Serves 4

1 pheasant
1 small onion
1 plump clove garlic
1 teasp crystallised ginger
2 tablesp olive oil
2 tablesp red wine vinegar
1 tablesp dry sherry
2 tablesp fresh orange juice
pinch of salt
8 turns black pepper
2 tablesp brown sugar
2 tablesp tomato purée
1 heaped tablesp cornflour

If your pheasant is young and tender, you may skip the marinade procedure, but if, as well as being well hung, you suspect that it is old and tough, then a marinade will be necessary. You can either choose a lusty one from the section on p. 159 or else use some of the above ingredients thus:

Chop the onion very finely and crush the garlic. If the ginger is not already in flakes slice it as thinly as you can. Mix these together with the oil, wine vinegar and orange juice, adding an extra tablespoon of wine vinegar instead of the sherry.

Check that the pheasant has no sharp bones protruding, and put it in a thick polythene bag with the marinade. This is advisable because the small quantity of marinade will not sufficiently wet the pheasant in a bowl. Gently turn the bird around in this marinade for 24–36 hours and then drain off the marinade into a bowl. Pat the pheasant dry.

Into the bowl of marinade add the rest of the ingredients, mixing the cornflour first with a little water to liquefy it.

If you are not marinading the pheasant, chop the onion, crush the garlic and slice the ginger thinly and mix them with the rest of the ingredients.

Put the pheasant, upside down, into a small roasting dish and pour the sauce all over it. Roast in a moderately hot oven (Mk 6, 400°F, 200°C) for 45 minutes, then turn down to moderate (Mk 4, 350°F, 180°C) for a further 45 minutes. This will make the pheasant fairly well-done, which is more appropriate to this sauce.

During the cooking turn the pheasant on to each of its sides for a period, finally turning it the right way up so that the top becomes nicely glazed. Every time the pheasant is turned, scoop up the sauce, which comes progressively more dark and glutinous, and baste the pheasant with it, making sure that the final basting is very thorough so that the top is well covered.

You will need to serve it in another dish because the roasting tin will look a little messy. Serve with plain boiled rice and a refreshing vegetable, such as marrow, or salad.

slow-roasted pheasant with mustard and beer

This is very similar to the venison recipe on p. 135, but it is a good way to cook pheasant. Unlike quickly-roasted pheasant, which should be served as soon as it is ready, this one can wait around a bit without spoiling.

Serves 4

1 large pheasant
2 oz (50 g) lard
4 heaped teasp French
    mustard
salt, pepper
¾ pt (450 ml) brown ale
rounded tablesp dark brown
    sugar

Cut the lard into thin slices. With your fingers, carefully ease the skin off the pheasant away from the breasts and legs—avoid tearing it. Distribute at least half of the lard under the skin, making sure that the legs are well covered as well as the breast. Do likewise with half of the mustard (this is a rather messy procedure). Pull back the skin to its original position and season with salt and pepper. Lay the remaining lard over the top of the pheasant and put it in an open roasting tin with the brown ale.

Roast in a moderately hot oven (Mk 5, 375°F, 190°C) for half an hour, basting at least twice with the beer. Then turn the oven down to cool (Mk 2, 300°F, 150°C) and cook for another hour, still basting from time to time with the beer.

Then spread the remaining mustard over the pheasant, and dredge with the dark brown sugar. If you only have one oven, pop the pheasant under a medium grill to cook the sugar and mustard (about 5 minutes), then baste gently. I just put the pheasant back into the hot oven of the Aga for 10 minutes, then baste.

The pheasant will sit happily in a cool oven for a while if need be, but give it an occasional baste. The beer has by now turned into superb gravy—all you need do is skim off the fat and check the seasoning.

Gallina Africana.

guinea fowl with black grapes

The combination of grapes and game birds is long-standing and very good. I like to use guinea fowl because the legs are less sinewy; somehow gnawing bones seems out of place when grapes are around.

Serves 4

1 guinea fowl
1 lb (450 g) black grapes
3 oz (80 g) mild fatty cooked
  ham
3 oz (80 g) butter
4 thin rashers streaky pork
2 glasses rosé *or* red wine
salt, pepper

Halve and stone the grapes and chop the ham. Mix the ham with 1 oz (25 g) of the butter and half of the grapes and stuff this into the bird. Spread the remaining butter over the top, season with salt and pepper and lay the pork over the breast.

Roast in a hot oven (Mk 7, 425°F, 220°C) for 30 minutes, basting frequently with the wine and butter. Then remove to a cool oven to rest and finish cooking. Skim the pan juices and reduce to a good strong gravy, adding the remaining grapes near the end so that they are warmed through but not cooked to a pulp. Season to taste and pour over the guinea fowl.

guinea fowl with a savoury zabaglione

In northern Italy roasted game birds are served with zabaglione poured over them. It is very sweet and not to my taste at all. I prefer this savoury version. The golden glaze is what imparts flavour, so if you are stuck, boil down equal amounts of white wine and chicken stock until very concentrated.

However, if you want to try the Italian version, roast the bird as described below, and make the zabaglione thus: Beat 3 egg yolks and 3 rounded teasp sugar together until frothy and pale. Add ½ wine glass of Marsala and stir over a very low heat until thickened.

Serves 4–6

1 large guinea fowl
3 oz (80 g) butter

Sauce
2 egg yolks
6 tablesp single cream
3 tablesp Golden Glaze
  (p. 164)
4 oz (110 g) butter
salt, pepper, lemon juice

Put the guinea fowl on its side into a casserole with the butter and roast in a hot oven (Mk 7, 425°F, 220°C) for 15 minutes, then turn the oven down to (Mk 4, 350°F, 180°C) for a further 40 minutes. From time to time, turn it over and baste with the buttery juices. When it is done, put it on to a serving dish and keep it warm while it rests for 15–20 minutes.

When the guinea fowl is nearly cooked, prepare the sauce. If you feel confident about making egg-yolk sauces, this can be done in an ordinary saucepan, but care must be taken, as the egg yolks will scramble if overheated. A safer but slower method is to use a bain-marie or a bowl over a pan of steaming water.

Make sure the butter is fairly soft. If you want to economise, pour the butter off the cooked guinea fowl and make up to 4 oz (100 g).

In the bowl or pan, beat the egg yolks and cream together, then beat in the golden glaze. A wire whisk will produce the lightest results. Continue to whisk over a low heat until you have a creamy coating consistency. Then draw the pan off the heat (or take the bowl off the steam). Bit by bit, beat the softened butter into the sauce, which will then thicken like a hollandaise sauce. Then season carefully, adding just a drop or two of lemon juice, and either pour the sauce over the roasted guinea fowl (this is the Italian way) or serve separately.

If it looks as though the sauce is going to be ready well ahead of time, keep it warm over lukewarm water. Hot water would continue to cook it. I sometimes reserve the last piece of butter and whisk it in at the last minute. Give the sauce an occasional stir while it waits just in case it should think of separating.

guinea hen à la numide

This is Alexis Soyer's suggestion for roasting guinea fowl, inspired by his delving into the gastronomic delights of Roman feasting. Worcestershire sauce is our most convenient substitute for 'garum', but garum was actually a fermented fish condiment and some of the oriental fish sauces are undoubtedly more authentic.

Serves 3–4

1 guinea fowl
3 juniper berries
2–3 shakes Worcestershire
 sauce
1 oz (25 g) butter
1 tablesp clear honey
1 tablesp Worcestershire
 sauce
salt

Although not essential, this dish is greatly improved if the guinea fowl is boned and rolled up first as it cooks more evenly.

Turn to p. 12 for boning instructions. When the floppy rag of skin and meat is lying on the slab, scrape the leg and wing meat to the centre to make an even layer with plenty of skin for rolling. Crush the juniper berries very finely (a little goes a long way) and sprinkle on to the meat. Moisten with 2 or 3 shakes of Worcestershire sauce and season with a pinch of salt. Roll up into a nice plump sausage, secure the end with a cocktail stick and keep it flat.

Melt the butter till it stops bubbling and brown the roll thoroughly all over. Turn the meat and butter into a hot roasting tin and bake in a very hot oven (Mk 9, 475°F, 240°C) for 10 minutes. Then drain off the butter and dissolve the honey and Worcestershire sauce in the tin. Over a gentle heat, turn the roll around in this liquid for another 5–10 minutes. Slice very thinly.

To cook it whole, put the juniper berries into the cavity, brown in butter and roast at Mk 7, 425°F, 220°C for 15 minutes, or until cooked to taste. My cooking times give moist rosy meat.

spiced guinea fowl

Even John liked this one (and he hates curries), because the spices are used in moderation and don't drown the taste of guinea fowl. There is not much in the way of gravy, so a sauce of some kind is necessary. Try the Red Wine Sauce (p. 170) or the Roman Honey Sauce (p. 175).

Serves 4

1 guinea fowl
1 lemon
fresh root ginger
2 cloves garlic
¼ teasp curry powder
¼ teasp cayenne pepper
½ teasp coriander
½ teasp ground mace
2 tablesp oil
salt

Grate the lemon peel and root ginger medium fine. A dessert-spoonful of the latter is sufficient. Crush the garlic. Mix these together with the rest of the spices and a pinch of salt. Stir in one tablespoon of oil and spread the ensuing paste all over the guinea fowl. Tuck half of the grated lemon inside the bird.

Put the other spoonful of oil into a small baking dish and lay in the guinea fowl. Cover the top and sides with foil and roast in a moderate oven (Mk 4, 350°F, 180°C). Baste once or twice with the spiced oil.

Once some juices emerge from the cavity of the bird, you may add the juice of the remaining lemon. If you do this too soon it simply burns on to the dish. An hour's cooking will be ample, then turn off the oven and leave the door ajar so that the meat can rest for 10 minutes. If you don't wish to make a sauce, serve instead with rice into which a lightly spiced vinaigrette has been stirred, and some juicy vegetables.

guinea fowl with chestnuts

In France, guinea fowl are reared commonly in the farmyard, very much as we rear chickens. Before killing them, they give the creatures a spoonful of cognac. This is not, alas, intended as a pleasant anaesthetic, though I daresay it helps, but to improve the flavour and texture of the birds. Chestnuts are also very common in parts of France, and many of the local recipes make use of them. Here is a good and simple example.

Serves 4

1 guinea fowl
1 lb (450 g) chestnuts
2 oz (50 g) butter
½ pt (300 ml) good stock
1 onion
2 cloves garlic

Slit the chestnuts, boil them gently until tender and then peel them. If you use dried chestnuts, soak them overnight, after bringing them to the boil in either water or, better still, some stock. Start off by roasting the guinea fowl upside down (this prevents the breasts from drying up) in the butter in a moderate oven (Mk 5, 375°F, 190°C), and basting two or three times with some of the stock.

Cut the onion into thin rings and when the bird has been in the oven for 20 minutes, take it out of its dish, put in the onions, chestnuts and crushed garlic and replace the bird, the right way up this time. Add the rest of the (warmed) stock and continue the cooking and basting for another 30 minutes or so, by which time the chestnuts should have absorbed some of the juices.

Slow Cooking

There are often times when we don't feel inclined to watch diligently over a carefully roasted bird. It is comforting, then, to be able to cook it slowly without undue worry as to timing. Many of these recipes are even better when neglected for an hour or so in a cool oven, or when reheated the next day—usually the longer you give them, the better the flavours marry together. They are also ideal for the bird of uncertain age which has lost the versatility of youth. Whereas the latter can be safely roasted in a moderate oven to past the pink stage, an older bird is simply too tough.

Grouse and partridge can be successfully cooked using these recipes. Because they are slightly smaller you will need to either increase the number of birds (1 bird for 2 people), or reduce the rest of the ingredients accordingly, but the cooking times remain the same.

good old pheasant casserole

I hesitate to call this goulash because it is not the genuine article, but the paprika and sour cream make it rather like one. Children enjoy pheasant cooked this way, rating the gravy higher than tomato ketchup—a rare compliment indeed. It is a good way to cook really old pheasants, though where children are present I wouldn't hang them (the pheasants, I mean) too high.

Serves 4

1 large pheasant
6 oz (150 g) bacon
2 onions
2 carrots
2 oz (50 g) dripping
flour
1½ pt (850 ml) good stock
1 glass red wine (optional)
heaped teasp sweet paprika
bouquet garni
4 big tomatoes
2 tablesp sour cream
  (optional)

Cut the pheasant into joints and remove loose bones. Cut thick slices of bacon into chunks, or roll up bacon rashers. Chop the onions and carrots. Brown bacon, onions and carrots in the dripping and remove to a casserole. Then roll the pheasant pieces in flour, brown them and add to the casserole. Stir a tablespoon more flour into the pan to absorb the fat and moisten with the stock. Bring to the boil and pour into the casserole.

If the stock is really good, wine is not necessary, but add a glass if you like. Stir in the paprika, bouquet garni and halved tomatoes, and cook in a slow oven (Mk 2, 300°F, 150°C) for about 3 hours. If you want to, swirl in the sour cream just before serving.

pheasant in a thick red wine sauce

Don't be fooled by the title—this is of course the classic Coq au Vin. With most modern chickens having so little flavour, I would venture to suggest that by using a pheasant instead, the end-result is more akin to the original dish. Most books on French cooking have a recipe and, though the method sometimes varies, the basics are always the same—the accompanying bacon, mushrooms and onions, the flambéing, the rich reduced sauce. It is not in the least difficult, and when correctly made it is superb.

Serves 8

2 pheasants
8 oz (225 g) chunk of streaky
    bacon, *or* 8 rashers
    streaky bacon
4 oz (110 g) butter
2 tablesp oil
24 pickling onions
12 oz (340 g) mushrooms
wine glass brandy
1 bottle red wine
1 pt (570 ml) Dark Game
    Stock (p. 165)
4 plump cloves garlic
2 bay leaves
sprigs thyme and parsley
1 tablesp tomato purée
2 oz (50 g) beurre manié
    (p. 15)
pepper, salt

Cut each pheasant into four joints, and remove any small bones (particularly ribs) that look as though they might detach themselves. If you are using bacon rashers roll them up and secure with cocktail sticks. Otherwise cut the bacon into sticks about an inch long.

In a small pan, melt half of the butter with the oil and roll the pickling onions around in it until they are nicely browned. Then remove them to a bowl for later. If the mushrooms are large, cut them in half—button mushrooms can be left whole. Sauté them in the same pan and keep them aside with the onions.

Into a large fireproof casserole, strain any butter/oil left from the mushrooms and gently brown the bacon. Eventually the bacon will exude its own fat. Remove the bacon and melt the rest of the butter. Brown the pheasant pieces all over—you will need to do this in batches. Return the bacon to the casserole, underneath the pheasant if possible, put the lid on and reduce the heat to cook bacon and pheasant together for 5–10 minutes, shaking the casserole so that they don't stick.

Then remove the lid, pour in brandy and ignite it. Be prepared to leap backwards—fast—as this can be a somewhat exciting procedure and false eyelashes are tedious to apply. Shake the casserole to burn off all the alcohol, but watch the cocktail sticks.

When the flaming has finished, pour the wine over the meat and add enough stock to cover. Add two crushed garlic cloves. Tie the other two into a little cloth with the bay leaves, thyme and parsley and throw them in. Add the tomato purée, give the whole lot a stir, then cover and bring to a slow simmer. (Sir Kenelme Digbie describes this process admirably: Directing us to cook it 'very leisurely and but simpringly . . . or it will not be tender but hard and tough', he conjures up a vivid picture of a pot steaming gently, giving the occasional bubble from time to time).

Cook like this for 1 hour, adding the onions after 30 minutes and the mushrooms 15 minutes later. Then remove the bag of herbs and pheasant pieces. Boil down the liquid to about 1½ pints (850 ml). Then draw it off the heat and whisk in the beurre manié. Simmer gently for a few minutes to thicken the sauce. Then replace the pheasant and for a further 30 minutes let it very slowly simmer as before. Sometimes I finish off the cooking in a slow oven (Mk 2, 300°F, 150°C).

Some people may maintain that the pheasant will be cooked to rags but this is not so. The pieces are firm but tender and imbued with the flavour of the wine. However, if you prefer meat less well cooked, and if you are sure that the bird is tender (most guinea fowl should be), then cut down the initial cooking to 30 minutes, reduce and thicken the sauce as described, and merely warm the meat in it for 5 minutes or so before serving.

pheasant with watercress

This is a refreshing way to eat a young pheasant. Crème fraîche is double cream which has been matured until thick but not actually sour (see p. 15). It should not be confused with soured cream which will curdle when boiled. Ordinary double cream will do instead. However, if you prefer the extra sharpness and lower butterfat of soured cream or yoghourt, you must forgo the final boiling.

Serves 4

1 pheasant
2 tablesp oil
¼ pt (150 ml) good stock
1 bunch watercress
¼ pt (150 ml) crème fraîche
salt, pepper

Heat the oil in a fireproof casserole and brown the pheasant thoroughly all over. Pour in the stock, cover, and simmer for 30 minutes, turning the pheasant from time to time.

Meanwhile wash and drain the watercress. Discard any yellowed leaves and chop the rest coarsely.

When the pheasant is done, lift it out and carve into four pieces. Keep them covered and warm in the serving dish.

Put the watercress into the casserole and let it soften gently for 10 minutes. If the stock has reduced to nothing, you may need to add a tiny splash of water. Add the cream and let it boil until the sauce is slightly thickened. Season to taste, then pour it over the pheasant pieces and serve immediately.

pheasant and blackcurrant casserole

This is what I call an Albert-type dish—slow cooked and fruity. Although it is not my favourite pheasant dish, I have put it in because other people enjoy it. Because of the slow cooking, older birds can successfully be used after marinating. My hungry eaters were surprised to learn that neither wine nor cream was used here.

Serves 4

1 large pheasant
well-seasoned flour
8 oz (225 g) blackcurrants
½ pt (300 ml) good game stock
1 tablesp brown sugar
butter

Cut the pheasant into four portions and marinate with a Cider or general marinade (see p. 161 or p. 160). Then pat the pieces dry and roll them in well-seasoned flour. Brown thoroughly and put them in a casserole with the blackcurrants, stock and sugar. Bring to simmering point and cook in a very moderate oven (Mk 3, 325°F, 170°C) for 2–3 hours depending on the age of the bird.

When the pheasant is tender, remove the pieces to a warm serving dish. Liquidise the cooking liquids to a purée. If you don't like the little bits of blackcurrant left in the sauce, then sieve it as well. Check the seasoning. If the sauce is a little thin, as it may be if a young pheasant not needing lengthy cooking was used, reduce it before pouring over the pheasant.

Perdix cinerea
The Comōn Partridge

slow-cooked pheasant with celery

This is an excellent way of cooking a pheasant when you feel uneasy about its age. The very slow cooking means that the meat never toughens up, and the bed of celery ensures that it keeps moist. As an informal meal, one pheasant will do four people, two of whom will have some finger-licking work with the drumsticks. For a more formal occasion it might be kinder to use two pheasants and discard the drumsticks, giving everyone a white and dark meat joint.

Serves 4

1 large *or* 2 small pheasant
flour, salt, pepper
2 oz (50 g) butter
12 oz (340 g) celery
2 wine glasses white wine

Cut the pheasant into four joints, and roll them in the seasoned flour. Heat the butter in a large frying pan and brown the joints well all over, making sure they do not crowd the pan.

Chop the celery into ½-inch (120-mm) pieces and line the bottom of a dish with it. This should accommodate the pheasant joints snugly in one layer. Lay the pieces over the celery, scatter a pinch or two of the remaining flour over the top, and sprinkle the wine over all. I generally use a medium dry wine, but a sweet one will give good, though different, results.

Cover the dish with foil and put it into a hot oven (Mk 8, 450°F, 230°C) for 10–15 minutes to warm through, and then turn right down to cool (Mk 1, 275°F, 140°C) for a further 3–4 hours. A slow cooker would be admirable for this job.

Gallina Guinea
The Guiny Hen.

game for all galantine

I thought I'd make an extravaganza to include all my game meats. You must have salmon and trout as a first course. We had this hot instead of a goose one Christmas, but it's actually easier to carve, and very good, served cold with Cumberland Sauce (p. 176) or Cold Green Sauce (p. 171). Make sure the pheasant skin is not torn or the filling may squeeze out; and the job is made easier if there is a long flap of skin left at the neck.

Serves 6

1 huge pheasant or guinea
  fowl
2 pigeons
oil and red or white wine (for
  marinade)
3 quails
2 oz (50 g) venison liver
4 oz (110 g) butter or bacon
  fat
1 clove garlic
1 tablespoon breadcrumbs
2 oz (50 g) petit-suisse
1 egg
cream or milk
6 dried apricots
1 large bacon rasher
1 shallot
1 dessertsp pinhead oatmeal
1 dessertsp chopped almonds
1 wine glass of water, wine or
  stock
ground mace
a few juniper berries
salt, pepper

Bone the pheasant or guinea fowl, removing the thigh bones but leaving the drumsticks intact (see p. 12). Take the breasts off the pigeons and slice three in half horizontally. Beat them very hard to tenderise, then marinade in a little oil or wine. Reserve the fourth. Lift the fillets off the quails. All the carcases can now be made into excellent game stock.

Chop the venison liver and gently fry it in 1 oz (25 g) of the butter or bacon fat. Season with salt, pepper and crushed garlic and pound to a paste with the breadcrumbs. Set aside. Chop the remaining pigeon breast finely and pound to a paste with half the petit-suisse, salt, pepper, and a little ground mace and crushed juniper berries. Moisten with half the beaten egg and a little cream or milk. Set aside.

Chop the dried apricots, shallot and bacon finely, and simmer them in a tiny amount of stock or water till soft. Mix in the oatmeal, almonds, and remaining egg. It should be fairly moist.

Now take the floppy pheasant and lay it out before you, skin side downwards. Pull it into a rectangular shape and rearrange the meat as evenly as possible. Spread it with the remaining petit-suisse and then with the venison liver paste. Lay on the marinated pigeon breasts and cover with apricot stuffing. Spread on the pigeon mousse and lay the quail fillets down the centre.

Then get ready a darning needle and some button thread, or a pile of wooden cocktail sticks. Very carefully reassemble the pheasant. Slightly overlap the edges of the skin so that they don't shrink apart in cooking. Secure firmly with thread or cocktail sticks. Press gently into a credible shape and tie the drumsticks neatly.

The galantine is cooked slowly so that everything is cooked through and the flavours develop. Carefully brown it all over in the remaining butter or bacon fat, then turn it, right way up, into a casserole. Pour all the fat over the top and add a wine glass of water, wine or stock. Cover and cook in a very moderate oven (Mk 3, 325°F, 170°C) for 2½–3 hours. Baste frequently.

There will be the makings of some excellent gravy in the dish which can be augmented by all that excellent stock made from the carcases. Slice the galantine crossways rather than in the conventional poultry fashion so that each person gets a bit of everything. You need a very sharp knife.

pheasant in a wine jelly

Here is a very refreshing way to have a pheasant. Despite the fact that it will look gorgeous when turned out, I'm afraid it won't cut into particularly neat slices, but it tastes so good that nobody minds. Potato salad and fresh green or tomato salads are all that is needed to round it off.

Serves 4–6

1 large pheasant
1 pig's trotter *or* calf's foot
2 tomatoes
1 large onion
3 carrots
1 leek
bunch parsley
2 whole garlic cloves
2 pinches salt
½ teasp black peppercorns
½ bottle dry white wine
1 egg-white (optional)
heaped teasp powdered
    gelatine

Put the pheasant, whole, into a large saucepan (a 7-pt one will be ideal) and tuck the pig's trotter, the vegetables, the herbs and the spices snugly in beside it. Pour in the wine and add enough water to barely cover, then clamp a lid on and bring to the boil. Simmer very gently until the meat is really tender and falling off the bones. This will take 2–3 hours depending on the age of the bird.

Retrieve the bird and carrots and put the pan back on to boil and start reducing the liquid. Take all the meat off the pheasant, being most diligent about removing the sinews from the legs. Throw the skin and bones back into the stock while it bubbles away and let it reduce until you have ½ pint (300 ml) of liquid left.

Meanwhile, slice the carrots into rings and divide the larger pieces of meat into strips. Strain the stock through a cloth into a clean pan. It should be pretty clear, but if not you may like to clarify it by whisking in a beaten egg-white and leaving it to simmer gently for about 15 minutes. Strain through a clean cloth. Scatter the gelatine over the stock and allow it to dissolve.

Take a couple of tablespoons of this liquid and swill it around a dish. One with a capacity of 1½ pts (850 ml) will do fine. Arrange a layer of carrots in a pretty pattern on the base. If you like, intersperse it with some parsley or other contrasting colour. Then pack in the meat, making sure that all the gaps are filled and scattering the remaining carrots throughout.

Once the gelatine has dissolved, cover the meat with the stock. Give the bowl a gentle tap to remove any trapped air, and leave to set. Wrap a hot wet towel round the dish to ease turning out. If you really object to the fact that it doesn't cut into neat slices, then you can increase the gelatine and chill everything more thoroughly, but I think the flavour is much better at room temperature, and it seems a pity to turn such a light and delicious jelly into rubber.

braised pieces of pheasant

Inevitably with pheasant, badly shot birds will occur. But do not despair! Although not suitable for roasting whole, they can nevertheless be used for countless other equally good dishes. Normally at least half a bird is usable and in this case I would quarter the carcase, discarding tough drumsticks and poach or braise the good bits. The rest can be made into stock, soup, or a terrine, depending on how battered it is.

Here is one braising suggestion: choose 2 oz (50 g) of mixed vegetables per person. Celery, bulb fennel and carrot go well together, or leeks and tomatoes or carrots. Cut them into strips and soften them in butter—1 oz (25 g) per person will do.

Cut some rounds of tinfoil and put a little bundle of vegetables on to each one. Lay a portion of pheasant on top, and moisten with a few drops of wine vinegar, plus half a small wine glass of wine. Red or white can be used—they are both good but different. Season with salt and black pepper, crimp the foil up into individual parcels and bake them in a moderate oven (Mk 4, 350°F, 180°C) for 20 minutes, and then a cool one (Mk 1, 275°F, 140°C) for ¾ hour.

Let everyone open their own parcel and savour the aroma.

poached pheasant legs

If you make a habit of whipping the supremes off your pheasants, there will be quite a lot of legs left over. I promised Ian Thomson that I'd find a use for them. Because of the sinews in the drumsticks, they are never going to make the most refined of dishes—a certain amount of gnawing is necessary—but the bones keep the meat (particularly the thighs) nicely moist. If feeling generous you might like to cut off the drumsticks and serve two thighs per person instead.

Serves 2–4

4 pheasant legs
1½ oz (40 g) butter
1 large onion
1 large carrot
2 sticks celery
½ pt (300 ml) water
½ oz (15 g) butter
½ oz (15 g) flour
salt, pepper

Brown the pheasant legs gently all over in the butter. Chop the vegetables finely and add them to the pan. Toss them around until slightly softened. Add the water and season with salt and pepper.

Bring to simmering point, cover, and cook gently for 35–40 minutes, by which time the pheasant pieces will be tender and still succulent. Mash the butter and flour together to a paste and whisk it into the gravy to make it smooth and thick.

pheasant legs with mushrooms

Serves 2–4

4 pheasant legs
1 oz (25 g) butter
6 oz (170 g) mushrooms
¼ pt (150 ml) wine
¼ pt (150 ml) water
3 juniper berries
thyme
salt, pepper

Brown the pheasant legs on both sides in a good knob of butter. Then add the mushrooms and toss them in the pan until they have taken up all the excess butter. If the mushrooms are tiny, they may be left whole, otherwise slice them thickly.

Add the wine (it can be red, white or rosé) and water. Crush the juniper berries and add them. Add a good handful of chopped fresh thyme (1 teasp dried) and season with salt and pepper. Bring to simmering point, cover, and cook slowly for 35–40 minutes. Don't use a cast-iron pan, as it will leave a metallic taste.

guinea fowl with fennel

The hint of aniseed in fennel makes it an appropriate accompaniment to guinea fowl, especially when you remember that in France Pernod is often used to flavour guinea fowl dishes.

Serves 6–8

2 guinea fowl
6–8 small heads bulb fennel
2 carrots
2 onions
4 cloves garlic
2 oz (50 g) butter and 2
   tablesp oil
⅓ pt (200 ml) stock
½ bottle white wine
3 tablesp whipping cream
seasoning
fresh fennel leaves (optional)

Cut the onions and carrots into chunks and brown them lightly in the butter and oil. Cut the fennel in half lengthways and brown them also. Put these vegetables with the peeled garlic cloves into a large flameproof casserole with the stock and wine, and simmer for ½ hour.

Meanwhile brown the birds nicely all over in the remains of the butter/oil mixture, and then put them into the casserole, pressing them down into the stock. Cover, and let them bubble away for another hour, then carefully remove the birds and the fennel and arrange them in a dish. Keep them warm while you complete the sauce.

Strain the remaining vegetables, reserving their stock, and purée them. Reduce the stock to just under ½ pint (300 ml), skim it, and then replace the puréed vegetables, seasoning to taste. Add the cream at the last minute. Anyone who is really keen on Pernod could add a capful to the sauce, but I don't consider this necessary.

You can serve the sauce separately or spoon it over the birds, as you wish, but arrange the fennel heads nicely round the dish and decorate with the fresh fennel leaves to relieve the somewhat monochromatic appearance. If you don't have fresh fennel, then blanch some very thin strips of carrot and criss-cross them over the top instead.

guinea fowl with bacon and prunes (two recipes)

Bacon and prunes are a traditional accompaniment to guinea fowl. Here are two methods, one for roasting and one for braising. The guinea fowl is kept moist in the first recipe by stuffing a layer of cream cheese and bacon under the skin. In the second, somewhat lustier recipe, the cooking process makes the meat very tender.

Recipe 1: Roasting

Serves 4

1 guinea fowl
4 oz (110 g) prunes (soaked beforehand)
¼ pt (150 ml) tea
4 oz (110 g) streaky bacon
3 oz (80 g) cream cheese
bunch fresh thyme
2 oz (50 g) butter
the giblets
2 oz (50 g) chicken liver
1 onion
2 carrots
1 leek
1 tablesp soy sauce
salt, pepper

Simmer the prunes in the tea until plump and tender. Drain, reserving the juice in a saucepan for stock. Remove the stones and chop the flesh of the prunes.

Cut the bacon into snippets and gently toss them in a pan until they have exuded some fat and are crisp. Remove from the heat and take out a quarter of the bacon, putting it into the stock pan with the prune juices. Mash the cream cheese into the remaining bacon so that it dissolves any pan brownings, and mix in the fresh thyme leaves.

While the cheese and bacon mixture cools off a little, start making the stock. Put the giblets, plus an extra chicken liver, the chopped vegetables and the soy sauce into the stock pan, bring to the boil, and leave to simmer for 1 hour.

Meanwhile take the guinea fowl, and using your fingers, part the skin of the breast from the meat. Stuff the cheese and bacon mixture under the skin, reaching as far as possible over the legs as well. Press firmly all over to smooth the surface, and pull the skin back to its original position so that it doesn't shrink and expose the meat during cooking. If the skin should be a little torn, secure it with a cocktail stick. Then spread the bird liberally with the butter and season with salt and pepper.

Roast in a moderately hot oven (Mk 5, 375°F, 190°C) for 40 minutes, basting from time to time. Then turn the oven to cool (Mk 2, 300°F, 150°C) to finish off for 10–15 minutes. During the final cooking, complete the sauce. Remove the giblets from the stock, but leave in the liver as it gives an interesting grainy texture to the sauce. Pass the vegetables, liver and juices through a sieve (this is speeded up if you first break them up a little in a blender). There will be quite a lot of residue, mainly from the bacon. If necessary, reduce the sauce to thicken it slightly, and then add the chopped prunes. Season to taste and warm the whole sauce thoroughly before serving it with the roasted guinea fowl.

Recipe 2: Braising

Serves 4

1 guinea fowl
6 oz (170 g) prunes
6 oz (170 g) smoked fatty
  bacon
2 oz (50 g) butter *or* oil
2 onions
¾ pt (425 ml) stock, wine *or*
  water
pepper

Soak the prunes overnight in water or wine. Reserve four or five slices of bacon for barding, and make the rest into bacon rolls, securing with cocktail sticks.

Brown the guinea fowl evenly all over in the butter or oil, being careful not to burn the butter. Remove, then brown the sliced onions in the same pan. Find a casserole into which the guinea fowl fits comfortably and make a layer of the onions on the base. Then lay the guinea fowl on its side, pressing it firmly down into the onions. Season well with black pepper. Arrange the prunes on either side, lay the slices of bacon over the guinea fowl to keep it moist, and pop the bacon rolls on top of the prunes.

Add enough stock, wine or water to come halfway up the bird, cover the casserole and braise in a very moderate oven (Mk 3, 325°F, 170°C) for 2–2½ hours. Halfway through the cooking turn the bird over, replacing the bacon on top. About half an hour before serving, take the lid off the casserole and gently turn the guinea fowl the right way up for carving. Check the seasoning and remove the cocktail sticks from the bacon rolls before serving.

poached guinea fowl with sweet-spiced yoghourt

A smooth creamy sauce which is lightly spiced counteracts the sweetness. You may prefer to choose your own combination of spices instead of using ready-made curry powder. Serve with Saffron Rice.

Serves 4

1 guinea fowl
½ pt (300 ml) dry cider
1 bay leaf
1 small onion
salt, pepper
2 large peaches *or* mangoes
8 fl oz (250 ml) natural
  yoghourt
curry powder
butter or oil

Cut the guinea fowl into four portions, removing breast and back bones. Brown the pieces gently in butter or oil for 5 minutes each side in a deep frying pan (not cast-iron). Then add the cider, the bay leaf and the onion, sliced. Cover, and simmer gently until the pieces are just done (about 20 minutes). Remove them to a warm dish and season with salt and pepper.

Meanwhile, peel and stone the peaches or mangoes, and blend the flesh to a smooth paste with the yoghourt. When the guinea fowl is cooked, add the now reduced cooking liquid (including the onion but not the bay leaf) and blend again. Return to the pan and warm through gently. Season to taste with salt, pepper and curry powder—a little pinch is enough for me, but I don't like over-spiced food. Pour the sauce over the guinea fowl pieces.

Grilling and Concoctions

sautéed pheasant breasts with a garlic cream sauce

There are many versions of this excellent way of cooking a pheasant or guinea fowl. Here is mine—unsophisticated but very delicious nonetheless. Remember that once garlic is cooked it loses some of its pungency. I enjoy garlic but if you have cold feet about it then blanch the garlic in boiling water first.

The only lengthy part of this dish is making the stock but, next to the pheasants themselves, it is the most important ingredient. If you are in a hurry and already have ½ pt (280 ml) of really good game stock then you are well away, but rather than give up altogether, you can get by with tinned consommé. This you can improve by simmering some vegetables, herbs and meat scraps in it for as long as you can manage. Half an hour should suffice. The remains of the two pheasants will then be available for stock-making so that you are well armed for another occasion.

Serves 4

2 pheasants
3 oz (80 g) coarse
    breadcrumbs
1 large clove garlic
butter and oil

For ½ pt (280 ml) stock
the 2 carcases
12 oz (340 g) vegetables:
    onion, carrot, celery,
    tomatoes, leeks
bouquet garni
water and/*or* wine to cover

Sauce
4 plump garlic cloves
1 oz (25 g) butter
scant tablesp flour
¼ pt (125 ml) cream
salt, pepper

Cut off the pheasant breasts, removing the skin and sinews (see p. 10). If you think you may have really old birds, you might want to tenderise them with a steak bat, but I only find this necessary when cooking for someone who refuses meat with the slightest trace of pink in it.

Now make the stock. Cut up the rest of the carcases. I sometimes reserve the thighs for another dish, but I would throw the drumsticks in—you have to have some meat to make a good stock. Brown the bones, meat and vegetables in a hot oven (Mk 7, 425°F, 220°C) for 15–20 minutes, turning them around from time to time so that the fat coats everything evenly, and the bones do not burn. It is not necessary to add extra fat unless the birds are really lean. Turn all this into a pan, rinsing out the pan to scrape up all the caramelised juices. Add the bouquet garni and cover with water, or a mixture of water and white wine. Bring to the boil and simmer for 12 hours. Then strain and reduce to ½ pt (300 ml).

To make the sauce, peel and crush the garlic. Melt the butter and soften the garlic in it without letting it brown (this can make it bitter). Scatter the flour on and stir until smooth, then pour on the hot stock, stirring all the time. Allow this to simmer gently for about 15 minutes to cook the flour and garlic, stirring from time to time. Add the cream and season to taste.

While the sauce simmers, cook the pheasant breasts. Crush the remaining clove of garlic into the breadcrumbs, which are best if slightly stale. Then press the pieces of meat hard into the breadcrumbs so that they are well coated on both sides. Heat the butter and oil in a large frying pan and sauté the pieces gently for 5 or 6 minutes on each side. The flame should not be too fierce or the breadcrumbs will simply burn before the meat is cooked. They should be nicely golden brown. Also, if cooked too fast, the thinner edges of the meat may toughen before the centre begins to cook. A moment or two's relaxation in a warm place will slacken the meat.

To serve, pour the sauce into a serving dish and arrange the crisp pheasant breasts on top.

pheasant with grapes in brandy cream sauce

Philippa Wheeler sent me this recipe from the depths of Sussex. The Wheelers rear a lot of pheasants among other delicious things, and she says that tender young pheasant are a must for this dish.

Serves 4

2 young pheasants
2 onions
4 sticks celery
2 carrots
bouquet garni
6 oz (170 g) black grapes
6 oz (170 g) green grapes
3 oz (80 g) butter
½ glass brandy
¼ pt (150 ml) double cream
croûtons *or* puff pastry
    shapes (optional)
salt, pepper

Remove the flesh from the carcases and cut into chunks. There won't be much meat on the drumsticks but they will improve stock no end. Put the bones and drumsticks into a pan with the onion, celery, carrots (all chopped), and the bouquet garni, and cover with water to make some well-flavoured stock. When it has simmered sufficiently, strain and reduce to about ¾ pt (425 ml). Check the seasoning.

While the stock cooks, halve all the grapes and de-seed them. With any luck your favourite radio programme will be on . . .

Heat the butter in a large pan and very gently cook the pheasant pieces for about 15–20 minutes, until just cooked through. Put them in a casserole to keep warm in a low oven.

Flame the brandy and pour it into the reduced stock. Add the grapes and cream and check the seasoning. Pour it over the cooked pheasant and serve pronto with perhaps croûtons or amusing puff-pastry shapes.

smoked ham with a pheasant filling

This is a lovely dish. We used to have it as children with just the ham and celery hearts, but I felt it wasn't quite substantial enough. The creamy pheasant filling completes it perfectly, and it is a good use for odd scraps of pheasant meat.

Serves 6

1 lb (450 g) pheasant meat
½ pt (300 ml) stock (from pheasant trimmings)
1 dessertsp tomato purée
1 oz (25 g) butter
4 oz (110 g) minced belly of pork
2 oz (50 g) fine white breadcrumbs
¼ pt (150 ml) double cream
18 slices raw smoked ham
6 celery hearts, braised *or* tinned
salt, pepper

First make some really good stock from pheasant trimmings and reduce to a good quality ½ pint. Stir in the tomato purée, butter and seasoning (not too much salt because of the ham).

Then mince or chop finely the pheasant meat and put it into a food processor with the pork, breadcrumbs, cream and seasoning, and blend to a smooth paste. Spoon this on to the slices of ham, leaving a gap at one end to ease the rolling up. Cut the celery hearts into three pieces and lay one on to each piece of ham. Roll them up and pack them into a dish, cover with the tomato-flavoured stock, and bake in a hot oven (Mk 7, 425°F, 220°C) for 20 minutes, basting the ham rolls once or twice with the stock.

devilled pheasant

The pheasants are part-roasted then coated with a peppered mustard and finished off under the grill. Young pheasants are best for this dish, but if using older ones I would marinate them first, then cut off the drumsticks, using these to make a little stock for a sauce. Also, beware of overcooking; the meat should remain slightly underdone, otherwise it will toughen.

Serves 4

2 small pheasants
melted butter
1 oz (25 g) butter
4 tablesp breadcrumbs
4 tablesp made-up English mustard
1 teasp Cayenne pepper

Cut the pheasants in half on either side of the backbone and breastbone. Remove any loose bones. Flatten the halves slightly with a rolling pin. This makes them cook more evenly. Brush with butter and half-cook them, insides-upwards, in a hot oven (Mk 7, 425°F, 220°C) for 15 minutes.

Melt the 1 oz (25 g) butter and stir in the breadcrumbs. I find this a lot easier and more successful than the proverbial 'sprinkle with breadcrumbs and dot with butter'. Mix the mustard and Cayenne pepper together. Put the pheasants, skin side uppermost, on the grill pan and coat them with mustard. Some people slash the meat before coating but I think it stays more succulent unslashed.

Sprinkle the buttery breadcrumbs over the top and finish off the cooking under the grill. If the pheasant has not cooled too much then 5 minutes should suffice; the juices should still run from the meat when pierced.

terrine of pheasant with chestnuts

This is good either hot, warm or cold. If it is to be hot, I prefer green leaves as a lining; if cold, bacon. A piquant accompaniment is good, perhaps Lemon Sauce (p. 173), Warm Green Sauce (p. 172) with Worcestershire sauce in it; if cold, try a salad tossed in a lusty sweet/sour vinaigrette.

You can use a whole pheasant for this, or use up odd joints.

1 pheasant, *or* equivalent
2 oz (50 g) butter
½ glass red wine
3 oz (80 g) cream cheese
2 egg yolks
2 tablesp thick cream
6 oz (170 g) chestnut purée
spinach leaves *or* thin streaky
    bacon
port *or* brandy (optional)
pepper, salt

Roast the pheasant in a tinfoil envelope with the butter and wine in a moderate oven (Mk 5, 375°F, 190°C) for ½–¾ hour. Leave it sealed until it is cool enough to handle. Remove all the meat from the carcase, making sure every scrap of gristle and sinew is left behind with the bones.

Put the meat into a liquidiser with the cream cheese, egg yolks, cream, some pepper, two good pinches of salt, and little of the roasting liquid. Blend until smooth and creamy. Butter a terrine or non-stick loaf tin and line it with spinach or bacon (or striped half and half).

If the chestnut purée is stiff, soften it with a dessertspoon of port or brandy, and some cream. Divide it into two parts. Divide the pheasant mixture into three. Fill the terrine with the five layers, starting and finishing with pheasant. Wrap the lining over the top, cover with foil, and place the dish in a tray of hot water.

Cook in a moderate oven (Mk 5, 375°F, 190°C) for 20–30 minutes until just set (a skewer comes clean out of the pheasant layers). An earthenware dish will need a little longer. If you have it hot, turn it out gently as it is fragile. If cold, weight it till cold and turn it out by heating the dish quickly.

quenelles of pheasant

These quenelles are so feather-light and smooth that it is hard to believe that they are anything to do with game. You can of course substitute any kind of game; it is an ideal use for some badly shot birds which are unusable for anything else. Port Wine Sauce (pp. 169–70) is ideal for pheasant quenelles especially when made from the carcase of the bird.

Serves 4

1 medium pheasant
5 juniper berries
½ pt (300 ml) water
2 oz (50 g) butter
salt, nutmeg, pepper
4 oz (110 g) sifted flour
2 eggs
2 egg-whites
3 or 4 tablesp double cream

Take all the meat off the pheasant, discarding all skin, bones and sinews—these can be made into stock. Dice the meat and blend or pound it to a completely smooth paste. If using a food processor you can hear any lead pellets pinging round, so remove them and keep blending till you can't hear any more. Crush the juniper berries as finely as you possibly can and blend them into the pheasant paste. You should have about 14 oz (400 g) which will be enough.

Put the water and butter into a heavy-bottomed pan with a generous pinch each of salt and nutmeg, and 6 or 7 turns of a pepper mill. Bring to the boil, then draw off the heat and add the flour. Beat hard till all the lumps have gone, then return to a gentle heat. Keep beating until it has formed a greasy-looking lump, and a whitish film begins to appear on the base of the pan. This does not want to be done too quickly because the flour needs a chance to cook, otherwise the quenelles taste a little pasty. Draw the pan off the heat again and one by one beat in the eggs and egg-whites. This is made slightly easier if they have been whisked a little first. Keep beating till you have a smooth thick paste. Then beat in the pheasant meat and chill thoroughly. If more convenient, all this part can be done the day before.

When you are ready to cook the quenelles, make sure that the cream is also well chilled. Tablespoon by tablespoon, beat in the cream. You may not need it all: the idea is to incorporate as much as possible without making the mixture too sloppy. Take a spoonful of the mixture and hold it on its side. It should just, but only just, stay on.

To poach the quenelles you will need two dessertspoons and an enormous frying pan, or even two. Fill them with 2 inches (5 cm) of salted water and bring to just under simmering point. The water should be barely moving—if it starts to bubble the quenelles will break up. Wet the spoons and take a spoonful of the quenelle mixture. With the other spoon, smooth the top, and ease it carefully into the water. As quickly as possible, form all the other quenelles—you should get about 20 from these quantities.

They will be done in 10–15 minutes, when they will roll over easily and look as though the surface is beginning to split. Remove them carefully with a slotted spoon to a large serving dish. Although they are best served quickly, they can be kept in a low oven for a while.

pheasant soufflé (two recipes)

Recipe 1

This is made in exactly the same way as the quenelle mixture, with the following alterations:

Serves 4

The ingredients from preceding recipe
2 extra tablesp cream

Instead of beating in the two egg-whites with the whole eggs, reserve them until the pounded meat and cream have been beaten in. You use a little more cream this time, which helps to keep the soufflé moist. 5–6 tablespoons instead of 3–4. Then beat the egg-whites to soft peaks and fold into the mixture. Turn it into a buttered 2 pt (1 litre) soufflé dish and bake in a moderately hot oven (Mk 5, 375°F, 190°C) for 15–20 minutes.

Recipe 2

This is made in the more conventional way, with a sharp cheese sauce as the foundation. A dessertspoon of whole grain mustard may also be beaten in if desired.

Serves 3–4

10 oz (280 g) pheasant meat
1 oz (25 g) butter
2 tablesp flour
½ pt (300 ml) milk
4 oz (110 g) Gruyère cheese
salt, pepper
3 eggs
a few juniper berries or
    chopped chives (optional)
2 tablesp double cream
    (optional)

Blend the pheasant meat to a smooth paste, removing any sinews and gristle. Make a white sauce from the butter, flour and milk and cook slowly for 10 minutes so that the flour has time to mature. Add the grated cheese and continue to cook for 5 minutes. Season with salt and pepper and, if liked, a few crushed juniper berries. Chopped chives are also a good addition.

Draw the pan off the heat and beat in the pounded pheasant meat. Separate the eggs and beat the yolks into the pheasant mixture. Adding a couple of tablespoons of double cream keeps the soufflé nicely moist but is not essential.

Whip the egg-whites till fairly stiff. Fold in a quarter of them thoroughly to slacken the mixture, then fold in the rest. Pour into a 2 pint (1 litre) buttered soufflé dish and bake at (Mk 5, 375°F, 190°C) for 15–20 minutes, when the soufflé should be nicely risen. Avoid prolonged cooking as the soufflé can become dry.

Suitable sauces for this soufflé are Port or Red Wine Sauce (pp. 169–70), or Francatelli's Venison Sauce (p. 176).

pheasant cock-a-leekie

Cock-a-leekie is one of Scotland's most famous soups but, as with many traditional dishes using older fowl, I feel that pheasants give a more genuine flavour to the dish. Traditionally it is served with the bird removed: a marvellous broth thickened with the leeks that have been virtually puréed by their long simmering with the fowl. However, it can also be served perfectly well with the pheasant cut into pieces and served with the broth. Soyer used to dish it like this, recommending it as his preferred Scotch soup, but suggesting that by rights it ought 'to have been the pride of Welch cookery'. Well it isn't.

The question of whether prunes should be served has been a subject of heated discussion for many a long year. F. Marian McNeill (author of *The Scots Kitchen*, surely the most authoritative book on Scottish cooking) thinks prunes should be served, one in each plate. Others, who are of the opinion that 'the man was an atheist that first polluted it with prunes', will prefer to discard them with the fowl.

Serves 8

2 small *or* 1 huge pheasant
3 lb (1.3 kg) leeks
4 pts (2 litres) good beef
    stock
salt, pepper
6 oz (170 g) prunes

Trim off any leathery old leaves and wash the leeks well, standing them upside down in a jug of cold water to remove any trapped earth. If they should be really big old chaps, blanch them in boiling water before proceeding. Then cut them into chunks.

Put the pheasants into a huge saucepan with two-thirds of the leeks and the stock. Traditionally beef or veal stock is used, but I would rather use any good home-made stock than a cube. Should you have neither, use water, but tie into a bag which can be discarded later a couple of chopped carrots, a tomato, some parsley, a clove or two, and 10 black peppercorns, and suspend them in the cooking pot.

Bring to the boil and simmer gently for 2–2½ hours, when the pheasants should be tender. Remove them carefully, skim any excess fat off the liquid and add the rest of the leeks. Season with salt and pepper and simmer slowly for 15 minutes. Then throw in the prunes and continue to simmer for a further 30 minutes until the leeks are tender.

If you want to serve the pheasants in the cock-a-leekie, cut them into usable pieces while the prunes and leeks simmer, remove any bones which might fall off into the broth, and warm them up in it a short while before serving. Discard the prunes or not, as you will.

guinea fowl with lemon and mushrooms

This is a wonderfully fresh-tasting dish, appropriate for summer or lunchtime. The herbs are an important ingredient and their choice will alter the flavour considerably. Fresh or frozen herbs are infinitely better than dried ones, which should be used much more sparingly. In fact I probably wouldn't make this dish at all without fresh herbs. It needs the inside of a day, at least, to marinate.

Serves 4

1 guinea fowl
salt, pepper
2 tablesp chopped chives
2 tablesp chopped parsley
2 tablesp chopped chervil *or* basil *or* tarragon
2 shallots
6 oz (170 g) mushrooms
2 lemons
1¼ oz (40 g) butter
¼ pt (150 ml) double cream
1 teasp sugar (optional)

Cut the guinea fowl into four portions—two with wings and breast and two with legs and slightly less breast. Discard the breastbone as it merely prevents even cooking. Slash the meat deeply on the underside so that the marinade can soak in.

Put the pieces into a bowl and sprinkle with a pinch of salt and some pepper. Add all the chopped herbs, and the shallots and mushrooms which should be thinly sliced. Squeeze all the juice from the lemons and add that too.

Make sure no pips go in because the marinade will be used for cooking. Turn the meat around so that it is well coated with marinade, cover with foil, and press the foil well down over the meat so that it is pressed into the marinade. I sometimes put a jar on top to keep it weighted down.

Refrigerate for at least 8 hours, turning the meat once or twice. Then remove the guinea fowl, scrape off the herbs, and pat them dry thoroughly. Strain the marinade off the mushrooms and herbs. Melt the butter in a large frying pan and brown the guinea fowl thoroughly all over—about 5 minutes each side. The heat should not be too fierce as the butter should not burn, only brown. Pour in the marinade liquid and scrape up all the tawny pan juices. Then add the cream and stir it in.

When the liquid boils, reduce the heat and cover the pan. I have no lid big enough to cover my large pan, so I use foil instead. Simmer slowly for 20 minutes, checking every now and then that nothing is burning. If it is getting dangerously dry, add a splash of water.

Then remove the pieces of guinea fowl to their serving dish and keep them warm. Add the marinated mushrooms and herbs to the pan and stir them around for about 5 minutes until they are nicely amalgamated. Check the seasoning. If the lemons were very acid you may like to add the sugar. Pour the sauce over the guinea fowl, and serve at once.

Mid 17th C. house in Auchtermuchty which has pigeon-holes in the gable ends.

"Lectern" style of doocott. V. common in Scotland but only seen there and in s. France — withstands the Mistral!

stringcourse, to foil rats

OISELLERIE OH

OISEAUX

Many French terms associated with Scots doocotes — c.f. "fuie" and "inside" there is an "arbre" & potence (Fr. for gallows) to climb up and catch the roosting birds.

Paris street pigeon wistfully regards his fancy caged cousins — who's the more fortunate?

4
Pigeons

There are definitely two schools of thought about pigeons. Some, like my cousin, regard them as inedible pests and will consider that I am stretching a point to include them in a book about game. Others look upon pigeons as a great delicacy, the more so because for many they are fruits of the land and therefore free. I feel quite unabashed about extolling their virtues. Although few are reared for the table nowadays, the rest are, like the Yonghy-Bonghy-Bo's fish, plentiful and cheap, and I think they deserve consideration.

Early Jews discovered in the pigeon 'the image of the sweetest virtues, of beauty, innocence and purity'. (I can hear a few sceptical snorts from crop growers here.) However, as Alexis Soyer the great Reform club chef wrote in 1853, 'Alas! the ancient prerogatives of this tender bird, its candour and innocence, could not preserve it from the fate common to almost everything which breathes. Its delicate flesh—fatal gift of Heaven!—recommends it to the epicure; not for its poetical qualities, but for its delicate flavour; and, after many songs of praise, it was condemned to be roasted.'

The Greeks used to trap immense numbers of live pigeons to stock up their pigeon houses, which they lovingly built as small towers, 'models of elegance and cleanliness'. The Romans, always keen to outdo that more civilised nation, refined their pigeon towers into luxury apartments with different designs for each kind of pigeon: 'a foolish and expensive taste which they continually attempted to embellish'.

It is only comparatively recently that pigeons, or squabs, as the young are termed, have ceased to be an important part of our winter diet. Most people will have seen the remains of old dovecotes in the fields, a clear indication of their importance. There were many dovecotes in the cities as well, being sufficiently important for Acts of Parliament to have been passed protecting the birds and their eggs from thieves. In 1589, the council of the city of Glasgow sent a drum round the town forbidding under severe penalties the shooting of pigeons and the breaking of dovecotes.

Those with neither space nor funds to build a 'doocot' had to adapt their homes to keep pigeons. Sometimes a little wooden construction was built on to the house. In Scotland this was called a 'fuie', one of many words assimilated during the days of our Auld Alliance with France (French *fuir*—to fly away). Crow-stepped gables made convenient landing places, and some old houses had holes made in the gable so that pigeons had access to the rafters. There is an old house in Auchtermuchty, at present uninhabited, which has both crow-stepped gables and circular holes, and every time I pass by I watch pigeons flying in and out just as they did centuries ago.

Once it became easier for winter rations to be kept, dovecotes declined in importance, and the pigeon lost his protection in the eyes of the law. There was a brief revival in pigeon-rearing in the nineteenth century, when many thousands were reared for trap-shooting but, due to the appearance of the clay pigeon for shooting practice, trap shooting became illegal in 1909.

The pigeon's lack of legal protection has hardly meant a diminution in numbers. With no close season, pigeons are available all year round from butcher's shops as well as from game-dealers.

A few enterprising people are fattening squabs once more. Seek them out, they will repay your effort. Addresses can be had from various guides now published listing specialist producers. Reared squabs are about the same size as wild pigeons, their flesh is a little paler and of course they are consistently tender.

Ageing

In order to decide how long to hang your pigeon, it would be valuable to know its age. Pigeons can live six or seven years, and young pigeons can be as large as well-grown ones. But a wood pigeon does not develop the characteristic ring round its neck until it is one year old, so if there is no ring you either have a young wood pigeon or a rock dove, whose descendants are found strutting about our parks, living off cigarette butts and the bounty of sympathetic humans. A squab is a pigeon under 4 months old and is not easy to distinguish from, say, an 11-month-old bird, but other signs of youth are downy feathers under the wing and soft red feet.

Pigeons provide a wonderfully lean and healthy form of meat which fits snugly into modern ways of cooking. I was told an Australian story about cooking pigeons which goes like this: 'Take a pigeon and a stone and put them into a hot oven. When the stone is tender, so is the pigeon.' Well, I hope they get a chance to read this book, for the oldest pigeon can be as moist and tender as you could wish, provided it is hung first, then cooked either very quickly indeed, or else poached/stewed extremely slowly at a low temperature.

Cooking Pigeon Breasts

It is becoming increasingly popular to serve just the breasts of pigeons. Perhaps it helps to overcome many people's innate resistance to pigeons *per se*. It is not surprising—the breast provides most of the eating—indeed many people can't be bothered with the rest, and when offering pigeons in this form, I find them accepted as a dish to be appreciated on its merits instead of eliciting a stifled sigh at the prospect of doing battle with sinewy little legs and wings.

There are three basic methods of cooking pigeon breasts—grill/sautéing, roasting or poaching. The first is the method to use when serving pigeon breasts like little steaks. The breasts are cut out and skinned before sautéing so that you have the carcases to make a little stock for an accompanying sauce. The roasting method is the one to use when serving pigeon breasts thinly sliced. I am sure from the diner's point of view it is the preferred method, but it is a little more fiddly and the carcases are not immediately available for stock. These two methods are for producing succulent pink meat and are cooked quickly. The poaching method is for those who refuse to eat meat unless it is well done as this is the best way of keeping it moist.

The methods are described in detail at the beginning of each section, and I recommend you to read them all before making your choice, as, particularly with the first two, they can be interchanged to suit what ingredients you have to hand. If you need stock to make a sauce, sautéeing or poaching are the methods to use, because it does seem rather a waste of time to burn your fingers neatly slicing piping hot pieces of meat only to surround them with an indifferent sauce.

There is a diagram on p. 10 describing how to cut off the breasts.

Grilling and Sautéing

This is the method to use when serving pigeon breasts like little steaks, either whole, sliced horizontally in two, or, if the leg is left on, like little cutlets. Here the breasts, or supremes, are cut out and skinned before cooking.

The supremes are then beaten with a spiked metal steak bat which both tenderises and flattens; this helps them to cook evenly. The sinews must be removed (see p. 10); this stops the meat from bunching up. I have found that sautéing unprepared pigeon breasts can lead to rather varied results, some being conspicuously more tender than others. And because of their shape, the outside edges tend to overcook and toughen long before the thicker centre has a chance to cook. Although my personal preference tends to be for fairly rare meat, I do like pigeon, especially when fairly well hung, and definitely when badly shot, to be cooked slightly longer till it is pink, not 'blue'. If you have a source of squabs, then the whole process is much more predictable.

pigeon breasts with chocolate sauce

Chocolate is a strange seasoning, but used in moderation it goes very well with game dishes, making them very powerful indeed. I find that cocoa powder gives the best results as the sauce should not be too sweet. On *no* account use drinking chocolate. If you already have some good stock, this dish takes only minutes—you might like to try it with venison steaks as well.

Serves 4

4 pigeons
1 onion
1 carrot
herbs for stock
2 teasp cocoa powder
¼ pt red wine *or* port
butter/oil for frying
salt, pepper

Cut the breasts off the pigeons, skin them, and set aside—marinate if you wish. Break up the carcases and brown them with the chopped onion and carrot. Cover with water and add some parsley and herbs, but not much seasoning as the stock will be reduced. Add anything else you have that will add flavour—celery, tomatoes, bacon etc. Bring to the boil, skim, and simmer gently for 1 hour or so. Then strain the stock into a clean pan and boil rapidly until it is concentrated and reduced to ½ pt (300 ml).

Add the red wine or port and reduce again to ⅓ pt (220 ml). Mix the cocoa powder in a cup with a spoonful or two of the liquid and, when smooth, stir into the stock. You must season this sauce very carefully indeed as it should not be over-sweet. Add salt and pepper, and if using red wine instead of port, the tiniest pinch of sugar might be needed, or a splash more port. Keep the sauce warm while you cook the pigeon breasts.

Flatten the meat with a steak bat, or score the skin side lightly with a sharp knife and beat with a rolling pin. Heat the oil/butter in a large pan and fry the breasts for about 1½ minutes per side. Remove and allow to rest for a few minutes before serving with the sauce.

wood pigeons in a ginger marinade

Here is a lovely way to eat wood pigeons. The inspiration came from a short visit to Japan where I was enchanted by the combination of strange tastes and exquisite visual form. This recipe is not really anything like Japanese cooking, but will be delicious however casually it may be presented. On leisured days I enjoy tying up little parcels of vegetables and the like, and I must say they do look pretty. Even if you are not fond of ginger, try some anyway; you can always discard it after cooking, by which time it will have given something special to the meat without being too obtrusive.

The leeks are not an essential adjunct, though I think them very good. Little bundles of carrot, parsnip or celery strips would do equally well. The first time I made this dish, I had some leeks that had gone to seed and I used the top part of the stalk—just the tender thin parts which snap easily in your fingers—as they go woody lower down. They were an interesting cross between leeks and spring onions and nicely crunchy. People who are apt to grumble at abstemious portions will need several bundles to keep them quiet.

Serves 4

4 wood pigeons
2 tablesp tomato purée
3 cloves garlic
1 large carrot
2 oz (50 g) leek trimmings,
    shallots *or* onions
⅓ cucumber cut into strips
16 very thin leeks
1 teasp cornflour
1 oz (25 g) butter

Marinade
2 tablesp fresh orange juice
1½ tablesp soy sauce
scant tablesp red wine
    vinegar
salt, black pepper
½–¾ oz (12–15 g)
    crystallised root ginger

Remove the breasts from the four pigeons, and take the skin off them. Break up the carcases and brown them quickly under the grill. Put them into a saucepan with the tomato purée, the garlic (no need to peel it, just cut the cloves in half), the carrot and the onions or leek trimmings. Cover with water, bring to the boil and simmer gently for about 3 hours.

Meanwhile, put the pigeon breasts to marinate, but first of all they must be beaten hard with a steak bat. The type with vicious metal spikes is the best because they will thoroughly pulverise the meat. Beat them on both sides. If you do not have a spiky bat and have to use a rolling pin or whatever, then slash the outer side in a criss-cross fashion with the point of a sharp knife. This stops them curling up in the pan when you sauté them later on.

Put these thoroughly flattened and somewhat starved-looking pieces of meat into a dish and sprinkle the orange juice, soy sauce and vinegar over them. Add a generous pinch of salt, about 10 turns of a pepper grinder, and the crystallised ginger, which should be sliced as thinly as possible. Turn the meat around in the marinade and leave for at least 3 hours. Both the marinading and the making of the stock can only be improved by being started the day before.

When the stock has simmered well and yielded its flavour, strain it into a smaller pan and start to reduce it. Drain the meat thoroughly. What little liquid remains from the marinade can go into the stock as well. Add the cornflour and reduce until you have about 8 tablespoons, then check the seasoning and, if necessary, strain again.

Cut the leeks, carrots, parsnips or whatever you have decided to use as a vegetable into sticks about 3 inches long, and tie them up in little bundles. In Japan they use seaweed for this type of job, but leek leaves, chives, or whatever your imagination extends to will be delightful. Sprinkle them with salt, and steam for about 15–20 minutes, making sure they are still crunchy. If you feel besieged with pans, then steam them in a sieve over the stock as it reduces, but cover loosely with a lid. Cut the cucumber into sticks or cut in half and slice into fan-shapes. They should be thick enough to remain crunchy even when warmed by hot plates.

When everything is ready, heat the butter in a large frying pan and, when it is beginning to brown, cook the meat and ginger slices very quickly on both sides. They must be so thin that about a minute each side should suffice. Rather than overcrowd the meat so that it stews, sauté it in batches. Remove from the heat, and arrange prettily on plates with 2 spoons of sauce, 2 sautéed pigeon breasts, a bundle or two of vegetables, a fan of cucumber, and a few slices of ginger for each person. Egg noodles or green tagliatelli are the best accompaniment.

Oenas Aldr
The Wood Pigeon

pigeon cutlets

This is more or less Escoffier's recipe for Côtelettes de Pigeonneaux. The birds are split in two and coated with a light forcemeat of pigeon before being shallow-fried. They are nicely succulent. Although squabs are recommended, I have made this successfully with wild pigeons.

Serves 4

6 pigeons
2½ oz (60 g) petit-suisse cheese
rounded tablesp breadcrumbs
1 tablesp cream
1 egg
pinch of nutmeg
black pepper, salt
4 oz (110 g) seasoned breadcrumbs
butter/oil for frying

Take two of the pigeons (the least tidy if there is any choice) and remove as much meat from the breasts and legs as possible, discarding all skin and sinews. This will give you about 8 oz (225 g) of meat. Set it aside to make the forcemeat.

Now prepare the 'cutlets'. Slip a sharp knife down either side of the breastbone and then cut the pigeons in two, cutting also either side of the backbone. Remove the small rib bones and any other sharp pieces and cut off the wings.

Flatten them slightly and fry them gently in butter, on the inside only, for 3–4 minutes. Remove them to a plate, placing another one on top to weight them lightly till cold. This keeps them flat so that they cook evenly.

To make the forcemeat, chop up the reserved pigeon meat and then pound it to a paste, or use a food processor or blender. Add the petit-suisse cheese, breadcrumbs, cream and egg, and beat thoroughly together to make a smooth paste. Season with a few turns of a peppermill, a pinch of salt and nutmeg.

Spread the forcemeat on both sides of the cutlets, pressing each side into the seasoned breadcrumbs afterwards. Melt a generous amount of butter and oil in a large pan and fry the cutlets on each side until well browned and cooked through. Do not fry too fiercely, otherwise the coating will be burnt to a cinder before the meat is cooked. Rest the cutlets in a warm place for 5–10 minutes before serving.

Escoffier recommends baking them in a moderately hot oven (Mk 5, 375°F, 190°C) for 20 minutes, but having tried both methods I prefer shallow-frying as being a little more juicy. However, baking would be a suitable way of cooking large numbers at once. Dribble melted butter over them, and cook in a buttered dish, basting once or twice to crisp the breadcrumbs. Rest as before.

Some sort of sauce or gravy is needed to go with the cutlets. There are plenty to choose from in Chapter 7, but Escoffier recommended mushrooms as an accompaniment. They are good lightly sautéed and then simmered in the stock made from the pigeon carcases, and sprinkled with fresh thyme.

grilled pigeons with fresh herbs

This is a very simple dish—the cream cheese stuffed under the skin keeps the meat moist as it cooks and it could equally well be roasted as grilled. Quite often, when grilling small birds, it is recommended to split them along the backbone only, flattening them out to make a 'spatchcock'. A skewer is passed through to keep them flat. This method has the advantage of leaving the skin intact all over the breast with the result that a little more stuffing can be inserted. However, they are impossibly ungainly things to eat, and to me look rather as though somebody ran them over. So I cut them in half.

Serves 4

4 pigeons
8 oz (225 g) petit-suisse *or* cream cheese
salt, pepper
3 tablesp fresh herbs
butter

Cut the pigeons in half, on either side of the backbone and breastbone. Remove the rib bones and wings.

Mix together the soft cheese with salt, black pepper and the fresh herbs (parsley, thyme, chives, or whatever takes your fancy). Starting at one end of each prepared pigeon side, part the skin from the flesh as far as you can reach, but if possible leave the skin attached along the top line of the breast (this prevents it from shrinking back during the cooking). Stuff the cheese mixture into the cavity, pressing it to cover as large an area as possible. Pull back the skin to its original position. If the skin was completely detached from the breast, secure it with a cocktail stick.

Melt some butter in a frying pan and fry the pigeon halves gently for 5 or 6 minutes on the insides only, pressing them down from time to time to ensure even cooking. Remove to a baking dish skin side uppermost and pour the butter all over them, melting a little more if necessary so that they are well-coated. Season with salt and pepper.

To grill them, place them under a moderate grill for 15 minutes, basting frequently with the juices. Rest in a warm oven for a further 15 minutes to disperse the juices.

To roast, put the tray in a fairly hot oven (Mk 6, 400°F, 200°C) for 25–30 minutes, basting frequently with the pan juices. Turn the oven off and, with the door ajar, rest for 10–15 minutes.

Roasting

This is the best method to use when serving pigeon breasts thinly sliced, whether they be cold, for a salad, or hot, surrounded by an exquisite sauce. Whatever the cook may think, from the diner's point of view it is undoubtedly the most sumptuous and popular way of presenting them.

It is obviously more wasteful since there is quite a lot left on the carcases, but consider this a bonus. Make some really good stock and freeze it in cartons for later use, or enjoy some excellent soup the next day. If it doesn't detract too much from the intended recipe, pop a few vegetables in the roasting tin to cook alongside the pigeons, *et voilà*, you are nearly there.

Roast the pigeons until they are slightly underdone, since they continue to cook whilst being served. Make sure that everything else is ready, for they should be sliced and served as quickly as possible.

Roasting times are obviously a matter of taste, but 15–20 minutes in a moderately hot oven (Mk 5, 375°F, 190°C) will give nicely rosy meat. Then carve the breasts diagonally into the thinnest possible slices. Some people find it easier to carve off the bird, others prefer to cut out the breasts quickly and slice them on a board. Whip out the sinews if possible, and discard the skin.

wood pigeons in a raspberry sauce

The raspberries in the sauce give the dish a superb colour and a flavour which is rich in an uncloying way. Blackberries may be used as an alternative when in season, though I prefer the slightly intriguing taste of raspberries.

Serves 4

4 pigeons
8 oz (225 g) raspberries
pinch of sugar
1 teasp water
¼ pt (230 ml) good stock
2 cloves garlic
2 oz (50 g) pork fat *or*
2 oz (50 g) butter

Put the raspberries into a pan with the sugar and water and stir them to a pulp over a low heat. It is not necessary to cook them, merely to extract the juice. Into a pan containing the stock, press the juice through a sieve so that only the pips remain. Start reducing the stock while the pigeons cook.

Put the pips inside the pigeons, this helps to keep them moist, crush the garlic over the pigeons and cover up the breasts with either the pork fat, in sheets, or else sheets of aluminium foil which have been liberally smeared with butter. Roast the birds for 15–20 minutes in a moderately hot oven (Mk 5, 375°F, 190°C), basting once or twice. The pigeons should emerge still juicy.

By this time the stock and raspberry juice mixture should have reduced considerably, to 2–3 tablespoons per person. Cut the breasts off the roasted pigeons, remove the skin and carve them, on the slant, into neat slices. Lay them on a dish or on individual plates, and spoon the sauce over the top.

The remaining carcases can be made into some excellent soup or stock with a fine flavour of raspberries and garlic. I think this dish is more successful when the pigeons have been quickly roasted, but if you need the carcase to make stock, you could remove the breasts first and sauté them instead. In this case, I would leave them steeped in the crushed garlic and raspberry pulp while the stock simmers.

roast pigeons with mushrooms and garlic

Leave out the garlic if you must, but I think it makes the dish.

Serves 4

4 squabs *or* pigeons
1¼ lb (560 g) mushrooms
6 cloves garlic
6 oz (175 g) butter
thyme
cream *or* stock (optional)
salt, pepper

Chop the mushrooms quite small, and crush the garlic. Melt half the butter and gently sweat the mushrooms and garlic until soft. Add a generous sprinkling of thyme and season with salt and pepper.

Stuff the mushrooms into the pigeons and spread the remaining butter on top. Roast in a hot oven (Mk 7, 425°F, 220°C), for 15–20 minutes, basting once or twice. At this stage the breasts will be nicely pink but the part by the legs may well be too rare for some tastes. So rest the pigeons in a cool oven for another 10–15 minutes until done to your liking.

Drain excess butter off the roasting tin, deglaze with water, stock or cream, and season this small amount of gravy to taste.

pigeon breasts with yoghourt and cucumber sauce

This is a good example of the roasting method (p. 95) because no stock is needed. The refreshing sharpness of the sauce makes a good contrast to the rich pigeons. They may be marinated beforehand if need be.

Serves 4

4 pigeons
½ large cucumber
salt
2 cloves garlic
3 oz (80 g) butter
¼ pt (150 ml) yoghourt

Peel the cucumber and cut into small dice. Sprinkle on two good pinches of salt and leave for an hour. Then rinse off the salt and drain. This improves cucumber no end and frequently removes any hint of bitterness.

Crush the garlic and tuck it under the pigeons' skin. It will flavour the meat as it cooks. Spread the butter over the pigeons and roast them in a hot oven (Mk 7, 425°F, 220°C) for 15 minutes, basting once or twice. Then keep the pigeons warm while you make the sauce.

Drain all excess butter from the roasting dish and stir in the yoghourt, scraping up any pan juices. Add the diced cucumber, season, and very gently warm through. It should not boil.

At the last moment, remove the skin and garlic from the pigeon breasts. Carve them diagonally into the thinnest possible slices. Serve at once with the sauce.

Slow cooking

The most successful way of cooking poached pigeon breasts is to poach the bird whole, and remove the breasts afterwards. The meat stays more succulent this way. Also, by adding vegetables to the pan, you will have some excellent stock to play with afterwards. One great advantage of this method is that the meat will happily sit around and wait for people.

Put the pigeons upside down in a pan, so that the breasts are always covered. Add the water, wine, or whatever, and simmer gently. An hour will be sufficient for squabs, older pigeons may need two.

The most important point to note is that the moment the meat is carved, it starts to dry out. This is easily remedied by spooning a little of the poaching liquid over the slices, which immediately restores their succulence. For this reason, I usually have the pigeon breasts sliced and moistened beforehand, pouring the sauce or gravy over them just before serving. Whole poached pigeons don't look all that appetising for carving at the table, but if you wish to do so, make sure that there is some poaching liquid in the serving dish. Tell the carver to drop the slices into it for a second before putting them on to plates. This makes all the difference in the world.

Once again, carving thin slices means the meat can absorb liquid easily, but if you wish to serve the breasts whole, keep them submerged in warm stock until ready either to cover with sauce, or to serve, hot or cold.

pigeons cooked in milk and mushrooms

A heavy non-stick pan is an enormous boon here, as the milk doesn't burn on the bottom during its slow simmering. Failing that, a heat diffuser will help, or else cook in a very slow oven (Mk 1, 285°F, 140°C) for 3 hours instead.

Serves 4

4 plump pigeons
6 oz (170 g) mushrooms
2 oz (50 g) butter
4 cloves garlic
1 pt (570 ml) milk
salt, pepper, nutmeg
1 oz (25 g) butter
1 oz (25 g) flour

Lay the pigeons breasts side down, in a heavy-bottomed pan.

Chop the mushrooms roughly, and pack them around the pigeons. Add the butter and peeled garlic, then pour in the milk. The pigeons should be more or less covered. Add a little salt, pepper and nutmeg (not over much or it will be too strong when cooked). Bring very slowly to simmering point. Then half cover the pan (it will boil over if completely covered) and simmer as slowly as possible for 2 hours, turning the pigeons around occasionally. By this time, the mushrooms and milk may look a little odd but it all comes right in the end.

Then take out the pigeons and remove the meat, discarding skin and bones. Slice the breast meat diagonally, and spoon a little of the cooking liquid over the slices to stop them becoming dry. Keep them warm.

Put the rest, including mushrooms and garlic into a liquidiser, and blend into a purée. Return it to the pan and check the seasoning. Mash the 1 oz (25 g) of butter and flour together and gradually beat little pieces into the mushroom sauce until it thickens, then pour it over the pigeon meat.

creamed squabs

I read an old French recipe which described braising an enormous joint of beef, hollowing it out to form a shell and filling it with creamed squabs. Whereas I decided the original recipe was somewhat complicated, the thought of creamed squabs sounded very appealing, so here is my version. It works excellently with pigeons; they merely require a little longer to cook. If you have no cream, use milk instead; it will still be good.

Serves 4

4 squabs *or* pigeons
2 carrots
2 onions
2 sticks of celery
2 bay leaves
10 peppercorns
small pinch salt
1½ pt (900 ml) water
1 oz (25 g) butter
2 level tablesp flour
milk if necessary
½ pt (300 ml) cream

Peel and chop the vegetables and line the base of a large saucepan with them. Lay the pigeons on top, breast sides downward. Ideally the pan should be wide enough for the four pigeons to sit side by side so that they are completely covered with water. Using more water is not a disaster, it will merely mean more boiling later on. Add the spices and cover with water.

Put the lid on, bring slowly to the boil, and simmer very gently. Squabs will take about 1 hour, pigeons will need 2 hours to be tender.

When they are done, strain off the cooking liquids into a clean pan, bring to a fast rolling boil, and reduce to ¼ pt (150 ml) of very concentrated stock.

While this is happening, take all the meat off the pigeons, discarding skin and bones. Slice the breasts diagonally and keep them warm in a serving dish. You will notice that they almost immediately become rather dry, so quickly trickle a few spoonfuls of the cooking liquid over them. This restores their succulence.

Melt the 1 oz (25 g) butter and stir in the flour. Cook for a minute or two, then gradually add the now reduced stock, beating well to remove any lumps. You should have a very thick sauce which now needs to be cooked for 15–20 minutes, barely simmering, over a very gentle heat. If the sauce is impractically thick, add a splash of milk. Stir from time to time.

Then thin the sauce with cream, adjust the seasoning, and pour over the pigeon meat. Serve with baked potatoes and a juicy vegetable.

wood pigeons with pork and broad beans

This is not an especially elegant dish, but it is tasty and filling. Because it uses the slow cooking method, it can be prepared well in advance and needs no last-minute adjustment.

Serves 4

4 wood pigeons
2 oz (50 g) streaky bacon (thin)
8 oz (225 g) belly pork (thick)
½ oz (15 g) butter
12 oz (340 g) broad beans
¼ pt (150 ml) stock
salt, pepper

Cut each pigeon in half, removing the breastbone, ribcage, and backbone so that there are two relatively bone-free pieces each. Make all the bones and scraps into your stock. Cut the bacon into snippets and the pork into chunks. Fry the bacon in the butter till crispy. Brown the pork all over in the same fat, and then do the same with the pigeons.

Mix the bacon, pork and beans together and line a wide dish with them. Arrange the pigeons on top, pressing them down well, and pour the remaining bacon fat over them. Add the stock and seasoning, cover, and bake in a slow oven (Mk 1, 275°F, 140°C) for 3–4 hours.

piccione al limone

This is an ancient recipe from Milan which I was given by a friend. As with so many old recipes, the details are rather sparse; so I hope that I have not adulterated the original too much. If you like the flavour of lemons it is well worth trying. It is extremely rich, so the vegetables should be rather plain.

Serves 4

4 pigeons
4 pigeon or 2 chicken hearts
4 pigeon or 2 chicken livers
2 oz (50 g) Italian sausage
seasoning
4 small lemons
8 tablesp olive oil
sugar or honey

Chop the hearts, liver and sausage finely together and season them. The original recipe includes the stomachs as well, but this is optional—I find it gives a bitterness to the dish. Stuff this into the four pigeons and tie the legs so that they stay close to the carcase. Prick all over with a fork so that the lemon and oil can permeate the flesh.

Peel the lemons, removing all the pith, and slice them. Pick out all the seeds. Arrange the slices on the base of a cooking dish and scatter with the sugar. The ideal is a clay dish with a clay lid, but any covered dish will do. Lay the pigeons on top and dribble the oil over them.

Put the cover on and bake in a moderate oven (Mk 4, 350°F, 190°C) for 1¼ hours. During the cooking, keep turning the pigeons so that each side is immersed in the lemons for a while, and baste each time you do this. Eventually the lemons will become caramelised and, when they are a really dark brown and verging on becoming burnt, add a good dash of water. The lemon pulp will sizzle and spit and become paler as the oil is emulsified. Keep turning the pigeons in this until they are done.

Depending on how ripe the lemons were, it may be necessary to add a little sugar or honey, though the original recipe doesn't mention this.

pigeon and orange casserole

Slowly cooked pigeons in a light orange sauce, not unlike Sauce Bigarade. I expect you could make it with marmalade as well, but it should not be oversweet or cloying.

Serves 4

4 pigeons
4 large bacon rashers
3 small sweet oranges
flour
salt, pepper
sugar

Cut the pigeons in half, trimming off the backbones and any loose bones. Cut the bacon into pieces and brown it. Brown the pigeons on both sides, pressing them down so that they brown evenly. Remove them to a casserole.

Scatter a tablespoon of flour into the frying pan and scrape up the juices and fat. Add some water, let it bubble for a moment, then pour it over the pigeons.

Wash the oranges and thinly pare the peel (no pith) off 1½. Cut the peel into strips (or use a lemon zester), and add to the casserole. Peel the oranges, removing all the pith and split them into segments. Remove the pips and put the segments into the casserole. Season with salt and pepper and add enough hot water to cover the pigeons. Give it a stir, then cook in a very moderate oven (Mk 3, 325°F, 170°C) until tender. Squabs will be cooked in around 1 hour, wood pigeons could take nearer 3.

When the pigeons are tender, taste the gravy. Depending on the sweetness of the oranges, it will probably need a little sugar. Start with a dessertspoon and taste again.

pigeons with olives

This is one of Jane Grigson's recipes from her book *Good Things*—an apt description of the book's contents and its author. My thanks to her for permission to use it.

I prefer to use the ripened black olives for this dish—they are more succulent and a better foil for the pigeons, but you may prefer the firm bite of green olives. Black olives preserved in oil are preferable to those preserved in brine, which sometimes spoils the taste of the olives. In this event, Mrs Grigson advises pouring boiling water over the olives and steeping them for 5 minutes before draining.

Serves 4

4 pigeons
4 oz (110 g) chunk fat bacon
1 large carrot
1 large onion
4 oz (110 g) butter
bouquet garni
wine
½ pt (280 ml) pale stock
1 heaped tablesp flour
4 oz (110 g) olives (unstoned)
extra wine *or* stock if
   necessary

Lard the pigeons with the bacon (see p. 10). Chop the carrots and onion, melt half the butter and brown the larded pigeons all over, removing them to a fireproof casserole. Then brown the carrots and onions and add them to the pigeons. If you prefer to cut down on butter, replace half of it with olive oil. Put in the bouquet garni and the wine and add enough stock to cover the pigeons. Season lightly and simmer gently until the pigeons are tender. Squabs will be cooked in ¾ hour but wild pigeons may need 1½–2 hours.

Half an hour before the end, ladle out a pint (500 ml) of the cooking liquid, making sure there is enough left in the casserole to keep the pigeons moist. If you are short, top up with stock or wine. Reduce the pint of liquid by nearly half. As Jane Grigson says, 'let flavour be your guide, remembering that the olives will add sharpness to the final result'.

In another saucepan make a roux of the remaining butter and the flour. Cook for a minute or two, then pour on the reduced stock gradually, beating all the time until the sauce is thick and creamy. Once the pigeons have finished cooking, stir the olives into the sauce and warm them through for a few minutes.

Remove the pigeons from their casserole and arrange them on a serving dish, pouring a little of the olive sauce over them and serving the rest separately. Serve with rice or noodles.

slow-cooked pigeons with beetroot

I wouldn't use precious young squabs here. This is for the tough old chaps that have been raiding the garden all year. It is one of those dishes that frequently tastes better the next day, after re-heating.

Serves 4

4 pigeons
4 oz (110 g) bacon
water *or* stock, salt, pepper
1 lb (450 g) cooked beetroot
beurre manié (p. 15) *or*
    cream (optional)

Marinade
½ bottle wine vinegar
1 large onion, chopped
3 tablesp oil
bouquet garni

Boil the marinade ingredients together for 5 minutes and leave to cool. Cover the pigeons with marinade and turn them around in it for at least 24 hours.

Then remove the pigeons and pat dry. Cut the bacon into chunks and brown it. Remove to a casserole and brown the pigeons all over. Put them upside down in the casserole with the marinade and enough extra water or stock to cover them. Make sure the bouquet garni can be fished out at the end, and season sparingly.

After 2–3 hours' cooking, chop the beetroot into little pieces and stir them into the casserole. By the time the pigeons are tender, the liquid will have reduced and darkened. Check the seasoning. If a slightly thicker sauce is wanted, remove the pigeons to a serving dish and whisk in a little beurre manié or thick cream.

Columba domeſtica major.
The great houſe Dove or Pigeon.

pigeons au soleil

'Pigeons à la Lune' and 'Pigeons au Soleil'—fancifully named dishes like these were popular in the eighteenth century. Chef/authors such as Vincent la Chapelle have many such recipes. Some use a great many ingredients not available nowadays but this one is comparatively simple. However, I first encountered this recipe in Jane Grigson's *Good Things* (she is one of the few modern authors who seem to appreciate the pigeon), and I remain indebted to her for permission to use it here.

Fried parsley was frequently used to accompany meat in those days and it is well worth trying. The nearest equivalent I have come across recently is the Chinese way of deep-frying seaweed —this too would make an appropriate side dish. There are plenty of sauces in Chapter 7 if you feel the need for one.

Serves 4

4 pigeons
8 oz (225 g) piece fat bacon
2 oz (50 g) flour
pinch salt
1 tablesp oil
¼ pt (150 ml) warm water
1 large onion
1 large carrot
bouquet garni
⅓ pt (200 ml) white wine
1 pt (570 ml) pale stock
1 egg-white
oil *or* lard for frying
4 oz (110 g) parsley
1 lemon
salt, pepper

Lard the pigeons with the bacon as described on p. 10. Then make a batter by mixing the flour and salt together and beating in the oil and water. Leave it to stand at room temperature while the pigeons cook. If you are using squabs, it is possible to partly roast the birds, for about 10 minutes in a hot oven, before removing the breasts and coating them in batter. With older birds, the following simmering method is more successful.

Brown the pigeons and vegetables and put them in a casserole with the bouquet garni, the wine, and enough stock to cover them. The breasts will keep more succulent if the pigeons are upside down and kept submerged. Season well and simmer gently for 1½–2 hours. Then gently remove the pigeons and cut off the breasts.

Beat the egg-white till stiff and fold it into the batter. Heat ¼ inch of oil, or a mixture of oil and lard, in a frying pan. Coat the pigeon breasts in the batter and fry them until golden brown and crisp. Drain, and keep warm on a dish.

In the same pan, quickly fry the parsley (or seaweed) until dark green and crisp, and serve alongside the pigeons with wedges of lemon.

You are left with the wherewithal to make some good stock with the carcases and existing stock. Useful stuff, stock . . .

pigeons in red wine jelly

Serves 6–8

This is another superb way to enjoy pigeons, whether young or old, for a cold first course or lunch. I wanted to write it out all over again because it is so good; but instead I shall direct you to the pheasant recipe on p. 75, and recommend that you replace the pheasant with four pigeons and the white wine with red. If appearance is paramount, make it in individual ramekin dishes; and, in the unlikely event of having any left over, it can also be warmed gently for a quick hot meal.

pigeon salami

If you should have a glut of pigeons, then you might like to try making salami. Pigeon meat is ideal, being so lean. Do not hang the birds overlong—a day is quite sufficient. There is no need to pluck, just skin and draw them. Remove the breast meat and as much of the legs as you can be bothered to pick off, discarding any sinews. You should get about 4 oz (110 g) from each bird. Then use the proportions and methods described for Venison Salami (page 155).

Columba tabellaria
A Carrier-Pigeon.

medallions of pigeon (cold)

This is a fiddly dish to do, on account of the boning and rolling of the pigeons, but I hope you will not be put off trying it, because the satisfaction of seeing and tasting the beautiful slices makes it all worthwhile. It is an admirable dish for a buffet. Suitable sauces, if you want one, would be Cumberland Sauce (p. 176) or a Béarnaise with Meat Glaze (p. 169). The meat glaze can be made from the remaining stock, boiled down. Make sure that the pigeons have not had their skins torn during plucking.

Serves 4–6

4 pigeons
vegetables and herbs for
   stock
3 oz (80 g) pistachio nuts
6 oz (170 g) cooked tongue
3 oz (80 g) petit-suisse cheese
pepper
cloth, string

Bone the pigeons carefully. Avoid cutting the skin, particularly over the breastbone, otherwise the filling will escape. Full instructions are on p. 12. Brown the bones and make about 1 pint (600 ml) of really good stock with the vegetables and herbs. A little bacon would not go amiss.

Shell the pistachio nuts and rub off the papery inner skin. Pound the tongue and petit-suisse together to a smooth paste. Salt is not necessary here, especially if the pistachio nuts are salted, but a few turns of the pepper mill are good.

Have ready four pieces of cloth (muslin or old sheeting is fine) about 8 × 6 inches (20 × 15 cm) and four pieces of string about 15 inches (38 cm) long. Lay the pigeons out, skin side downwards and arrange them as near to a rectangular shape as possible. Loose bits of meat can be laid along the middle where the breastbone was. The idea is to make them as even as possible. Divide the tongue and cheese filling into four and lay a sausage-shape of it along each pigeon. Stud the filling with pistachio nuts. There will probably be some left over. You are in luck. Eat them.

Roll the pigeon up around the filling to make a somewhat bulky sausage shape. Tuck the ends in as you roll to prevent the filling squeezing out. It doesn't matter which way they are rolled —whichever you find the easiest. Just make sure the filling is contained all round. Then roll them as tightly as you can in the cloth, once more tucking in the ends as you go. Bind the rolls tightly with the string and tie securely. Do not be discouraged by their lumpy appearance at this stage.

Put the rolls into a pan or casserole in one layer. Cover with the strained stock, put the lid on, and simmer very gently for 3–4 hours. Or cook them in a very slow oven (Mk 1, 275°F, 140°C) for 4–5 hours. Let them cool completely in the stock.

Then lift them out and unwrap them. They still look horrible. But now cut them with a very sharp knife into ½-inch (1-cm) slices and your efforts are rewarded. Slice them not too far in advance of serving lest they dry out. Use the stock to make meat glaze if wanted (p. 165). They may be served with mayonnaise, perhaps flavoured, or else with a vinaigrette drizzled over them and sprinkled with a little finely grated orange peel.

insalata di piccione

This is one of the best ways I know to eat cold pigeons as the meat stays so beautifully succulent. It is ideal for people who don't like rare meat, which is how a pigeon salad is normally presented. You could use any game bird—in Italy they cook partridges like this too. The recipe will stretch to do eight people as an hors d'oeuvre.

Serves 4

4 pigeons
4 plump cloves garlic
1½ pt (900 ml) clear stock

Dressing
4 teasp Dijon mustard
8 pinches salt
black pepper
4 teasp sugar
4 tablesp lemon juice
4 tablesp white wine vinegar
12 tablesp good olive oil
4 tablesp chopped herbs

lettuce hearts *or* salad leaves

Pop a clove of garlic into each pigeon and lay them in a pan, breast downwards. Pour in enough stock to cover them and season if necessary. If you don't have stock, pack some browned vegetables in beside the pigeons and cover with water. Bring to the boil and simmer very gently for 2 hours until the birds are really tender. The stock will reduce, but as long as the breasts are kept covered there is no need to dilute with water.

Make up the dressing—stir the mustard into the salt and a generous amount of pepper. Beat in the sugar, lemon juice, wine vinegar, olive oil and herbs till well amalgamated.

Lift the pigeons out of their stock and prick them deeply all over with a fork. While they are still hot, immerse them completely in the vinaigrette. They should be turned around in this till cool. I find the easiest way to keep them covered is to put each one into a double polythene bag with vinaigrette and tie them tightly.

The pigeons can be eaten while still warm but they keep quite well in their bags for a day or two in the fridge. Serve at room temperature.

To serve, arrange the salad leaves on a plate, sprinkle them with the pigeon's vinaigrette, and lay the pigeons on top. They may be served whole or cut in half, or else just the breasts can be taken off.

The left-over broth is now a sumptuous consommé so don't throw it away.

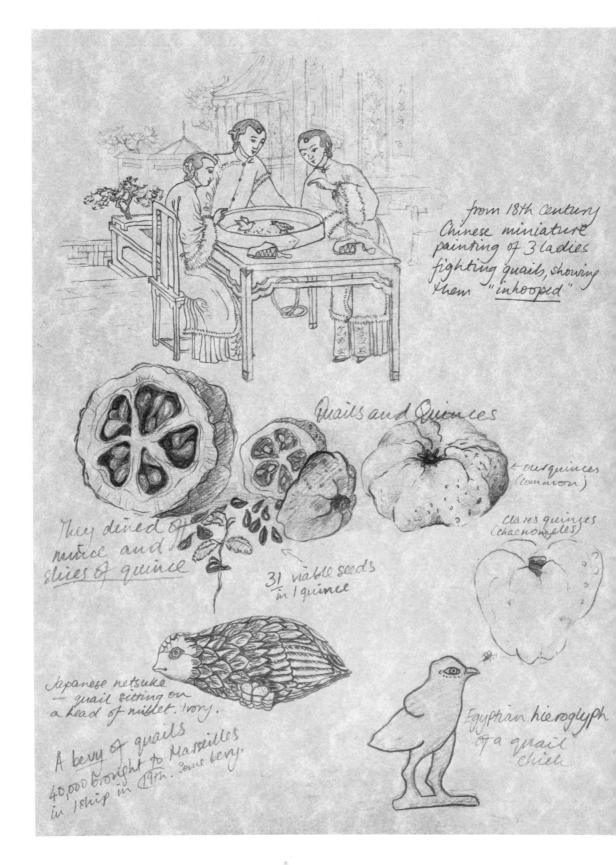

from 18th century
Chinese miniature
painting of 3 ladies
fighting quails, showing
them "_inhooped_"

Quails and Quinces

← our quinces
(common)

They dined off
mince and
slices of quince

Clares quinces
(chaenomeles)

31 viable seeds
in 1 quince

Japanese netsuke
— quail sitting on
a head of millet. Ivory.

Egyptian hieroglyph
of a quail
chick

A bevy of quails
40,000 brought to Marseilles
in 1 ship in 19th. Some bevy!

5
Quail

Quails are migratory birds in the wild, covering vast distances in their travels. It was once believed that they carried three stones in their mouth whilst in flight, to hear by dropping them whether they be over land or sea.

Despite their subordinate appearance they are pugnacious little creatures and in many countries are kept as fighting birds. Antony and Caesar had quail fights, but Antony was not very successful: 'and his quails ever beat mine inhoop'd at odds'. And on the North West Frontier of India it used to be a common sight to see a Pathan boy bouncing a quail up and down on the palm of his hand to strengthen its legs. In Japan, however, quails were kept as songbirds. The male's shrill whistle seems rather a minimal form of music to my ears, but it takes all sorts.

There are ancient accounts of phenomenal numbers of migrating quail: Pliny for instance tells of a ship that was overturned due to the density of exhausted quails alighting on the rigging.

The most famous historical account of quails is of course the Israelites' flight from the Egypt when the Lord provided them in abundance: 'at even the quails came up and covered the camp', followed in the morning by manna. Whereas to begin with manna had the appearance of coriander seed 'and the taste of it was like wafers made with honey', later on, when the ungrateful Israelites had had an unrelieved diet of manna, it was described as tasting like fresh oil, which must have been rather monotonous. In John Dryden's words, the Israelites protested, crying 'we loathe our manna and long for quails'. They got their just rewards in the form of another prodigious shower of quails 'two cubits high on the face of the earth', followed closely by a plague.

The medicinal properties of quails were a cause of some dispute to our forebears. Despite the fact that Aristotle speaks most highly of them, and that quails' brains were at one time an ancient cure for epilepsy (Hercules was reputedly resuscitated from a fit, even death, some believed, by a quail), Pliny noted that quails are resistant to certain poisonous plants. Eventually they were for a period banned from the Roman table in the belief that they actually caused epilepsy. Even the physician Galen confirmed this strange prejudice. Later on in France, certain types of migrating quail were believed to cause a deadly illness called coturism.

I wouldn't pay undue attention to all this, because those who cared more for their stomachs than for reading continued to catch quail by the thousand, using whatever means they could think of. Mirrors, nets, a kind of scarecrow, and snares were all used, though the latter was frowned upon as 'not being a gentlemanly-like pursuit.'

Nowadays quails are farmed extensively both for their delicate flesh and for their tiny speckled eggs. Because of their small size they are obviously less versatile than, say, pheasants. Early books abound with dishes made from the fillets of a couple of dozen quail, and very sumptuous they are too. And highly practical, should you have two cubits of quail to deal with, but I have not included any because I didn't think anyone would use them. If you want to try, read Escoffier's culinary bible.

Quails are not usually hung for more than a day. I have hung them two or three days and found them improved, though the flavour is always rather delicate. Presentation is particularly appropriate to quails, though appearance should never take precedence over taste.

Quails can be poached, quickly casseroled, or roasted. Spit roasting is deemed the best method, but a moderately hot oven is perfectly good. 20–30 minutes plus 5–10 minutes resting should see unstuffed quails amply cooked. Stuffed quails will need an extra five minutes or so, depending on the stuffing. They are often wrapped up to prevent them drying out, but I have always found them remarkably resistant.

As a general rule, if quails are not going to be stuffed, leave them whole, but I would strongly advise boning them out if they are to be stuffed. It really is a little tantalising trying to extricate such a minute titbit. Boning quails is no more difficult than boning any other bird. To be sure you'll have to do more than one, but remember that quails after all, were a lover's gift. If that doesn't cheer you up, bear in mind that one beautifully plump boned and stuffed quail per person will normally suffice, whereas left intact without stuffing you may need two. The tiny carcases will make some lovely stock.

Whatever the decision, ensure that all other ingredients are of good quality so that you end up with a perfect combination of flavours. Quails deserve this treatment.

quails with grapes on a little mat

Quails cooked simply with grapes are delicious, but served on this crisp mat of potatoes, they are even better. I read about it in one of Paul Bocuse's books; he tells us that it came from G. Pleynet, who was Meilleur Sommelier de France in 1963. Such is the evolution of cooking.

Serves 4

4 plump quails
2 oz (50 g) butter
1 lb (450 g) potatoes
salt, pepper
8 oz (225 g) green grapes
1 tablesp clarified butter
1 tablesp brandy

Peel the potatoes, grate them coarsely, and rinse under cold water. Season with salt and pepper. Halve the grapes and remove pips.

Season the quails and brown them all over in butter in a small pan. Lower the heat and cook to taste (20–30 minutes), turning them round in the butter from time to time.

While they are cooking, melt the clarified butter in (preferably) a non-stick frying pan. Scatter in the shredded potatoes and, over a fierce heat, cook until they have stuck together and are crisply brown on the underside. Then deftly flip the 'mat' over, either by using a plastic spatula or else tossing it like a pancake. Cook the other side until crisp and golden, then slide the mat on to a large round serving dish. If you manage this—well done! I can't pretend to find this procedure easy, so I now resort to dividing the potatoes and making four small mats.

When the quails are cooked, drain off most of the butter, but no precious juices. Add a generous tablespoon of brandy and the grapes. Swirl them around with the quails until the pan juices are dissolved and the grapes are well heated. Lift the quails on to the mat, adjust the seasoning, and tip the grapes and the juice over the top. They will slightly soften the potatoes. This is as it should be.

quails stuffed with pheasant

This is not quite so absurd as the title suggests—the pheasant takes the form of a mousse. It sounds extravagant to buy a whole pheasant to obtain such a small amount of meat, but you can use the leg meat for this dish and cook the breasts some other time. As long as it is well-flavoured, the meat from any game bird can be used in lieu of pheasant.

If you refuse to bone quails, don't stuff them. Instead, wrap the spinach parcels in well-buttered foil and cook them alongside the quails, serving them separately. Increase oven temperature to hot (Mk 7, 425°F, 220°C) and reduce the time to 15–25 minutes. But in this case I would double all the ingredients.

Serves 6

6 quails
6 oz (170 g) raw pheasant
1 oz (25 g) petit-suisse
2 tablesp cream
1 small egg
salt, pepper
mace
2–3 juniper berries
6 spinach leaves
butter *or* bacon fat
brandy (optional)

If you decide to bone the quails—well done! Allow 10–15 minutes per bird and listen to the radio. Then take the pheasant and remove the skin, bones, and every scrap of gristle and sinew. You should be left with at least 4 oz (110 g) of meat. Cut it up fine and pound to a smooth paste with the cheese. Beat the cream and egg together and moisten the paste. You may not need all the liquid, but the paste should be fairly floppy as it stiffens when cooked. Season with a pinch of salt, milled black pepper, a small pinch of ground mace and 2–3 finely ground juniper berries.

Blanch the spinach leaves in boiling water for a minute, then drain and refresh in cold water. Divide the mousse into six and wrap in the spinach leaves. Lay the quails skin side downwards, place a spinach parcel on to each, and reassemble into nice plump little birds. 'Sew' them up with cocktail sticks, keeping the base flat.

Pack them into a well-buttered dish and secure the legs so that they are tucked neatly beside the bodies. Brush the tops with butter or preferably melted bacon fat, season with salt and pepper and add a dessertspoon of brandy if wished.

Roast in a hot oven (Mk 6, 400°F, 200°C) for 25–35 minutes. It is important to baste the quails frequently since they are roasted for longer in order to cook the stuffing. Red Wine Sauce (p. 170), Francatelli's Venison Sauce (p. 176), or a quick gravy made from the pan juices can be served with the quails.

quails on a bed of spinach

The taste and colour of quails and spinach complement each other beautifully, and this quick dish makes a good first course. More colour can be added with little strips of carrot and red pepper, quickly plunged into boiling salted water till slightly softened.

Serves 6

6 large quails
3 oz (80 g) butter
1 lb (450 g) spinach leaves
4 tablesp water
1 oz (25 g) butter
4 tablesp whipping cream
salt, pepper

Brown the quails all over in hot butter, then put them in a roasting dish and pour the butter over the top. Roast in a hot oven (Mk 7, 425°F, 220°C) for 20 minutes and baste them. Then leave the quails to rest and finish cooking in a cool oven while you prepare the spinach.

Chop the spinach leaves roughly and gently sweat them in the water and butter till soft. Put them in a blender and purée. Then return to the pan and stir in the cream and seasoning. The purée should not be too liquid, so let it reduce a little if necessary.

Just before serving, remove the quails from their dish, drain off the fat, and add the purée to the juices. Stir them together, replace the quails and serve at once.

quails provençales

My aunt Begum cooked quails like this in the south of France. They were so good that Jack Fry ate six, so perhaps my quantities are a little niggardly.

Serves 6

12 quails
1 large aubergine
4 fl oz (125 ml) olive oil
2 onions
2 sweet peppers
2 courgettes
3 cloves garlic
¼ pt (150 ml) red wine
  (optional)
3 ripe tomatoes
salt, pepper
parsley, basil

Slice the aubergine, sprinkle with salt, then leave for at least 30 minutes. This removes excess moisture and any trace of bitterness that might be there. Then press them dry.

Meanwhile, brown the quails briskly all over in hot oil, then set them aside. Lower the heat, then slice the onions and soften them in the same casserole. Add the aubergines, sliced peppers, courgettes and garlic and stir them. If you want to use wine, add it at this point. Cover the casserole and simmer gently for 40 minutes.

Then add the chopped tomatoes. Press the quails into the vegetables, season with salt and pepper, and cook gently for another 30 minutes. Then stir in some freshly chopped parsley and basil. Check the seasoning and serve from the casserole.

quails with plums

The combination of quails and sharp plums is good. Choose fruit that is just ripe and firm, otherwise it turns into a sickly mush. The stock should be well-flavoured; if necessary boil some down beforehand till well-concentrated.

Serves 4

8 quails
3 oz (80 g) butter
8 plums
small glass brandy
½ pt (300 ml) good stock

Brown the quails all over in hot butter, then arrange them neatly in a large dish. Cut the plums in half and remove the stones. Then, using the same hot butter, seal the cut side of the plums quickly and arrange them round the quails.

Drain most of the butter from the pan, then add the brandy and set it alight. It doesn't have to be brandy—whisky or gin are just as good. Shake the pan till the flames go out, then add the stock and scrape up all the juices. Pour them over the quails and plums, season, and bake, uncovered, in a hot oven (Mk 7, 425°F, 220°C) for 25 minutes.

Now check the seasoning. If the plums were very sharp, a tiny sprinkling of sugar might be necessary. Return to the oven for another 10 minutes by which time the quails will be cooked and the plums still intact. Serve from the dish.

quails in bread nests

Depending on the rest of your meal, you may want to double the quantities here.

Serves 6

6 plump quails
6 large cloves garlic
thyme
butter
salt, pepper
½ lb (225 g) mushrooms
2 oz (50 g) butter
¼ pt (150 ml) thick white
    sauce
salt, pepper, nutmeg
6 large slices brown bread

Put a crushed garlic clove, some thyme, and a small knob of butter inside each quail. Rub the skins with salt and pepper. Spit roast, grill, or oven roast to taste, basting frequently with butter.

Meanwhile, prepare the mushroom purée as described on p. 178.

To make the nests, you will need two six-holed bun sheets. If you have the larger tartelet sheets, so much the better as they are a more suitable size. Perhaps you can improvise something. Butter the bread very thinly on both sides. Cut the largest possible circles. Press a circle on to each bun hole and press the other bun sheet on top, squashing the bread into shape. Bake in a hot oven (Mk 6, 400°F, 200°C) for about 10 minutes, until the nests are crisp. Then carefully remove them.

At the last moment, fill the nests with mushroom purée and lay a quail on top.

quails with olives

Vine leaves are not always easy to buy in this country. In recipes like this where they are discarded before serving, I often use blackcurrant leaves instead. Although smaller, they serve very well and are nicely perfumed. Blanch them for a minute first so that they are limp enough to wrap round the quails. Blackcurrant leaves can also be frozen for later use, and then don't need blanching.

Serves 4

8 small quails
6 oz (150 g) green olives
8 vine leaves
8 thin slices fatty pork
8 tablesp oil *or* butter
salt, pepper
8 cloves garlic
2 *or* 3 tablesp hot water
8 slices bread

Stone the olives and plunge them in boiling water for 2 minutes, then drain. Heat half of the oil or butter in a casserole and brown the quails quickly. Then envelop them in vine leaves and put a piece of fatty pork over the top, securing it with string.

Brown the wrapped quails once again in the casserole, then drain off all the fat and season with salt and pepper. Add the olives and garlic (no need to peel it, just slash the skin). Sprinkle in 2–3 tablespoons of hot water, cover the casserole and let the quails cook very gently for 40 minutes. Add a little extra water if necessary.

Trim the bread into neat shapes and brown the slices in the remaining oil or butter. Depending on the bread, a little extra may be needed. When the quails are cooked, take off the pork and vine leaves. Place the quails on their fried bread. Discard the garlic cloves, adjust the seasoning, then pour the olives and their juice over the quails. Serve very hot.

quails and quinces

Quinces are worth growing for the smell of their fruit alone. Try putting some ripe yellow quinces into a pot with a lid. Next day open it and enjoy the most exquisite perfume, one of those simple discoveries that make life worth living.

Serves 4

1 lb (450 g) ripe quinces
8 quails
4 tablesp brandy
sugar
3 oz (80 g) butter
salt, pepper

Slice 6 quinces crossways into thinnish slices. Hundreds of plump little pips will fall out: hooray, you can grow some more quinces. Discard the ends and lay the pretty slices in a deep dish with the quails. The quails should not be touching or they won't cook evenly. Sprinkle the brandy all over them and seal the dish so that it is airtight. Leave for 2–3 days.

Make a little jelly with the remaining quinces and trimmings. Chop them roughly, cover with water and simmer till soft. Strain through a thick folded tea towel and weigh out ½ lb (225 g) sugar for every ½ pt (300 ml) liquid. Dissolve the sugar, then bring to a fast boil and skim until the jelly reaches setting point (test on a cold plate). Pour into a clean warm jar.

When ready to cook the quails, dot them with the butter, season lightly with salt and pepper and cover the dish so that it is airtight again. Two or three layers of foil crimped over the edge will do, or seal the lid with flour and water paste. Bake in a very hot oven (Mk 9, 475°F, 240°C) for 30 minutes. Serve from the dish, with quince jelly and the brandied buttery juices.

quails with drambuie

Given this book's subtitle, you might expect to see a drop of Drambuie featured somewhere. Quails may not spring readily to mind as a partner, but their delicate flavour and the sharp dusky taste of raspberries are well-complemented by Drambuie. You would have to hypnotise Mrs McKinnon to find out what the spices are; they are subtle and I have not presumed to add more.

The stock must be well-flavoured but not overpowering—good homemade chicken stock will just do. The honey I suppose ought to be heather, but unless you heat it up it will hardly trickle off a spoon, so I use clear flower honey instead.

Serves 6

12 quails
2 oz (50 g) butter
dessertsp honey
salt, black pepper
1½ pt (850 ml) pale poultry
    stock (p. 164)
6 tablesp Drambuie
4 oz (110 g) raspberries
spring greens or dark green
    12 oz (340 g) cabbage
    leaves

Toss the quails all over in the well-heated butter until they are golden brown. Arrange them in a roasting tin, spooning most of the butter on top. Trickle the honey over the birds, season lightly with salt and pepper, and put them to roast in a moderately hot oven (Mk 5, 375°F, 190°C) for 40 minutes, basting once or twice.

While they cook, boil down the stock rapidly to ¾ pt (425 ml). Re-heat the pan in which the quails were browned, spoon in the Drambuie and set it alight. Add the stock and scrape up the pan juices. Bring to the boil to amalgamate the flavours, season very delicately, then keep warm until the quails are cooked.

Shortly before serving, add the raspberries to the sauce and warm them through gently. They should not be cooked, just slightly softened so that their sharpness contrasts with the sweetish sauce.

Cut the spring greens or cabbage into strips and boil in salted water. Drain as soon as it is cooked.

Serve the quails on their nest of shredded cabbage with the sauce and raspberries spooned over the top. The honey juice from the roasting tin may also be used. The honey may make the dish too sweet for some tastes, so serve it separately.

lemon quails

This is a cold dish, suitable for a lunch or buffet. The quails are stuffed and poached, then set in a crystal-clear jelly.

Serves 4

4 quails
2 small juicy lemons
4 oz (110 g) petit-suisse
   cheese
salt, black pepper, chives
4 spinach leaves
1¼ pt (700 ml) clarified
   poultry stock (p. 164)
a little sherry (optional)
2 rounded teasp gelatine

I'm afraid you must bone the quails for this dish. Allow 10–15 minutes per bird and use a small pointed knife. Grate the rind off one of the lemons and mash it into the soft cheese with a pinch of salt, some milled black pepper and snipped chives. Divide into four and wrap in the spinach leaves. If you blanch the leaves first they become limp and easier to handle.

Lay the boned quails untidy side upwards and put a spinach parcel on each one, untidy end next to the meat to make a better seal (that's the point of the leaves). Reassemble the quails and secure with a cocktail stick. Tie the legs neatly so they stay in place. Pack them into a small pan and pour ½ pt (300 ml) of the stock over them. Bring to simmering point, cover, and poach for 45 minutes. Lift out the quails to cool slightly, then remove cocktail sticks and trussing string.

The poaching liquid will be cloudy because of the cheese and is unsuitable for clear jelly. So warm the remaining stock with seasoning and lemon juice. Quite how much you use depends on the flavour of your stock. A little drop of medium sweet sherry is good. When you have a well-flavoured crystal clear stock, dissolve the gelatine and stir it in.

Arrange the quails in a white dish with the golden jelly poured over them. Or lay them upside down in a decorated mould, pour the jelly over, and turn them out when set.

quail's eggs

When this book was first mooted, I had grandiose ideas about filling many pages with recipes for quail's eggs—after all nobody else has. I now realise why—quite frankly I'd just as soon use a free-range hen's egg. Of course children love quail's eggs because they are so tiny, and they do make a pretty addition to a perfectly collated salad. I suppose the slimmer could have a wee poached quail's egg in his consommé.

If presenting them as a starter, here's one idea that will entrance all your friends except the ones who can't be bothered with such frippery.

Serves 6

2 dozen quail's eggs
heaped teasp turmeric and
    1 tablesp oil
heaped teasp paprika and
    1 tablesp oil
½ pt (300 ml) strong tea and
    1 dessertsp soy sauce
a bunch of spinach leaves
salad leaves
mayonnaise

Cover the quail's eggs in cold water, bring slowly to the boil and simmer for 1 minute. Drain, then roll them all over on a hard surface so that the shells craze. Plunge 12 into cold water, then shell them.

Simmer six of the remaining crazed eggs in the strong tea and soy sauce for 1 hour. Chop the spinach finely and simmer in ½ pt (300 ml) water with the other six crazed eggs for an hour. Peel when cold to reveal the marbling.

Prick the 12 shelled eggs all over with a needle. Mix the turmeric and oil together and roll six eggs in this paste. Do likewise with the paprika and oil. Leave for 1 hour, then rinse to reveal the speckling.

Shred the salad leaves and make into six little nests. Pour a dribble of runny mayonnaise into each (bought mayonnaise can be improved and liquefied by beating an egg yolk (hen's) into it). Pop four pretty little eggs into each nest and admire your handiwork. Fiddly, isn't it?

Coturnix.
The Quail.

Coturnix fæmina.
A Hen Quail.

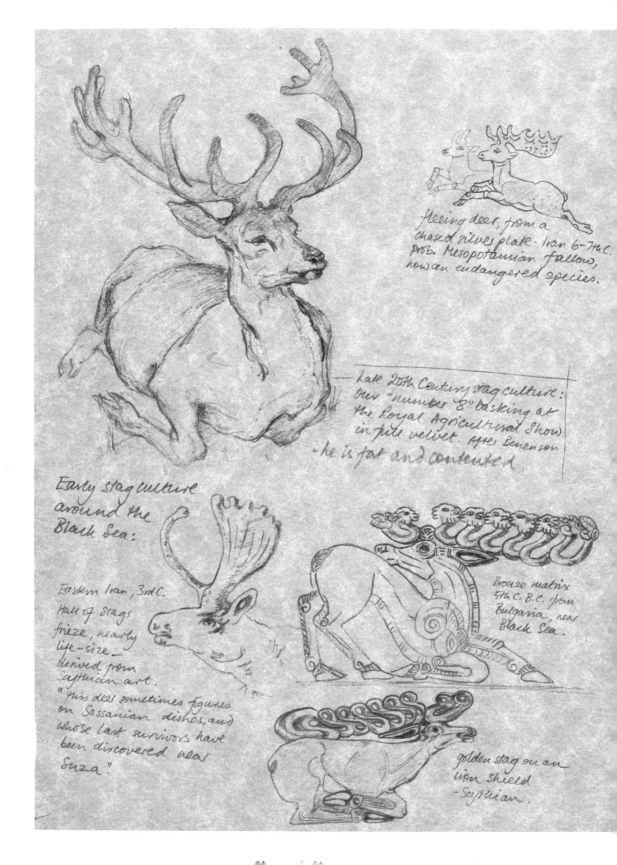

fleeing deer, from a
chased silver plate - Iran 6-7th C.
prob. Mesopotamian fallow,
now an endangered species.

Late 20th Century stag culture:
our "number 8" basking at
the Royal Agricultural Show
in full velvet. After Benenson
- he is fat and contented.

Early stag culture
around the
Black Sea:

Eastern Iran, 3rd C.
Hall of Stags
frieze, nearly
life-size -
derived from
Scythian art.
"this deer sometimes figures
on Sassanian dishes, and
whose last survivors have
been discovered near
Suza."

Bronze matrix
5th C. B.C. from
Bulgaria, near
Black Sea.

golden stag on an
iron shield
- Scythian.

6
Venison

'And Solomon's provision for one day was 30 measures of flour, and three score measures of meal, ten fat oxen and 20 oxen from the pastures, and an hundred sheep, beside harts, and roebucks, and fallow deer, and fatted fowl.' We start off with Solomon's seal of approval —venison must now resume its place in our everyday diet.

The Egyptians seem to be among the first to have enclosed deer to provide meat for their great banquets, and indeed would roast whole carcases in their huge ovens. The Greeks further refined their husbandry and observed deer's habits in great detail. Aristotle noted with interest how deer apparently ate serpents, though modern sceptics would say that the unfortunate beast had probably just sneezed out some nostril maggots.

Ever ones to feed their gluttony, the Romans kept deer inside wooden palisades 'so that when the custom of giving feasts called for game, it might be produced, as it were, out of store.' Columella gives sensible advice on suitable feedstuffs, especially important when rearing young, and recommended introducing hand reared animals to quieten the herd.

The Romans loved their venison, so brought fallow deer with them to Britain to stock their parks. Mediaeval deer parks were remarkably common considering the population at the time, some 1,900 were recorded in England alone, with as many as 300 head enclosed in some cases. Husbandry was well organised, with areas fenced off to grow hay or oats for winter feeding and to conserve coppices. Perhaps the keepers of Falkland Palace in Fife had read Columella's advice, for there is an account of two cows being purchased to provide milk for orphan deer calves in the fifteenth century.

The parks contained both red and fallow deer and were used as a convenient source of fresh meat as well as providing a measure of sport. Queen Elizabeth I was particularly fond of hunting deer, continuing the sport until over 75. At Cowdrey one day, she rode in to find 'a delicate bowre prepared, under which were her Highness' musicians placed; and a crossbow, by a nymph with a sweet song, was delivered into her hands to shoot at the deere; about some thirty were put into a paddock, of which number she killed three or four'.

The Civil War occasioned the decimation of many parks, those left being retained mainly for decoration. After this period, the whole idea of husbanding deer virtually disappeared; from thenceforth they were regarded either as landscape gardener's props or creatures to be hunted by generations of sportsmen. When they ran out of wild deer Englishmen took to hunting carted stags. This was not quite so unsporting as it sounds. The stags were reared in paddocks, and on the appointed day, the chosen stag was led into a specially made cart (some hopped in themselves with alacrity), trundled out into the countryside, and released. Horsemen and hounds would then give chase, but once the stag was harboured the dogs were called off. Some stags appeared to enjoy this, becoming celebrities. One such, named Winchelsea, had such an affinity with his keeper Mr Crust, that whenever Winchelsea had tired of running, he would give himself up and there, miraculously, would be Crust and his cart, ready to take him home for tea.

In Scotland the deer 'forests' provided the more rugged sport of stalking. MacPherson of Cluny was reputedly the first Highland gentleman to stalk deer for no other reason than the sheer thrill of it—a very different matter from the procurement of venison and hides, however exciting that may prove to be. This happened just a few months before Bonnie Prince Charlie's defeat at Culloden, followed closely by the influx of sheep and the Highland clearances—dark days of Scottish history. The controversial promotion of deer stalking in the nineteenth century was an economic necessity for lairds whose sheep had suddenly become of little value when cheaper Australian wool came on the market.

Deer stalking quickly became popular, encouraged by the writings of William Scrope and Millais and a great outpouring of romantic painting. With his proud demeanour, Landseer's 'Monarch of the Glen' epitomises the ideal of the stalker. The home comforts of horse and hound were spurned —crawling through bog and tick-ridden heather was the thing.

Romantic and spartan this life may be, but I believe that the decline in deer husbandry and the prolonged period of sport at all cost is largely responsible for many people's belief that venison is *per se* tough and dry and over-strong. This sad state of affairs occurs when aged beasts have, because of the rough terrain, been shot, retrieved, and hung under far from ideal conditions. Although the Victorian sportsman naturally preferred a mature eight- to ten-year-old with a fine head, once seated at the dining table, he proclaimed a young yeld hind afforded the best eating.

Having said this, I'd better point out that venison's unfortunate reputation has earlier beginnings. When John Manwood wrote his *Treatyse of the Laws of the Forest* in 1615, he mentions that, although venison was the privilege of the nobility, 'those deer that are not sweet nor meet to be eaten by the best of people. . . . The flesh shall be given to the poor and lame and the head and skin shall be given to the poor of the next Town.'—a statement hardly likely to leave the common people enamoured of such a delicacy. Even the middle classes were not immune—venison sent into town from the country often arrived in less than perfect condition. Pepys mentions with disgust 'a damned venison pasty that stank like the devil', and John Johnston recalls sending a venison pie to Antwerp for his brother's wedding. It too arrived in a sorry state.

Strangely, though, the passion for deer stalking was indirectly responsible for the emergence of modern deer farming. In the late 1870s a shipment of deer from Invermark in Angus was imported into New Zealand. Several others followed suit and were released for sporting purposes. The deer thrived and multiplied in the lush forests, eventually causing serious destruction, and ultimately were classed as vermin to be slaughtered by any means possible. However, the price paid for the by-products of the extermination campaign (tails, pelts, velvet antlers) by Oriental medicine-makers was such that one or two entrepreneurs decided to farm these pests, much to the derision of their neighbours.

That was in the late 1960s. Deer farming in Britain started only a year or so later, for different reasons. The Hill Farming Research Organisation in Kincardineshire was looking about for alternative land uses for high ground, and considered deer worthy of consideration. Over in the west, a handsome young veterinary surgeon, researching the behaviour of wild deer on the Isle of Rhum, wondered what to do when his PhD was finished. After all, his enclosed deer bred successfully and were easy to manage, and a growing awareness of animal fat meant that venison should have great potential. My dear husband sent his newly-wed young wife back to Edinburgh and told her that he wouldn't come off his island until she had found a suitable farm. It took me three weeks to find Reediehill, but thereby hangs another tale.

Having spent all my married life involved in the emergence of deer farming, it is perhaps not surprising that I have strong views on the subject. I realise that we are in a privileged position: in starting again, we can look selectively at modern agriculture; and we can observe the behaviour of wild deer in order to work with these delightful creatures, not against them. Venison's appeal lies in its taste, its lack of fat, and its freedom from the more unsavoury aspects of modern farming. Let's keep it like that. (End of sermon—you may now sing a jolly song.)

Venison: The Meat

Alexis Soyer rated venison as 'the second great pedestal . . . of English cookery'. Since turtle soup (his first great pedestal) has met its demise, that elevates venison to first place, exactly where I should have put it myself.

Venison is a highly desirable meat for today because of its marvellous flavour which exists without the help of fat. I don't wish to pursue too vigorous an anti-fat campaign, for many meats lose their flavour without it, but in today's climate of cholesterol-conscious consumers it is worth taking a closer look.

Young venison (most farmed venison is sold at around eighteen months) may have only 5 per cent fat, though admittedly a fully mature stag of five or six years may have 20 per cent by the end of a good summer. Beef has around 20 per cent and lamb 25 per cent. Furthermore, half of venison's fat consists of polyunsaturates (that's the less harmful sort) as opposed to beef and lamb's mere 5 per cent. Another advantage is that all venison's fat is distributed on the exterior of the carcase—there is no marbling—and is easily trimmed off if so desired.

But in case you think me hopelessly biased, I'll mention a disadvantage. Like mutton fat, it has a high melting point, so where venison fat is around, serve it piping hot and skim the gravy diligently or your enthusiasm may congeal. An almost total lack of cholesterol may be an enormous advantage for diabetics and dieticians, but it does mean that sympathetic cooking is required in order that it should remain moist. This is particularly so with roasting, and I do urge you to read that most important section.

Enough of fat—what of taste? Red deer are naturally forest animals, grazing mainly on grass in the clearings, with small amounts of leaves, apples, acorns etc. In the Highland glen he does his best with heather and grass, and a few raided trees or potatoes if he can find them. Frequently there is nothing at all and then he dies. On farms, deer grown for venison graze on grass, supplemented by hay, potatoes, apples etc when necessary: in other words, a fairly natural diet. They are, by and large, healthy creatures and grow well enough without growth stimulants and antibiotics. So the meat is good.

In the section on hanging game, I have pointed out that the conditions under which a deer lives, be it wild, park or farmed, have far less bearing on the final flavour of its meat than the conditions imposed on the carcase after dispatch. Age has a far greater effect, for old venison needs much longer hanging to make it tender, and this affects the flavour. Young venison can be hung to acquire a good venison flavour or else hung until gamy, but it will always be tender. It is up to you to ask for what you want.

Since deer farming is a new industry and its venison relatively scarce, considerable amounts of wild venison are also consumed. When you know its origin and likely age, you can deal with it accordingly, but once the head is removed it is almost impossible to age a carcase. That is why so many people have had unfortunate experiences with wild venison. However well-meaning, the vendor simply doesn't know what he is selling and can therefore offer little helpful advice.

Very briefly, there are exceptions, I know—here are the wild species most commonly sold in this country: roe deer generally produce the most reliable wild venison. Roe are tiny, have a relatively short life, and fine-textured meat. Fallow deer may be wild or from a park (they are also farmed in small numbers). The meat is a little darker and at some times of the year has considerably more fat. It can be excellent, but beware the old buck! Sad to say, wild red deer, the majority of which comes from the Highlands, are the least reliable, due mainly to the difficult terrain over which they are stalked. When well shot and carefully handled, though, the young Prince of the Glen has a great deal to offer.

Grilling and Sautéing

Generally speaking, venison steaks and chops are perfectly straightforward, but bear in mind: because it is lean, venison does not take kindly to being fiercely cooked past the medium rare stage. But all trace of pinkness can be eliminated by cooking quickly to medium rare so that both sides are well browned, then resting the meat in a plate-warming oven. This process also relaxes the steaks and keeps them juicy. The length of time depends on thickness.

Unless you like very rare or 'blue' steaks, thick steaks also need to be rested after initial fierce cooking, rather like small roasting joints. Otherwise the outside will have dried up long before the centre has cooked.

If you need to cut down on fat, brush the meat with a thin coating of oil and quickly brown in a pan or under the grill. Thin pieces cook quickest and therefore need less oil, but *do* undercook, then rest as before or the meat will be very dull. The unhealthily delicious taste of grilled butter can be replaced by pressing a few spices or fresh herbs on the surface. But without any additions, venison is healthier and tastier when not overcooked.

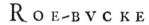

venison steaks with red wine sauce

This is the simplest red wine sauce of all. It should be made speedily so that the steaks don't dry up. It doesn't work quite so well with smaller quantities since there is not much in the way of pan juices to give flavour. I actually prefer the red wine sauce on p. 170, but for that you need stock.

Serves 4–6

2 lb (900 g) venison steaks
dessertsp butter
dessertsp oil
3 shallots
¼ pt (150 ml) red wine
3 oz (80 g) butter
parsley (optional)
salt, pepper

Heat the butter and oil in a large pan till very hot and seal the steaks on both sides. Then reduce the heat and cook to taste. Remember to undercook the steaks slightly, since they will continue their cooking while you make the sauce. Remove the steaks to keep warm and drain most of the fat from the pan.

Chop the shallots very finely indeed and cook them gently in the steak pan until transparent. Add the wine and let it bubble away until it is thick and syrupy and much reduced. Then draw the pan off the heat and beat in the butter, a little at a time, until it has thickened the sauce. You may not need the full 3 oz (80 g). Season to taste and add a good handful of chopped parsley if wished. Serve immediately with the steaks.

venison in blackberry sauce

We were delighted when we heard that one of our customers, Sheila Harrison from Aberdeen, had won a national cooking competition using our venison. When she came to stock up her freezer I asked if I could include her recipe in this book, as it is simple but very good. As with so many recipes of this sort, good stock is vital, and if you buy your venison on the bone, then you have the main stock ingredient already there. Mrs Harrison served her prize-winning dish with her Vegetable Terrine (see p. 184) and Juniper Potatoes (p. 188).

Serves 3–6

1½ lb (675 g) venison fillet (6 chops could also be used if you cut out the noisette of meat and use the rest for stock)
¾ pt (425 ml) excellent venison stock
6 tablesp blackberry vinegar
some blackberries for garnish
salt, pepper

Cut the venison into six steaks and sauté them without fat in a non-stick pan for 1 to 2 minutes per side. This makes them very rare. (4 minutes per side would make them medium—I wouldn't recommend well-done steaks for this recipe.) Keep the steaks warm in a low oven.

Add the stock to the pan juices, then stir in the blackberry vinegar and reduce this rapidly to a syrup. Check the seasoning, then pour a little puddle of sauce on to each plate and place the noisette on top. Garnish with the blackberries.

pitmedden forest mushroom steak

Our neighbour's daughter Trishie, at the grand old age of 11, dreamt up (with only a little help from her friends), exhaustively tested, and finally cooked this dish in front of a panel of judges for a children's cookery competition. She was quite remarkable: while her mother and I knocked back gin with trembling hands, Trishie calmly coped with blazing TV lights, a babble of questions from the press and various other distractions, grinning cheerfully throughout. She won the Scottish final and went on to a repeat performance at the Savoy Hotel.

Trishie's theme was local and wild food and all her ingredients came from within a few hundred yards of her home. Except the rice, even with a soggy summer like 1985 our paddy fields wouldn't grow that. The steaks must be cut into a half-circle with any sinews trimmed off the edges to prevent curling in the pan. Topside steaks are admirably shaped.

Serves 2

2 × 6 oz (170 g) venison
  steaks
8 oz (225 g) blackberries
¼ pt (150 ml) good venison
  stock
2 oz (50 g) rice
4 oz (110 g) horse-
  mushrooms *or* shaggy
  caps
3 oz (80 g) butter
2 wild garlic cloves
3–4 oz (80–100 g) sorrel
  (a good bunch)
¼ pt (150 ml) stock *or* water
fennel
salt, pepper

Stew the blackberries for 10 minutes and make them into a smooth purée. Add this to the good venison stock and boil to reduce. Put the rice in a greased dish, add the stock or water and a good pinch of salt, and cook with the lid on in a moderate oven (Mk 4, 350°F, 180°C) until all the liquid is absorbed. This takes about 30 minutes.

Select 4 small mushrooms and 2 large stalks and keep these aside for later. Chop the rest really fine and soften them in 2 oz (50 g) of the butter with the crushed garlic.

Slit each steak to make a pocket with the flat side having the opening. Use a very sharp pointed knife for this job and take the cut as near to the edges as you dare. Stuff the mushroom mixture into the pockets, stitch them shut, and fry in 1 oz (25 g) hot butter, turning to brown both sides.

Rinse and cook the wet sorrel in a saucepan with a tiny pinch of salt.

Now assemble the dish. Coat the bottom of each plate with the blackberry sauce. Make a line of sorrel on the bottom, then put the steak about half way up, giving it a mushroom stalk and placing the other two appropriately to form a clump of mushrooms. Carefully arrange the rice in a semi-circle round the top of the mushroom steak, strew a little chopped fennel over it, et voilà! a pretty pastoral scene which tastes as good as it looks.

venison chops with gin and yoghourt

Grenville Foster gave me this recipe and it has proved very popular. Gin is a fairly obvious choice of spirit to use with game, since it has the pungent flavour of juniper berries. There are a lot of flavours here, and it is a filling dish.

Serves 4

4 big *or* 8 small venison
    chops
Yoghourt Sauce (p. 173)
2 cloves garlic
2 oz (50 g) butter
1 medium onion
1 tablesp tomato purée
sea salt
½ wine glass gin
regani (Dutch oregano)
paprika

First make the Yoghourt Sauce. Then chop the garlic finely and fry it in 1 oz (25 g) of the butter until it is just beginning to brown. Chop the onion, add it to the pan and cook gently until soft and golden. Stir in the tomato purée and remove to a side dish.

Melt the butter in the pan and sprinkle some sea salt in it. When it is very hot seal the venison chops on both sides, then cook to taste. Pour in the gin and set fire to it (stand well back!). When the flames have died down, remove the chops and return the tomato/onion mixture to blend in with the pan juices and warm through. When nearly warm, replace the chops on top and sprinkle a pinch of dried regani on to them. Marjoram or ordinary oregano can be used instead but use more sparingly if the latter. Just before serving, add the Yoghourt Sauce (p. 173) and dust with paprika.

korean bulgogi

When Tim Wallis, New Zealand's pioneering deer farmer, first gave me this recipe there was much less sesame salt in it, as he couldn't believe the quantities. But now he tells me that there really should be this much and so here is the more authentic version. This is a good open-air recipe since the actual cooking is so quick—the Wallises have served it countless times at New Zealand venison promotions, with great success.

Serves 4–6

1 lb (450 g) venison shoulder
    or neck in large slabs
2 tablesp soy sauce
1 tablesp sugar
1 tablesp sesame oil
1 cup sesame salt (see below)
4 medium green onions,
    chopped
3 cloves garlic
1 teasp fresh ginger, finely
    chopped
water *or* white wine to cover

Cut the venison across the grain into slices as thin as possible (this is much easier to do if the meat is half-frozen). Stir all the marinade ingredients together and steep the meat in it for 2 hours. Then drain the meat and sear it over a good barbecue grill.

To make sesame salt
Spread a cup of sesame seeds on to a large non-stick frying pan and stir constantly while they brown and pop. Do not plan to do anything else while they cook; they know exactly when your attention is elsewhere and will burn immediately. When they are an even dark golden brown, completely pulverise them in a pestle and mortar. Then add ½ cup of salt to every cup of crushed seeds and blend again.

marinated heart with fresh herbs

Venison heart is rather an unusual dish, but it is becoming extremely popular with our customers—gone are the days when we and our cat used to have them all. You can buy whole hearts to stuff and bake, or simply cut in half and grill, but most people seem to prefer them ready-sliced. Here are two quick ways of cooking them. Those who have an aversion to pink meat should stick to the slow-cooking method because if overcooked the meat will be like rubber bands instead of succulent rosettes with an interesting bite to them.

Serves 4

1½ lb (675 g) sliced heart
1 medium onion
2 cloves garlic
chopped fresh herbs
olive oil
red wine *or* wine vinegar
butter and oil to cook
more herbs to serve
salt, pepper

Trim any fat off the slices and remove any gristle from the centre. Chop the onion and garlic finely and put them into a bowl with the heart. Add a good quantity of fresh herbs—parsley, chives, thyme or lovage—though use the latter in moderation as it is very strong. Sprinkle enough oil and wine (in roughly equal quantities) to cover the meat. Mix in well, cover the bowl and leave to marinate. Overnight is fine, but it will improve for several days. Stir everything around from time to time so that the oil is mixed in.

When ready to use, lift out the meat and pat it dry. Heat some butter and oil in a large pan till beginning to brown a little. Then brown the slices for about 2 minutes per side. Remove to a warm oven to rest for 10–15 minutes.

While the meat rests, strain the marinade and skim off as much oil as possible. Add a few spoonfuls of the remainder to the pan and dissolve the pan juices. If you used wine for the marinade you can add more, but go easy with wine vinegar. A little rowan or redcurrant jelly, yoghourt or cream may be added to extend the sauce if desired. Season to taste, add a good handful of herbs, and pour over the sliced heart.

venison hearts with cucumber sauce

Serves 4

1½ lb (675 g) sliced hearts
½ small cucumber
butter
¼ pt (150 ml) cream *or* yoghourt
salt, pepper

Peel the cucumber and chop it into small dice. Sprinkle with salt and leave for at least 1 hour, then rinse it under the tap. Pickled gherkins may be used instead for a sharper taste.

Trim the slices of heart as before, then beat them hard on both sides with a metal steak bat to flatten and tenderise them.

Heat a good knob of butter till turning brown, and quickly sauté the slices on both sides. Do a few at a time so that they brown quickly. Remove to a warm oven to rest for 10 minutes, seasoning with a little salt and pepper. This period of resting slackens the meat and disperses the pink juices evenly.

Drain excess butter from the pan, then stir in the cream or yoghourt to dissolve the pan juices. Add the cucumber and heat gently until it is warmed through. Season, and serve with the sliced heart.

roe venison with pine kernels

Sophy Weatherall sent me this recipe for roe venison. The 'secret ingredients', she says, are the pine kernels and the grinding of the pepper 'till your arm aches'.

Serves 6

6 loin of venison steaks
just over 1 pt (570 ml) rough
   red wine
2 fl oz (55 ml) olive *or*
   sunflower oil
2 teasp fresh thyme (*or* ½
   teasp dried)
1 sliced onion
1 tablesp flour
1 tablesp cornflour
¾ pt (425 ml) stock
6 slices bread
2 oz (50 g) butter
1 tablesp brandy
2–3 tablesp Worcestershire
   sauce
black pepper
2 oz (50 g) pine kernels

Reserving 1 glass of wine, put the venison into a plastic bag to marinate with the rest of the wine, oil, thyme and onion. Shake them together and leave in a cool place overnight. Next day, drain and dry the meat. Boil the marinade for 5 minutes, then strain out the onion etc, and reduce the liquid to 4 fl oz (110 ml), half of which should be the oil.

In a separate bowl, mix together the flour and cornflour and stir in the stock slowly so there are no lumps. Add the stock and flour to the reduced marinade and cook until the mixture thickens. Allow it to simmer for another 5 to 10 minutes and then set aside.

Meanwhile trim the slices of bread to fit the steaks, fry these croûtes in butter, and drain them well. Brown and cook the steaks in the same butter. I would slightly undercook them since they will finish themselves off while keeping warm. Add the brandy and ignite it. After it has stopped burning, remove the steaks and place them on the croûtes, keeping them warm.

Pour the remaining glass of wine into the pan, scraping into it all the pan juices. Reduce this to practically nothing, then add the sauce you have already made and reduce a little more. Then add the Worcestershire sauce and grind in pepper until your arm aches. Reduce still more, scraping the edges of the pan until the sauce goes a very dark brown and looks as if it may separate. Throw in the pine kernels and taste the sauce.

The final sauce should amount to about 6 tablespoons—enough to coat each steak. Serve with a purée of chestnuts (see p. 178).

Roasting

Most of us feel at home when grilling a venison steak or making a venison stew. But when it comes to roasting, many people feel less confident. In fact it is very simple once the whys and wherefores are understood, and I hope now that I can finally dispel all worries.

I have already explained on p. 121 that venison is an extremely lean meat without a marbling of fat. Because of this I have given you two different methods of roasting which should cover all eventualities. In general, most people are agreed that venison is at its best when, in Soyer's words, it is 'underdone, red in the middle, and full of gravy, but not raw'. But equally I know that some people dislike pink meat, preferring it really well-done and melting off the bone. All stages from rare to well-done can be achieved, but before you start you must make up your mind which result you want to achieve.

fast cooking method

This is the way to roast venison if you like it rare, medium-rare, or just no longer pink, but not really well-done. It is the best method for those anxious about consuming too much fat. Because we use a high oven temperature here, the meat *must* be cooked with speed so that it has no chance to dry out. Prolonged cooking at a great heat will cause any meat to harden, and because venison is also lean it would dry out badly.

The Method Explained. To explain the theory, here is the Parable of the Baked Egg. Sorry about all these eggs which keep popping up, but they make good examples. Imagine an egg, if you will, broken into its buttered dish and put into a hot oven. In only a few minutes the white has become opaque and the yolk starts to solidify. It is delicious—soft and curdy. But supposing the phone goes and the unfortunate egg is roasted for too long, what happens then? You take it out and what do you find? The white (albumen) has become like a squeaky piece of rubber with an almost impenetrable skin, and the yolk is completely dry. Exactly the same principle applies to meat, which among other goodies contains albumen.

So—when using a high temperature, don't cook for long. The procedure is to brown the joint, then roast it, then rest it. All three stages are important.

Preparation. Using this method, it is not necessary to lard venison unless cooking a really large joint of, say, over 8 lbs/3.5 kg. The slow cooking method gives easy larding instructions. But it is advisable to brown the joint before roasting, particularly if it is small, since the quick cooking leaves little opportunity for browning in the oven. Browning also seals the juices into the meat.

Heat some fat or oil, or a mixture, in a frying pan till very hot but not burning, and brown the meat thoroughly on all sides. The fat can be dripping, lard, butter or margarine—use ½ oz per pound plus 1 oz over (30 g/1 kg + 50 g). If using oil, less is needed but use one of good quality as it will impart flavour.

Then lift the joint into its roasting tin and pour the fat over the top. You may season with milled black pepper and crushed juniper berries, but only a light sprinkling of salt. To compensate for the lack of pan juices (small joints do not produce much with this method) a few spoonfuls of beer, wine or orange juice may be put in the base of the pan and used to baste the joint. Don't use too much or the joint will start stewing. Alternatively, serve one of the sauces in Chapter 7. Only very large joints need to be covered.

Roasting Times for Fast Cooking. I am wary of giving exact cooking times, because they are determined by the thickness of the joint as well as its total weight. A 5 lb/2.3 kg piece of haunch could be anywhere from 3–6 inches/8–15 cm thick, depending on the cut, and obviously the thick piece will take longer to cook. But as a general guide, the oven should be very hot (Mk 8, 450°F, 230°C) and cooking times are as follows: 10 m/lb (20 m/kg) for rare venison, and 15–20 m/lb (30–40 m/kg) for medium rare, after initial browning. Very large joints need less minutes per pound than small ones, for example, a whole haunch weighing 20 lbs/9 kg will only take 3–4 hours to become medium rare. A meat thermometer is a great help—use beef temperatures but *always* slightly undercook to allow time for resting.

The longer venison is in the oven, the better it will be if basted at intervals, and if you don't have a meat thermometer you can check progress by piercing the joint deeply with a skewer and observe the juices that run out. Bright red juices indicate rare meat, rose red indicates medium rare. Remember to take courage and undercook so that you can rest your joint.

Resting. The period of resting completes the cooking and relaxes the meat. The larger and thicker the joint, the more important this is. When the joint is taken from the hot oven into the cool or plate-warming oven it is rather unevenly cooked. The outside is comparatively well-done while the centre of a big joint may be almost raw. Resting the meat for 10–15 minutes (30 or more for a large joint) means that the heat travels on toward the centre and at the same time the redder juices in the centre are drawn back towards the edge. The result is a more evenly cooked and tender joint.

To produce venison that has just lost its pink tinge, but is still beautifully moist, cook to medium rare, but rest for at least 30 minutes in a cool oven. Once again, you can test the colour of the juices which should be clear with the faintest tinge of pink. This is how I do venison when I have an unknown visitor because if you like pink venison you can just call it pink, but if you like brown venison you can pronounce it brown! And don't forget that hot plates cook meat too.

slow roasting method

This is the way to roast venison when you want it really well done. Cooked this way, venison gains full benefit from being left on the bone as it stays more succulent. Carving is simple because the meat comes off the bone easily. It produces the most marvellous gravy, but since that gravy comes out of the joint it is necessary to lard the meat in order to keep it succulent. After the meat is sealed it is then cooked at a low temperature. Returning to the eternal egg analogy, this method is similar to baking an egg custard. Because it is baked in a slow oven, the egg never becomes hot enough to harden and the custard, though cooked, stays moist.

Preparation and Larding. Lard the meat. The conventional way of larding is to chill some pork fat, cut it into strips, and 'sew' it with a larding needle under the surface of the meat. It looks wonderful and gives a tremendous feeling of satisfaction, but quite honestly I find that my method (which is easier) is far better for venison.

Take a small knife and stab the meat all over at 1½-inch/4-cm intervals, pressing a knob of fat deep into the holes as you go. The fat may be dripping, lard, butter or margarine. Garlic or any other flavouring may be introduced as well if you wish. The advantage of this method is that the fat goes deep down into the meat (remember venison has no marbling of fat), and keeps it succulent as it cooks. Another advantage is that most of the fat melts out during cooking, so there is very little left in the meat—it is easy to skim the gravy.

Once larded, the meat should be sealed by browning in a frying pan or putting it into a hot oven for 15–30 minutes depending on size. If the latter, spread a little more fat over the joint. Then season with milled black pepper, crushed juniper berries and a sprinkling of salt. A little moisture of some sort (water, red wine, beer, orange juice etc) may be put into the tin, and a few onions roasted beside the joint are traditionally delicious. Now cover the tin with a lid or foil and lower the oven to slow (Mk 3, 325°F, 170°C).

Cooking Times for Slow Roasting. Everybody knows that it takes just as long to stew two pounds of meat as it does to stew six. It is not so different for a slow-roasted joint; the only variation being that thick joints will need longer because there is more to heat up.

On average I would allow 40 minutes per pound (85 m/kg) plus an extra 40 minutes for joints up to 6 lb/2.7 kg. Above 7 lbs/3 kg, 30 minutes per pound (65 m/kg) in total should suffice, and really huge joints will need proportionately less. During this time the venison should be basted at intervals. The more often you baste, the better your venison and gravy will be. It is not necessary to rest slow-roasted venison.

Cold Roast Venison

Cold roast venison is delicious, but only when it has not been overcooked in the first place. Well-done venison, though delicious when hot, can be rather dry and crumbly when cold. So use the fast-cooking method and roast to the rare side of medium (less if you like, but no more). Then leave to cool, preferably uncut to keep the juice sealed. If you want to use the remains of a roast cold, ask the carver to turn the joint cut side uppermost when he has finished, and spoon a little gravy on top. This will keep the venison moist as it cools.

variations

There are exceptions to every rule. I mention the first three because people have asked for them, the fourth is a curiosity.

Variation 1. Occasionally, customers in our shop announce that they are going to roast their venison in a paste because their book told them to. It is not a bad method, but unless you are experienced in roasting venison you will probably want to see how it is getting on. A meat thermometer is invaluable here as the venison is hermetically sealed in paste and keeps its juices intact, though a certain amount is lost in the discarded paste. There is no gravy, and the joint needs to be browned at the end.

Thus, the great Soyer roasts his haunch of venison in a stiff paste of flour and water an inch thick, but he also says that at the end of the cooking you must take off the paste and test the meat with a skewer. If it is not cooked you have to wrap it up all over again—what a palaver! You can bet your boots that had aluminium foil been around in the nineteenth century M. Soyer would have downed his rolling pin and belted off to get some p.d.q. Because of the thickness of paste, the venison will take a little longer to cook, but may be done quick or slow after the paste has set.

Variation 2. Occasionally I am caught unawares with impromptu visitors who expect to be given venison when they stay here. So I whip a generous-looking piece of haunch out of the freezer, smear it all over with fat, and put it in a cool oven (Mk 2, 300°F, 150°C) to thaw. I cover the top with bacon rashers or foil and baste every now and then so that the surface does not dry out. When the joint is defrosted I slam it into a very hot oven (Mk 8, 450°F, 230°C) and baste like mad. Because the meat is already warm it cooks very quickly indeed. Then I rest it for a good while to make sure the centre is done to a turn. The slow-cooking method doesn't work well here because you can't lard the meat.

Variation 3: Microwaving. Prime venison can be microwaved as successfully as other meats. Bear in mind that microwaves are attracted to fat and bones, the meat nearest to these cooking quicker. So a piece of unlarded boneless venison, because it is lean, takes a fraction longer than a similarly shaped piece of beef. If you wish to cook venison to well-done, lard it at closer intervals and then it will cook as beef. As with all microwaved meat, and large joints in particular, it is always best to undercook slightly and then leave to stand. A minute is a long time in a microwave. If you use the flavourings suggested in this book and the techniques recommended by your handbook you will manage fine. Remember, though, that herbs and spices keep more flavour in a microwave, and anything with sugar cooks ultra-quick, so modify these ingredients a little.

Variation 4. Last summer a Gallic visitor told me that at the most chi-chi dining tables in northern France, venison haunches are now roasted with the skin and fur left on, just in case anybody thinks they have been fobbed off with a piece of imported kangaroo meat. Paranoia in the extreme, I should say.

In theory it is not unlike the flour-and-water paste method. The haunch is wrapped in paper to protect the fur (presumably it is cleaned first), but don't ask me how you carve it. Paul Bocuse modifies this slightly, recommending that just a furry foot be left on. Perhaps it makes a good handle for the carver, but I suspect that a wavering demi-veg would be fully converted to vegetarianism when faced with such a sight, so reserve this method for ghouls and Gauls.

jura venison

A distinct disadvantage of being a so-called venison expert is that sooner or later someone is going to dump a frozen lump of anonymous venison on the table and say, 'Okay then, do it'. That's what happened to me a year or two ago on the island of Jura and this is how I dealt with my block of meat. I took a gamble and guessed (correctly, luckily) that, being a sensible household, they would have kept some of the best young venison for themselves, so I treated it as I would farmed venison, perhaps taking a little more care over the larding. However, if you are uneasy about the source and age of the beast, play safe and marinade it for a day or two.

Serves 8

6 lb (2.7 kg) haunch *or* saddle
 (on the bone)
¾ pt (425 ml) excellent stock
2 lb (900 g) mixed
 vegetables—carrots,
 onions, celery, courgettes,
 tomatoes, etc
sour cream
beurre manié (optional)
sour cream (optional)
salt, pepper
juniper berries
parsley

First produce the stock. If you have bought ready-boned meat, then you may have to make do with tinned consommé. Although I generally think that meat cooks better on the bone, I sometimes bone it for ease of carving and to give me some stock bones, and I put the tougher shank ends into the stock pot for extra flavour.

Brown the bones and meat with some onion in the oven and then scrape them into a pan, rinsing out with 1½ pts (850 ml) water and a little tomato purée to dissolve all the brown bits. Simmer and reduce to ¾ pt (425 ml).

Lard the meat by sticking a small knife into it at 1½ inch intervals and inserting some fat (the better the fat the better the flavour) deep into the holes. Spread more fat, plus salt, pepper, and crushed juniper berries over the top, cover with a lid or foil and roast in a moderate to hot oven for about 15 minutes to the lb, basting frequently. This will yield meat that is rare to medium. A flat slab of meat will of course cook quicker than a square chunk. If this is how you like your meat, then rest it in a cool oven for 10 minutes. But if you dislike pinkness, leave it in a warm oven for ½–¾ hour, by which time the very pink part in the centre will have diffused into the brown at the edge and vice-versa so that you have a joint that is just brown but still nicely succulent. If you overcook it it will be dry and you have only yourself to blame.

While the meat cooks, make the sauce by cooking the vegetables in some of your excellent and concentrated stock. When they are tender, purée them. If the result is watery, then reduce it or add some beurre manié to thicken. If it is extremely thick, then add more stock until it is a good consistency. Add the pan juices after the meat has been removed and season to taste.

To serve, either put the meat into a shallow dish and pour the purée over it, or go Nouvelle and deftly carve the meat into picturesque slices, and arrange them fan-shaped on top of the purée on individual plates. A little sour cream swirled through the purée is pretty and delicious. Garnish with a few strips of vegetable or parsley.

saddle of venison with cream cheese and liver

The cream cheese keeps the venison beautifully moist here, and the liver provides an interesting contrast to its flavour. If you can't abide (or get) venison liver, then poor you, but this is still a dish worth trying if you leave it out.

Many of you may buy your venison boned and rolled. If this is the case, choose as long and thin a shape as possible so that you are able to roll it up again round its filling. Page 14 will give instructions on how to bone saddle—do try because it really isn't difficult.

Serves 6

4 lb (1.8 kg) saddle on the bone
6 oz (170 g) cream cheese *with* 2 large cloves garlic crushed into it
4 oz (110 g) venison liver
3 oz (75 g) butter *or* dripping
6 rashers belly of pork
1 medium onion, chopped
6 oz (170 g) mushrooms, chopped
salt, pepper, paprika, parsley
3–4 tablesp sour cream *or* yoghourt (optional)

Turn the boned or unrolled meat skin side downwards. It will probably look rather strange now, but it doesn't matter. Slice about three-quarters of the way through the thickest part of the meat and spread the cream cheese along the slit.

Toss the sliced liver in a sauté pan with a little butter so that it is nicely browned but still pretty raw. Then lay it alongside the cheese, pressing well in so that it doesn't pop out when you start rolling.

Roll up the meat, starting with the most solid end and using the flap to finish it off. At this point many butchers keep everything in place with a skewer while they tie the first string. It doesn't matter if the string is not perfectly placed since it will be removed before carving. The important thing is to bind everything as tightly as possible.

Heat the dripping in your roasting pan and brown the roll all over. Then lay the strip of belly pork over the top and roast in a very hot oven (Mk 8, 450°F, 230°C) for 45 minutes, basting frequently. Then take it out and let it settle for a few minutes before removing the pork and gently pulling off the strings. Rest the meat in a cool oven while you prepare the trimmings.

Fry the onion till golden brown and soft in the roasting tin, then drain off as much fat as you can. Add the mushrooms and slightly soften them in the onions; they should absorb any fat left. Season with salt, pepper and paprika, and if you can stand the thought of any more delicious cholesterol, stir in three or four tablespoons of sour cream. If not, use yoghourt or water, scraping up all the brownings from the tin.

Pour this over the saddle and dredge with fresh green parsley. The meat should be rosy pink throughout, because its spell in the cool oven will have diffused any really red juices.

a sweet and sour roast

The sweet and sour sauce baked on to the venison makes a very rich and filling course, so choose simple vegetables of the watery kind to go with it. Some will find just a simple green salad quite ample, but you could ring the changes by serving crispy Chinese leaves tossed in a warm not-too-sweet vinaigrette.

Serves 6

3 lb (1 kg) haunch, saddle *or* shoulder
a little fat for browning the meat
¼ pt (150 ml) tomato sauce *or* diluted purée
1 heaped teasp salt
2 tablesp Worcestershire sauce
2 oz (50 g) butter
2 tablesp vinegar
1 sliced orange
1 medium onion, grated
½ teasp ground ginger
pinch allspice

Brown the venison all over in a frying pan. Put all the rest of the ingredients into a saucepan and boil them together for 10 minutes, stirring so that they don't burn.

Put the seared meat into an open roasting tin and pour the sauce over the top. Cook in a medium oven to your liking (see pp. 129/130 for cooking times), and baste the meat frequently with the sauce. It is a good idea to turn the meat occasionally.

The final result will be a thoroughly sticky brown coating on the joint—quite delicious.

saddle of venison with blackcurrant sauce

The success of this dish is determined largely by the quality of stock and by using belly pork not bacon. If you have to use bacon then remove it before serving, otherwise it will drown the other flavours. And if you can't make good stock in time, then use tinned consommé instead.

Serves 6

5 lb (2 kg) saddle
⅔ bottle red wine
8 oz (225 g) pickling onions
8 oz (225 g) belly pork, thinly cut
2 oz (50 g) butter
1 onion ⎫
1 carrot ⎬ diced small
2 sticks celery ⎭
1 heaped tablesp flour
¾ pt (425 ml) excellent stock
3 tablesp blackcurrant purée

Marinate the saddle and peeled onions in the wine overnight. Next day, remove the saddle and bone it out so that you have two small cylindrical joints (see p. 14). Wrap the rashers of belly pork neatly round each joint, securing it with cocktail sticks pressed well in (count them so that you know how many to remove later). Set the stock on to boil with half of the marinade wine and onions.

Melt the butter and oil in a large frying pan and when hot, brown both the joints together all over for 10 minutes. Remove them to a roasting tin and roast in a hot oven (Mk 7, 425°F, 220°C) for 10–15 minutes. Remove the cocktail sticks carefully. The meat should still exude nice red juices at this point. Keep warm in a cool oven for about 10 minutes.

While the meat roasts, gently soften the vegetables in the frying pan, then sprinkle them with the flour to absorb the fat. Add the boiling stock and onions, and stir till smooth. Let this bubble away uncovered for 20 minutes to cook the flour and substantially reduce the sauce. Stir occasionally and top up with more wine as and when necessary.

Once the sauce has thickened nicely, remove the onions and put them round the joints. Add the blackcurrant purée to the sauce and simmer for another 3 minutes, then season and pour it around the meat.

shoulder of venison with mustard and ale

Hearsay has it that Frederick the Great was an exuberant experimenter with bizarre flavourings. Apparently he once made his coffee with champagne and mustard in it; not, I imagine, one of his most successful attempts at gourmandising. Perhaps if he had substituted venison for the coffee he would have found something more to his liking; anyhow I hope that he would have approved of this excellent way of cooking a shoulder.

Although I generally think that venison is at its best when cooked rare, this is a dish which I have to confess is far better when cooked long and slow; so that the meat is melting off the bones with the advantage of being able to slip out the bladebone before the final spreading of the mustard.

Either English or French mustard may be used, each has its merits, but remember that mustard loses its potency when cooked so don't be alarmed at the proportions.

Serves 6

4 lb (1.8 kg) shoulder on the bone
4 tablesp mustard
fat and seasoning for larding
1 pt (570 ml) brown ale
3 tablesp Demerara sugar
salt, pepper

Stick a thin knife into the meat at 1½-inch intervals and squirt a blob of mustard deep into the hole. The easiest way of doing this is to buy a small tube of ready-made mustard and use that, but if you should be on friendly terms with a doctor or a vet then beg a jumbo-sized syringe for the job. Press a good knob of fat into the hole, spread some more over the meat, and season it.

Put the joint into a covered roasting tin with half of the beer and roast in a very hot oven (Mk 8, 450°F, 230°C) for 45 minutes, and then turn the oven down to slow (Mk 3, 325°F, 170°C) for a further 2½ hours, basting frequently and topping up with the beer.

About 30 minutes from the end, take out the meat. Spread the remaining mustard over the meat, dredge with the Demerara sugar, and return it to the oven for the final cooking.

The joint will have a gloriously sticky glaze and the gravy is a ready-made sauce with a most distinctive flavour.

rosettes of venison with stilton and chicken mousseline

Alan Hill, the big white chef at Edinburgh's Caledonian Hotel, sent me this recipe and I thought it rather intriguing. However, since it is to appear in this book, I feel bound to say that a pheasant mousseline might be even better. Use the one on p. 111.

Serves 4

4 × 6 oz (170 g) loin steaks
2 tablesp oil
2 oz (50 g) walnuts
2 oz (50 g) Stilton cheese
½ oz (15 g) mixed fresh herbs
3½ oz (100 g) chicken mousseline
4 fresh basil leaves
a piece of crépine (caul fat)*
¼ pt (150 ml) Port Wine Sauce (p. 169)
salt, pepper

Season the venison steaks and seal them in very hot oil, then remove them from the pan and allow them to cool. Blanch, peel and chop the walnuts (they taste better like this rather than using stale ready-chopped ones) and mix them with the Stilton, fresh herbs, and mousseline.

Place this on the sealed steaks and put a fresh basil leaf on top of each one to decorate. Cover with the crépine and put the steaks into a hot pan and bake in a hot oven (Mk 7, 425°F, 220°C) to taste (anywhere between 10 and 20 minutes depending on how thick they are).

Arrange them on plates and spoon the warm Port Wine Sauce over the top to finish.

venison en croûte with juniper and coriander

This dish is good either hot or cold and it has the advantage of being prepared well in advance, leaving the final cooking until the last minute. If you should want to freeze the joint when part-cooked, then do not wrap it in the pastry as it produces a rather soggy crust.

Serves 6

3 lb (1.4 kg) boned and rolled saddle or haunch
dripping
heaped teasp coriander seeds
heaped teasp juniper berries
2 cloves garlic
salt, pepper
1 tablesp oil
1 lb (450 g) puff pastry
egg yolk to glaze the pastry

Partly roast the joint with a little dripping in a moderately hot oven (Mk 5, 375°F, 190°C). The time will depend on the shape of the joint, but the juices should be still running pink. About 30 minutes is a guide. Leave the joint to cool completely (remember that it will continue to cook a little as it cools). When the joint is quite cold remove the strings.

Crush the coriander seeds, juniper berries and garlic together with a good pinch of salt and black pepper. Mix to a fine paste with the oil. Spread this evenly all over the joint.

Roll out the pastry thinly so that the meat can be easily enveloped

* Caul fat (crépine) isn't the easiest of ingredients to get hold of in this country. If you are stuck, ask the butcher to cut some belly of pork in paper thin slices and drape them over instead. Discard them before serving.

and wrap up the joint carefully, making sure that all the edges are sealed. Put it seam-side downwards in a dish and brush the surface with egg yolk. You can score the pastry with the point of a sharp knife, but make sure that you don't break the pastry seal.

Bake in a hot oven (Mk 6, 400°F, 200°C) for 15 minutes or until the pastry is golden, and then turn the oven off for another 5–10 minutes before serving to make sure the meat is warmed all the way through. If you plan to serve cold, then remove from the oven as soon as the pastry is cooked.

filet of venison in a cream sauce

Here is a richer way of cooking venison. It comes from Austria. It is interesting, when gathering recipes from all over the world, to see how cooking practices merge from one country into another. Austrian cooking is a lovely half-way house between Germany and Italy; while retaining much of the Germanic influence, the use of lemons and various forms of pasta show the Italian thought processes being assimilated. I expect my Austrian friends will be filled with righteous outrage when reading this, and will maintain that it is the Austrian genius which has influenced Germany and Italy. But that's Europe for you.

Serves 8

4 lb (1.8 kg) haunch
4 oz (110 g) uncooked ham in large slices
4 oz (110 g) fat
¾ pt (425 ml) good stock
juniper berries
salt
a small root parsley
a smaller piece celery root
a very small carrot
½ onion
1 oz (25 g) flour
¼ pt (150 ml) red wine
½ pt (300 ml) cream
20 black peppercorns
10 pimento seeds
1 bay leaf
thyme, ginger, nutmeg (a pinch)
dessertsp redcurrant jelly
juice of 1 lemon
salt, pepper

Rub the haunch with salt and juniper berries and wrap it up in the ham. Tie it on with string or fix with cocktail sticks, but remove them before serving! Fry the sliced roots and onion in the fat and then add the haunch to the pan, turning it round in the vegetables. Put all of this into a roasting tin and roast in a hot oven (Mk 7, 425°F, 250°C) for 45 minutes, basting with a little of the stock from time to time. Then remove the joint and add the flour to the gravy. Allow it to cook for a few minutes and then add the rest of the stock, the wine, cream, all spices, the redcurrant jelly and the lemon juice.

Put the joint back into all this and cook in the oven for another 30 minutes, or longer if you prefer the meat better done. Then remove the venison to a serving dish, skim the sauce if necessary, and purée it. This should be served with rice or pasta, and it is nice to stir the sauce into either, making them very moist.

venison haunch 'fiorito'

This delightfully frivolous recipe was given to me by Professor Franco Rambotti of Perugia University. He lives up above Assisi and runs a marvellous mediaeval restaurant in a grotto carved out of the mountainside. His home-produced olive oil is the best I have ever tasted, perhaps because he stores it in ancient earthenware crocks. He knows a lot about good living and is definitely a Good Thing. Cheers, Franco!

Serves 8

4½ lb (2 kg) boned haunch*
1 onion
3 cloves garlic
1 bunch fresh parsley
6 mint leaves
1 handful sweet violet flowers
petals 6 dog roses
petals large scented carnation
1½ oz (40 g) rosemary
    flowers
1 small chilli
juice 5 lemons
6 oz (150 g) ox marrow
3–4 whole cloves
5 crushed juniper berries
2 glasses red wine
2 ladles vegetable stock
10 ripe tomatoes
salt, pepper

Finely chop the onion, garlic, mint, and three-quarters of the parsley. Cut the petals into strips, reserving a few flowers for decoration at the end. Add the chopped chilli, the juice of one of the lemons, some seasoning, and 2 oz (50 g) of the marrow, and mix all this together to make the filling. Stuff this into the cavity in the haunch, and tie a string round it, end to end, to prevent the stuffing from escaping.

Brown the joint quickly all over and then put it into a large casserole, moistening it with the wine. Mix the remaining marrow (excellent dripping will do if you're stuck) with the lemon juice, cloves and juniper berries and tip this over the meat.

Roast in a moderately hot oven (Mk 5, 375°F, 190°C) for 1½ hours, basting every now and then and adding a little hot water if it looks dry. About 15 minutes from the end add the sliced tomatoes and stock. Then remove the string and leave to rest for 15 minutes before serving. Strew the fresh flowers on top.

roast shoulder, roman style

This recipe is derived from a book written by a Roman gourmand called Marcus Apicius. His work was called *De arte coquinaria* (All about Cooking) and in it is a wealth of spicy recipes.

The Romans used honey lavishly in the cooking of their meat (they had no sugar), as well as prodigious quantities of herbs and spices many of which were very powerful and alas not often used nowadays. One flavouring to which they seem to have been addicted was called 'liquamen'. It was a liquid made from salted fish fermented with vinegar and a great many spices, and the resultant black liquor was used ubiquitously. It must have been formidable stuff to have fed such successful legions of Empire-seeking Romans. The nearest modern equivalent is Worcestershire sauce or one of the many Chinese fish sauces.

* For this recipe it is best to use a piece of haunch with the bone tunnelled out. It gives a better shape than a rolled piece and is easier to control the stuffing.

Serves 8

4 lb (1.8 kg) rolled shoulder
salted water *or* stock, to
   cover
3 oz (80 g) good dripping
5 tablesp honey
salt, pepper
2 dessertsp Worcestershire
   sauce
all or any of the following:
juniper berries, coriander,
lovage, pennyroyal, mint,
cumin, ginger, celery seed,
raisins, cloves, pine kernels

Put the meat into a pan which fits it neatly, just cover it with water or stock, and bring to the boil. Simmer for 1 hour, and then lift out the joint and put it into a roasting tin. Spread the dripping over it (this is easier if it is a little warm), and the honey as well. Sprinkle it with salt, pepper and your 'liquamen'.

At this point you will have to decide just exactly how authentically Roman you want to be. Some recipes have many more herbs and spices than I have put in, but I must confess that I find quite such a cacophony of tastes a little confusing. It would be a fine test for a spice expert. So make your choice of herbs and spices and strew them over the honeyed venison.

Roast in a moderate to slow oven (Mk 4, 350°F, 180°C) for 1½ hours, basting frequently with the spiced honey. If necessary moisten the joint with a little of the initial stock.

venison with sorrel and carrots

The venison here should not be of the very gamy variety as this is quite a delicate combination of flavour and colour.

Serves 4

2 lb (900 g) venison shoulder
   or shin
3 oz (80 g) butter
1 lb (450 g) carrots
1 pt (570 ml) mixture of good
   stock and white wine
bunch sorrel
lemon and sugar (optional)

Brown the venison, which can be cut into chunks or left in larger pieces, thoroughly all over in the butter. Remove the meat to a casserole and add the wine/stock mixture and also the carrots which should be scraped and cut into chunks. Season with salt and pepper and cook gently in a moderate oven (Mk 4, 350°F, 180°C) for about 2 hours until the meat is tender. Shin will need rather longer than shoulder, but cooked slowly it will be delicious.

Chop the sorrel up fairly fine and add it to the stew about 10 minutes before serving up. At this point you can decide whether you like it as it is or whether you would prefer to add just a suspicion of sugar and lemon.

It should emerge as tender morsels of venison in a pale bouillon, contrasting well with the sweetness of the carrots and the acidity of the sorrel i.e. the kind of thing which used to be described dismissively as 'good for invalids', but to which I am very partial.

venison stewed in beer

Here is a completely different proposition to the delicate bouillon: a lusty rich and extremely filling stew which is excellent for ravenously hungry people in the winter time. If you cook some herb dumplings in the stew you will be even more popular.

Serves 6

3 lb (1.4 kg) diced shoulder *or* shin
1 head celery
flour and dripping for browning
2 tablesp black treacle
2 oz (50 g) brown sugar
1 pt (570 ml) bitter beer
½ pt (300 ml) good stock
salt, pepper

Chop up the celery and brown it lightly. Roll the venison in seasoned flour and brown it thoroughly. Remove both these to a casserole. Then dissolve the treacle and sugar in the same pan with the beer. Add this and the stock to the meat and celery, season, and bring slowly to the boil. Remove to a moderate oven (Mk 4, 350°F, 180°C) and cook gently for at least 2 hours, topping up if necessary with more stock or water. This is the kind of stew which often tastes better the second time round, so it will happily simmer away for longer, improving all the while. If you do add the dumplings, thin down the gravy first or the whole lot may become solid and too much of a good thing.

venison in a red wine sauce

I practically never cook venison like this, but so many people say they want to cook venison in red wine that I thought it should be included.

There are scores of ways of serving venison with red wine, and there is of course no definitive recipe. It could be roasted, with red wine used as the basting liquid; and, while the meat rests, the pan juices can be reduced with more red wine to make a clear gravy. Steaks and chops can be grilled and served with the red wine sauce on p. 170. Slices of shoulder or shin, or with an aged animal I might substitute haunch, can be gently braised or simmered in red wine. This is what most people seem to have in mind.

Serves 6

2½ lb (1.1 kg) venison shoulder
2 large onions
2 large carrots
bouquet garni
8 crushed juniper berries
⅔ bottle red wine
3 oz (80 g) butter
1 oz (25 g) flour
rowan *or* redcurrant jelly (optional)
salt, pepper

Tough old venison should be marinated for a day or two before proceeding (see p. 159). Depending on the marinade, it can be used for cooking, but if a strong one were necessary, discard it.

Put the venison into a bowl with the sliced onions and carrots and the spices. Pour over the red wine and leave overnight. Then lift out the meat and pat it dry. Reserve 1 oz (25 g) of the butter and use the rest to brown the venison all over. Put it in a casserole. Pour the marinade into the frying pan and scrape up all the browning. Let it boil for a minute or two, then pour it over the meat. Season with salt and pepper. Don't overseason as it will becomes stronger on reduction. Bring to the boil, cover, and simmer very gently for 2–2½ hours until the meat is tender. Older venison may need a little longer, and can be cooked in a slow oven.

Lift out the meat and keep it warm. Reduce the liquid by about two-thirds. There should be enough left to coat the meat liberally without completely drowning it. Quality is better than quantity. If a slightly sweet sauce is wanted, then now is the time to stir in a tablespoon or so of jelly to taste.

Mash the remaining butter and flour together to make a smooth paste (beurre manié) and whisk this into the reduced sauce. Let it simmer and thicken for a few moments, adjust the seasoning, and return the venison. Gently warm through before serving.

ingrid's austrian venison

Ingrid's grandmother's venison recipe is based around the herbs in the marinade, but on the day she wanted to cook this dish for us, we encountered certain linguistic difficulties translating local Austrian names for the herbs, particularly the key one. Eventually, after much waving of hands and little pictures, we decided it must be fennel.

The result was extremely good. Parsley roots are widely used there, though not enough in Britain, but perhaps this is to do with the old superstition which says that someone will die if you dig up a parsley plant. Anyway, the roots and the fennel made a very distinctive sauce.

Serves 8

4–6 lb (1.8–2 kg) venison
    shoulder
fat for browning
2 oz (50 g) flour
¼ pt (150 ml) cream
⅛ pt (75 ml) red wine
peel of 1 lemon
3–4 sugar lumps

Marinade
3 pt (1.7 l) water
¼ pt (150 ml) red wine
    vinegar
10 oz (280 g) vegetables
    (carrots, celery, onions
    and parsley roots)
1 bay leaf
5 peppercorns
3 juniper berries
salt
fresh thyme* (or fennel!)

Bring all the ingredients for the marinade to the boil and allow it to cool before pouring it over the venison in a big bowl. Leave it for 24 hours, turning once or twice. Then take out the meat and wipe it dry before browning it all over in 4 oz (110 g) of the fat. Put the joint in a deep pan, cover with the marinade, and simmer for 2½–3 hours. Then take out the joint and remove the meat in large pieces from the bone.

Fish out the bay leaf, peppercorns and juniper berries (if you can find them), and purée the rest of the vegetables and liquid together. Then heat another 4 oz (110 g) of the fat in a saucepan and stir in the flour until it is browned. Add the puréed marinade and bring slowly to the boil, stirring all the time. Cook the flour for 15 minutes or so. By this time it should be smooth and thick; if not reduce until it is, then add the cream, red wine, lemon peel and venison pieces. Keep all this warm but do not now let it boil.

Finally make a caramel from the last ounce (25 g) of fat, the sugar lumps and a little water. Pour this into the sauce and bring it up to nearly boiling point before serving.

* We later discovered that the elusive herb was thyme.

venison flank

Venison flank is not often offered in shops, as it is generally used for processing. However, if you are dealing with a whole carcase then it will be there and, apart from stocks and soups, you may wonder what to do with it. On a young animal there will be minimal fat, but off a late summer-shot older stag there will be a lot, so remove as much as possible. There is also a layer of fascia, but since the flank does not really enter the realms of haute cuisine it is hardly worth the bother of removing it. In order to roll the meat satisfactorily, it is best to roll both flanks together.

I find these dishes an economical way of feeding hordes of hungry students who are more interested in a tasty and hearty meal than great finesse. A rolled shoulder can be cooked like this too.

Serves 6

3 lb (1.4 kg) rolled flank
2 large onions
1 red pepper
3 cloves garlic
1 large tin tomatoes
water *or* stock
salt, pepper

Brown the flank thoroughly all over and remove to a casserole. Chop the onions and pepper and brown them in the same pan. Remove them to the casserole and add the crushed garlic and the tomatoes, roughly chopped.

Deglaze the frying pan with the stock or water and nearly cover the meat and vegetables with it. Season to taste, bring slowly to the boil and either simmer for 2–3 hours, or cook in a very moderate oven (Mk 3, 325°F, 170°C) for 3–4 hours. Top up with water if necessary.

fairlie bennet's stuffed venison flank

In New Zealand the flank is called by the rather unappetising name of flap (pron. flep), but I suppose it is quite a descriptive term. I was interested in Mrs Bennet's recipe because it is one of the very few which mentions venison tongues. She said you could treat a boned haunch in the same way. A whole flap from a two-year-old beast weighs about 4 lbs (1.8 kg) after boning. This includes breast.

Serves 8

1 whole flank, boned
6 venison tongues
2 medium onions
sage
salt, pepper
stock *or* water to cover

Trim the flank so that it is rectangular and will make a better shape when rolled. Boil the tongues and trimmings from the flank together for about 1 hour. If you also include a few vegetables, this will give you a rudimentary stock. As soon as you can handle them, skin the tongues, as it is a lot easier when they are hot.

Chop the onions and sage and sprinkle them over the inside of the flank. Season with salt and pepper. Lay the tongues, packed as tightly as possible, along one edge of the flank. Then roll it up, starting at the tongue end, as tightly as you can. Wrap the roll up firmly in sheeting and stitch securely.

Cover with water or stock and bring slowly to the boil. Simmer for 3–4 hours. If serving hot, unwrap the roll, but if serving cold, leave the meat still wrapped to cool in the stock, as it will keep its shape and be more succulent that way.

roe deer with rice

This is another of Franco's recipes, typical of a rich Italian stew. Any type of venison can be substituted as long as you remember that roe venison is in general more tender than wild red or fallow venison.

Serves 6

3 lb (1.25 kg) roe venison: shoulder *or* haunch
12 oz (340 g) butter
2 tablesp oil
1 glass white wine
¼ pt (150 ml) cream
¼ pt (150 ml) béchamel sauce
2 tablesp rich stock *or* consommé
juice of 1 lemon
1 glass cognac
2 bay leaves
salt, pepper

Melt the butter in a casserole with the oil and add the venison cut into chunks. Brown the meat nicely all over, then add the wine and continue to cook over a lower heat for about 1 hour, stirring occasionally to prevent it sticking. Then stir in the cream, béchamel sauce, stock and the bay leaves and continue the cooking for another 30 minutes.

Just before serving, add the lemon juice and cognac and adjust the seasoning. Serve very hot with rice.

braised venison shoulder in a creamy sauce

Rolled shoulder may be used here, but I think the sauce is all the richer for having the meat left on the bone. I also think that the bones keep the meat sweet and moist. If you bone the shoulder yourself, then of course you can compensate by using them to make a really good stock.

Serves 6

4½ lb (2 kg) venison
    shoulder, on bone
good fat for larding
salt, pepper, nutmeg
12 crushed juniper berries
1 medium onion, sliced
1 medium carrot, sliced
4 sticks celery, sliced
1 teasp French mustard
grated rind ½ orange
¾ pt (425 ml) stock *or* water
½ pt (300 ml) thick fresh *or*
    sour cream

Lard the meat (see p. 130) and rub it all over with the salt, pepper, nutmeg and juniper berries. Brown the vegetables and remove them to a casserole, then brown the meat thoroughly in the same pan. Put the meat into the casserole, adding the mustard, orange peel, and stock.

Cover the dish and let it simmer in a moderate oven (Mk 4, 350°F, 180°C) until the meat is nicely done (about 2½ hours), adding a little more stock if necessary. When it is ready, remove the joint and keep it warm in a deep dish (you can remove the blade-bone at this point if you want).

Purée the vegetables with the stock in a Mouli or coarse sieve, reduce if necessary to a fairly thick sauce. Add the cream and adjust the seasoning. Warm this sauce, but don't let it boil, then pour it over the joint and serve.

venison tongues in a grape sauce

The cream in this dish is optional but completely alters its character; it is equally good with or without.

Serves 6

6 small venison tongues
1 pt (470 ml) pale consommé
1 wine glass sherry *or* white
    wine
6 oz (170 g) small seedless
    grapes
4 tablesp thick cream
    (optional)
salt, pepper

Plunge the tongues into boiling water to seal them and then lower the heat and simmer gently for 1½–2 hours until tender. Take off the skin, trim off the ends, and slice the rest into ¼ inch thick slices across the grain. Keep them warm.

While the tongues are cooking, put the consommé and sherry into a pan with 4 oz (110 g) of the grapes. Simmer gently for 15 minutes and then pass all this through a sieve or Mouli to remove the grape skins. Reduce to just under ¾ pint and throw in the rest of the grapes which you have laboriously cut in half (you should do this) and peeled (only saints or lovers do this). Warm them gently in the sauce and at this stage add the cream if you are going to. Season delicately and pour this sauce over the prettily arranged slices of tongue.

venison tongues in a cream and parsley sauce

Despite a pretty normal 8-year-old's taste in food, my daughter Stella is passionately fond of tongues cooked this way, so I am reassured that there is still hope stuck in the rim of her gastronomic box.

Venison tongues are small and because of their delicate flavour (I never pickle them) they benefit from sympathetic cooking. I expect lambs' tongues done like this would also be good.

Serves 4

1½ lb (675 g) venison
    tongues
3 large carrots
2 onions
1 oz (25 g) butter
heaped tablesp flour
stock from the tongues
¼ pt (150 ml) thick cream
a good handful of parsley
salt, pepper

Wash the tongues and pack them into a pan with the onions (quartered) and the carrots (cut into ½-inch chunks) tucked in close beside them. Just cover them with water, add a pinch of salt, and bring slowly to the boil. Simmer very gently and skim the broth for about 2 hours, or until they are tender. Remove the tongues, skin and trim them, cut into ½ inch rounds and keep warm in a dish.

Fish out the chunks of carrot and keep them with the tongues. Purée the onions with the stock. Make a roux with the butter and flour and gradually add the oniony stock. Bring to the boil and simmer for 20 minutes to cook the flour, stirring from time to time to stop it burning on the bottom of the pan. The sauce should be thick and smooth.

Add enough cream to let the sauce down to a good consistency. Adjust the seasoning and stir in the well-chopped parsley. Add the tongue and carrots to this sauce, warm them through gently and it is ready to serve.

the Roe-bucke

braised venison heart

A simple and homely dish for a cold winter's night.

Serves 4

1½ lb (675 g) venison heart
2 large onions
3 oz (80 g) butter
salt, pepper

Trim any fat off the heart, as it is not very pleasant to eat, and also any gristle. Chop the onions. Melt the butter in a small casserole and soften the onions. You could use good dripping instead, but margarine only if you actually like its flavour.

Add the chopped heart and stir continuously for a few minutes so that nothing sticks to the bottom. Season to taste. Once some juices have formed, cover the pot, turn the heat right down and let it bubble away gently for about 1½ hours. Check once or twice during the cooking that there has not been too much evaporation, and top up with a splash of water if necessary.

You could top it up with orange juice or wine or even add a tablespoon of jelly, but I think it perfectly good as it is. Check the seasoning and serve with mashed potatoes.

venison kidneys

As long as they are from a young beast (and on no account from a rutting stag!) venison kidneys are delicious and can be treated like lambs' kidneys. Here are two recommendations. Two or three kidneys per person should suffice.

Recipe 1
Split the kidneys in half and remove the fine layer of skin if this has not already been done. Grill them, cut side uppermost, with a knob of butter on top, but don't burn them to a crisp. Serve with Black Butter Sauce (p. 177) or else with some chopped parsley and lemon juice. They could also be sautéed.

Recipe 2
Cut the kidneys into dice and sauté them in butter, once again being careful not to overcook. Remove the kidneys to a warm serving dish. Sauté some mushrooms (sliced) in the same pan, then remove them to the serving dish. Add a dash of brandy or vermouth to the pan and dissolve the juices. Pour in a little cream or yoghourt and let it bubble for a moment. Season to taste, then return the mushrooms and kidneys briefly so that they are all coated with the sauce. Serve at once.

venison nickie fletcher

A few years ago I put this recipe on a leaflet in our farm shop, and it became so popular that people started buying larger joints in order to make this dish with the left-overs. I was suitably gratified. It is a good way to use up cold meat, though like the classic salmis it is even better when the meat has been roasted specially to make the dish. Meat roasted by the slow method (p. 129) is particularly suitable as it yields plenty of gravy to make the sauce.

cold roast venison
1 oz (25 g) butter
heaped tablesp flour
left-over gravy
milk if necessary
sour cream
salt, pepper

Remove every scrap of meat from the bone and dice the large pieces. Melt the butter in a saucepan and stir in the flour. Cook for a minute or two then, bit by bit, add the gravy, beating all the time. Use the minimum amount of milk necessary to cook the flour in the sauce without burning.

Stir this thick sauce over a low heat for 15–20 minutes and then thin it with the sour cream. Season to taste with salt and pepper and then stir in the meat, warming it gently. On no account allow to boil (particularly if the meat was fairly pink) because this would toughen the meat.

salmis of venison

This is a good way to use up venison which has been roasted nice and rare. The best results are obtained when a joint has been specially roasted to make the dish, since all the juices are sealed into the meat. However, don't let that put you off making it. If, at the end of your hot meal, you have the foresight to up-end the joint and spoon any remaining juices over the top, then the meat will be considerably improved.

Follow the method for Salmis of Pheasant (see p. 63), bearing in mind that a pheasant will yield about 12 oz (340 g) of meat. If your venison was boned, leaving you with nothing to enrich your stock, then that stock will have to be especially good.

venison or game consommé

The only hurdle you need to leap over to make the most divine consommé is the mental block which tells you it is desperately complicated. It isn't in the least, though it does take place over several hours, but most of these you can spend reading, sleeping or 'getting on with things'.

It is well worth making a decent quantity because you can freeze it in cartons and ensure that you always have the basis for countless good soups and sauces as well.

The only bones I would not use are from pigeons or from really high game as they can impart a bitter taste. You will need some trotters to help it gel, and some extra meat if the bones are well-scraped. Now you know what to do with all those pig's feet and sinewy pheasant drumsticks! I remain convinced that farmed venison gives the best flavoured consommé in the world, but there you are, I'm prejudiced.

meaty bones—neck and
    shoulder from venison
drumsticks and wings from
    pheasant *or* guinea fowl
pigs' trotters and
    marrowbones to help it set
some extra scraps of venison
    if necessary
some good dripping for
    browning
a selection of
    vegetables—carrots,
    onions (unskinned),
    tomatoes, leeks and celery
    (all good for flavour and
    colour)
a bag of herbs with a few
    peppercorns
2 egg-whites for every 3 pts
    (1.75 l) of liquid
Madeira *or* sherry

Put the bones and meat into a roasting pan with some dripping and roast, turning them around occasionally, until they are tawny brown all over. Then tip the bones and meat into a huge pan, not forgetting the precious pan juices, and add the vegetables and herbs. Do not add any salt at this stage. Cover with water, bring slowly to the boil and simmer gently for 4 hours or so. Rapid boiling will make it difficult to clarify at the end. Skim occasionally to prevent bitterness. Then strain off the liquid through a cloth-lined colander to eliminate as much murk as possible, and leave the unpromising-looking bowlful to cool. If you now add water (less, this time) to the bones and boil them up again, you can glean a useful secondary stock.

Next day, remove every scrap of fat from the surface of what should now be a jelly, and then scoop the clear part of the jelly into a perfectly clean and fat-free pan. (The sediment at the bottom can go back into the number two stock.) Melt the jelly, and before it starts to heat up much, whisk in two or three stiffly beaten egg-whites. Bring the panful slowly to simmering point and let it remain barely simmering for 20–30 minutes. On no account disturb the rather dirty looking scum which will have risen to the surface during this process.

Line a colander with a dampened and folded tea towel and place it over a clean bowl. Gently ladle the consommé into the cloth, being careful not to swirl the scum about lest it yields the sediment it has so cleverly removed. Some people recommended adding a little minced shin to the egg-white process to aid clarification, but I have always found it unnecessary, the consommé appearing from the horrid-looking sieve as a beautiful clear amber liquid.

It is only at this point that you add salt, remembering that cold consommé will need a bit more than hot. Add the Madeira or sherry by the spoonful rather than sloshing in great quantities which is overpowering and wasteful.

Consommé can be served in its own natural simplicity, with quenelles, with a few shreds of *al dente* vegetables, or else little pieces of a delicate curd made from egg yolks and some consommé which is gently baked in thin sheets and cut into shapes.

quenelles of venison

Venison quenelles can make a delicious starter or main course, as the quality of the sauce served with them can drastically alter the character of the dish. Suitable creamy sauces are consommé cream sauce, tomato cream sauce, or Mushroom Purée (p. 178). Traditional Port Wine Sauce on p. 169 would be a good rich dark one.

Serves 4–6

6 oz (170 g) Venison Liver
     Pâté (p. 152)
¼ pt (150 ml) water
pinch salt, also nutmeg
1 oz (25 g) butter
2 oz (50 g) sifted flour
1 whole egg, beaten
1 egg-white, beaten
4–6 dessertsp cream

First make a choux paste by putting the water, salt, nutmeg and butter into a heavy-bottomed saucepan and bringing them to the boil. Remove from the heat and quickly beat in the flour. Return to a lower heat and keep beating until you have a cohesive lump which leaves a film on the bottom of the pan. Take it off the heat again and beat in gradually first the whole egg and then the pâté. When this is quite smooth, gently beat in the egg-white, and then chill. The cream must also be chilled so that more can be incorporated into the paste.

Beat the cream gradually into the paste until it is light, but just stiff enough to keep its shape when moulded with two wet spoons.

Bring 4 inches (10 cm) salted water to just about simmering point in a large deep frying pan. Several saucepans could be used in lieu to speed up production. Form the quenelles into nice egg shapes with two wet dessert spoons, slipping them into the water carefully to preserve their shape. Keep the pan uncovered and allow the water to barely bubble for about 15 minutes. If the water agitates overmuch the quenelles will disintegrate.

Lift them out carefully with a slotted spoon and keep them warm. Serve as soon as possible. This quantity makes about 12 quenelles. Instead of serving them with a sauce, these quenelles are also good poached in perfect venison consommé (see p. 148) which is then strained and served with the quenelles floating in it. I'd make them a little smaller in this case.

a raised venison pie

This is a most spectacular dish to serve hot or cold, and tremendous fun to make. The ideal mould to use is one of those fluted edged ones which are clipped or hinged together. They are however rather expensive, and a cake tin with a removeable base will do fine; you still have the top to decorate. The amounts you need are obviously determined by the size of the tin. If you have any pastry and filling left over then you can have great fun making little individual pies by moulding the pastry around a floured jam jar; a strip of paper pinned round the case before it is removed from the jar will prevent its collapse during cooking.

There is much debate as to whether the meat should be minced or chopped. Mince makes it easy to cut the pie into neat slices, but somehow lacks 'pieness'. If the meat is chopped, then it should be in very small pieces of about ⅓ inch (1 cm) so that there are not too many air spaces. I usually use half of each which means that the gaps are filled but there is still a bite to the pie.

Serves 6

2 lb (900 g) lean venison
1 lb (450 g) minced belly of
    pork
2 wine glasses red wine *or*
    port
1 wine glass olive oil
½ wine glass wine vinegar *or*
    brandy
1 dessertsp crushed juniper
    berries
salt, pepper, nutmeg, ginger
small pinch ground cloves
a large bunch parsley

Pie crust
1 lb (450 g) plain flour
7 fl oz (220 ml) water
6 oz (170 g) lard
pinch salt and nutmeg
pinch sugar
beaten egg yolk to glaze

Mix all the ingredients in a large bowl and add the liquor. The amount depends on how strong it is and how generous you feel. Go easy with the wine vinegar and brandy—a little goes a long way. The mixture should be pretty moist but not swimming. Leave this for several hours for the ingredients to become acquainted, preferably overnight.

Next make the hot water crust. Mix the flour, salt, nutmeg and sugar in a warm bowl. Bring the water and fat to the boil and stir them, still bubbling, into the dry ingredients. Mix them well together until you have a rather unappetising greasy-looking paste. This paste is only workable while warm so keep the bowl covered and warm after you have removed the first ⅔ for lining the tin so that the remainder is still malleable when needed to roll out the top.

Pack ⅔ of the paste into the mould making sure it is evenly distributed. I find the easiest way is to put a lump into the bottom of the tin and work it up the sides with my fingers. At first the paste may slip down, but as it cools it will stay put. Make quite sure there are no cracks to allow your precious juices to escape. And try not to make it too thick (not more than ¼ inch). The crust is really just a case for the meat and in bygone days it was apparently discarded (don't know what's good for them, mutter some hungry pie-eaters). Pack the meat in firmly right up to the top, rounding it off nicely. Then roll out the rest of the crust, and seal it on to the top with beaten egg yolk. Brush all over the top with beaten egg, crimp the edges with a fork, and decorate as the fancy takes you. Make at least one hole in the top to avoid the pie splitting and pop a roll of paper into the hole to keep it open.

Bake the pie in a fairly hot oven to brown the top, and then turn the oven down to cool (Mk 2, 200°F, 150°C) to cook for a further 3–4 hours. About 1 hour before the end, I often remove the roll of paper and top up the pie with a mixture of olive oil and red wine to keep it really moist.

Let the pie cool completely before removing the tin, as this avoids splitting the delicate pastry and precipitating a deluge of juice, which is most distressing I can assure you! When it is quite cold, return the pie to the oven for a few minutes to heat the tin which can now be eased off.

At this stage the pie will happily mature for a day or two in a cool place, but don't serve it icy cold. If you want to serve the pie hot, then put the mould back round the pie and slowly warm it for about 1 hour.

You will need a lot of hot Cumberland Sauce (p. 176) to go with this, creamed potatoes, a moist vegetable such as celery, and of course a good quantity of lusty red wine.

THE FALLOW DEERE

smooth venison liver pâté

This is an exceedingly popular pâté and it is extremely easy to make. But before I pronounce it foolproof I must make an important proviso—on *no account* use liver from a rutting stag (it has been done!) or liver that has been left hanging with a carcase. Liver must be dealt with immediately, so stick to farmed venison in this case.

8 oz (225 g) venison liver
3 oz (80 g) butter
2 tablesp red wine vinegar
2 cloves garlic, crushed
1 egg
3 oz (80 g) fine white
    breadcrumbs
salt, black pepper

Chop the liver into ¾-inch cubes and put it into a small fireproof dish with the chopped butter and the wine vinegar. Cover with a buttered paper and braise in a moderate oven (Mk 4, 350°F, 180°C) for 25 minutes. Halfway through the cooking, take it out and stir the contents around so that it cooks evenly. Meanwhile crush the garlic into a food processor and add the egg, a good pinch of salt, and 8 turns from the pepper grinder.

As soon as the liver is cooked (it will be nut brown all over, but still exude a little pink juice if pricked), tip the whole bubbling contents of the dish into the food processor, and blend with the egg etc. at top speed until it is completely liquid. Then add the breadcrumbs and blend again until the pâté is smooth. At this stage it can be put into little dishes and used as it is, but if a still creamier pâté is wanted, then it can be processed again once it is cold.

This pâté freezes very well for a week or so, but if kept frozen for a long time it will become dry and crumbly. If this should happen, blend it with a dash of brandy or cream and it will jump back to life again. This recipe is the base for Quenelles of Venison (p. 149).

pâté en croûte

Here is a fine little starter which is also made from the Venison Liver Pâté (above). It goes well with either of the tomato sauces on p. 174. It is quite rich, so a small amount is adequate (usually!).

Serves 4

6 oz (170 g) Venison Liver
    Pâté
4 large spinach leaves
6 oz (170 g) puff pastry
beaten egg

Blanch the spinach leaves in salted water, refresh in cold water, then cut out any tough stalks which would not roll up easily. Put a quarter of the pâté on to each spinach leaf and fold it up to make a little parcel. Proceed with the rest.

Roll out the pastry thinly and cut into four. Place a spinach parcel on to each piece of pastry and fold the pastry around to seal it completely. Use the beaten egg to moisten the pastry.

Place the pastries, sealed side downwards, on to a baking tray and brush them with the beaten egg. Decorate with pastry scraps. Cook in a moderately hot oven (Mk 5, 375°F, 190°C) for 10–15 minutes, or until the pastry is puffed and golden. Serve at once with fresh tomato sauce.

crazy paving venison galantine

This galantine comes from an excellent charcutier in Provence, and is rather unusual in that it uses other meats with the normal pork. It is good for a buffet lunch as a little goes a long way. Don't be put off by the sheets of pork fat. You will need to order them, but if I can get it in Auchtermuchty then I'm sure your butcher will also oblige. Ask him to cut it extremely thin: as near to ⅛ inch as possible. This gives a beautifully professional finish as well as being necessary to hold everything together.

You will need a rectangular terrine or bread tin, and a former for it so that the galantine can be pressed; so try and find something suitable before you start. A small piece of thick plywood is ideal. If you resort to foil and tin cans, take extra caution in slicing.

Serves 8–10

8 oz (225 g) venison steak
8 oz (225 g) venison liver
6 oz (170 g) belly of pork
12 oz (340 g) sheets of pork back fat
1 wine glass brandy or red wine
5 juniper berries
black pepper
butter
sea salt

Marinate the steak, liver and belly of pork (but not the sheets of pork fat) overnight in the brandy or wine, juniper berries (crushed) and ground black pepper. Next day, take them out and pat them dry. Cut into long strips ⅓ inch (1 cm) square in cross-section. Heat some butter in a pan and quickly brown the meat all over. Do this in batches so the butter remains really hot.

Line the bread tin or terrine with the sheets of pork fat making sure there are no holes. Lay the sautéed strips of meat lengthways down the tin, alternating the three kinds and filling in the gaps so that it is packed tightly. Season well with the sea salt in between each layer. Sprinkle a tablespoon or two of the marinade over the meat. Most of this will ooze out during the pressing but it flavours and moistens the meat as it cooks.

Fold the remaining pork sheets over the top to make a lid and press on some folded foil to keep it in place. Then encase the whole tin in foil and stand it in a tray of warm water. Bake in a very moderate oven (Mk 3, 325°F, 170°C) for 1½–2 hours. Remove all the foil and stand the terrine in a dish in case of spillage, and fit the former. Weight heavily till cold.

To turn out the galantine, stand the dish in hot water for a few moments to melt the fat slightly. Use a very sharp knife to cut slices, and you will see the neat white rim with a crazy paving of the different meats inside.

two venison terrines

There must be hundreds of recipes for terrines, but the golden rule with game terrines is to include a good proportion of fatty pork, otherwise it will be dry. Here are two, the first is a simple no-nonsense one which, as an enthusiastic correspondent rather ambiguously wrote, is 'excellent for shooting sandwiches'. The other is a little more special.

Recipe 1

1 lb (450 g) raw minced venison
½ lb (225 g) minced belly of pork
1 teasp crushed juniper berries
½ teasp ground ginger
salt, black pepper
1 glass red wine
2 tablesp olive oil
6 oz (170 g) thin-cut streaky bacon
1 egg
1 tablesp chopped lovage (optional)

Marinate the venison and pork with the juniper berries, pepper, salt, and ginger, in the wine and olive oil. Line a terrine (a bread tin will do) with the streaky bacon, reserving some for the top. Stir the egg and lovage into the meat mixture and pack it into the dish, pressing down firmly. Put the rest of the bacon over the top, tucking it down the sides to prevent shrinkage, and cover with foil.

Bake in a moderate oven (Mk 4, 350°F, 180°C) for 1½–2 hours or until a skewer comes out clean. Weight the dish lightly until cold. It can be served straight from the dish or else turned out, in which case stand it in hot water for a moment to make this job easier.

Recipe 2

1 lb (450 g) raw minced venison
10 oz (280 g) minced belly of pork
6 oz (170 g) venison steak
2 cooked venison tongues
2 glasses red wine *or* port
salt, black pepper, ginger, nutmeg, juniper, cloves (all ground)
fresh herbs to taste
1 small onion
2 cloves garlic
½ oz (15 g) butter
½ glass brandy *or* sherry
8 oz (225 g) thin cut streaky bacon *or* pork fat

Put the minced venison, pork and steak to marinate in the red wine with the spices (3 pinches of salt, one each of the rest) and fresh herbs. Leave this overnight for the flavours to mingle.

Next day, chop the onion and garlic and soften them in the butter. Remove the steak from the marinade and cut it into long strips about ¼ inch in cross-section. Peel the tongues and do likewise. Put the onions and garlic into a blender with the minced pork and venison, leaving behind the marinade liquid for the time being. Blend at top speed for a few seconds to make a smoother paste, or else mince it again. Then stir in the brandy, and if needed, some of the marinade liquid.

Line a terrine with bacon, keeping some back for the top, and put in a layer of your delicious forcemeat. Then lay some strips of steak and tongue in, leaving a space all round the edges, and cover with forcemeat. Whether this operation is done in three or five layers depends on the shape of the terrine, but it should begin and end with forcemeat. Fold the bacon strips over the top and arrange the rest in a pretty criss-cross fashion over them. Cover with foil and tie it down so that the flavour is sealed in.

Put the terrine in a tray of hot water and bake in a very moderate oven (Mk 3, 325°F, 170°C) for 2–3 hours. When it comes out of the oven, weight the terrine until cold.

venison salami

Salami is surprisingly easy to make. It can lose up to 40 per cent of its weight during the maturing process, which makes it extremely sustaining as well as being delicious. Venison used for salami should not be very gamy as the maturing process takes place with the rest of the ingredients. Like cheeses, I find that salami is best made in the autumn or spring as you are more likely to encounter the right conditions, i.e., cool and airy, after their first few days' drying in a warmer temperature. If you have a cold smoker, they can be cold-smoked after their initial drying.

2½ lb (1.2 kg) lean venison
1½ lb (675 g) lean pork
1 lb (450 g) hard pork back fat
dessertsp black peppercorns
dessertsp juniper berries
3 large cloves garlic
3 oz (80 g) salt
dessertsp brown sugar
pinch saltpetre
pinch nutmeg and ginger
small glass brandy (optional)
natural casings

Chill the hard back fat. Mince the venison and pork well together. Crack the peppercorns and crush the juniper berries and garlic. Mix them with the salt, sugar, saltpetre and spices. The saltpetre helps the meat to keep its colour as well as acting as a preservative. Mix all these seasonings very thoroughly into the meat. Cut the chilled pork fat into little dice, wet with the brandy, and stir them into the seasoned meat.

Pack the mixture tightly into lengths of natural casing. The large intestine is best because the salami shrinks so much. Normal sausage casings can be used but they give rather spindly salamis. However, they have the advantage of slipping nicely into a coat pocket and they will mature a little quicker than larger ones. Tie the ends and hang them up to dry, making sure they don't touch each other so that air can circulate around them.

The temperature for the first four or five days should be a fairly constant and well ventilated 60°F (16°C). We hang ours on a rail above the Aga which is ideal, though a lot of steam from cooking should be avoided, as should direct sunlight. After this period of initial drying, the salamis may be smoked if you wish. Then hang them in a cool and dry place to mature for at least a month. They will, given the right conditions, improve for two or three months. During that time, a white bloom will probably (though not always) appear on the skin. You may congratulate yourself—all is going well, so don't wipe it off.

The salami will shrink considerably during this time, so every once in a while squeeze it from the ends to keep it firm. It's not the end of the world if you don't do this, but they won't slice so well, and paper-thin slices are the order of the day.

a hungarian venison salami

Bryan Green sent me this recipe which his friend Gabor Molmar makes, and Bryan assures me it is quite excellent.

12 oz (340 g) lean venison
12 oz (340 g) lean pork
11 oz (310 g) pork fat
1 oz (25 g) salt
1¼ oz (30 g) paprika
black pepper and garlic
    (optional)
casings

Mince the meat and mix it all together with the seasonings. Use sweet or hot paprika to taste, but don't under-season—it is meant to be spicy. If using sweet paprika, add ¼ oz (7 g) crushed black peppercorns, and four crushed cloves of garlic are about right.

Stuff this mixture into the skins. Then, says Mr Molmar, it helps if you freeze the sausage, presumably because the skins are dried a little. Then smoke for 4–5 days over a slow cold smoke, and hang in a dry place to mature.

venison sausages

You don't need to have a sausage filler to make venison sausages. They can just be rolled into shape, dusted with flour and cooked as they are. Sausages need a lot of fat to keep them moist—I don't believe a healthy sausage exists!

2 lb (900 g) lean minced
    venison
1 lb (450 g) minced pork
    belly
¾ oz (20 g) salt
½ oz (15 g) cracked pepper
egg, oatmeal, red wine, mace,
    sage, garlic, juniper (all
    optional)
casings (optional)

The basic idea is to mix the minced venison and pork together with the various flavourings and then fill the sausage skins. If you aren't using sausage skins, bind the mixture with an egg.

It is the optional bits which make the sausages interesting. Pin-head oatmeal gives a good nutty flavour, but needs to be soaked overnight: 6 oz (170 g) is about right. The meat can be marinated in red wine to give a richer flavour. Darker sausages can be made by substituting a little venison heart or liver for some of the venison. And herbs and spices can be added to taste.

Before filling the skins or rolling into sausages, it is best to check the seasonings by frying a little sample. Then you can adjust at will. These will be meaty sausages and they take longer than normal to cook.

barry burns' venison haggis recipe

Barry, our butcher, is justifiably proud of his haggises—they are quite the best I have tasted and I had to twist his arm hard to make him divulge the recipe.

We find that there are three vital points which if followed should prevent the skins from contracting and bursting. First, fill the skins only half-full to allow for the contents swelling. Secondly, prick the skins all over with a needle before, and occasionally during, cooking. Thirdly, when using ox bungs (which are like very thick and wide sausage casings), do not cut into individual haggises until after cooking. In other words, make them like a string of giant sausages with two strings tied between each haggis. Admittedly you need an enormous pan to cook them in, but it saves a lot of frustration.

1 lb (450 g) lean venison
1 lb (450 g) venison heart
1 lb (450 g) venison liver
1 lb (450 g) venison lights
1 lb (450 g) beef suet
8 oz (225 g) pinhead oatmeal
½ pt (300 ml) water
4 level tablesp salt
4 level teasp ground black
   pepper
4 level teasp ground ginger
4 level teasp nutmeg

Soak the oatmeal in water overnight. Mince all the meat, offal, and suet and mix them well together with the soaked oatmeal and seasonings. Fill the skins, tying the ends securely as described, and pricking all over with a needle. Cover with cold water in a large pan, bring to the boil and simmer gently for 3 hours.

After cooking, the haggises can be frozen or will keep in a fridge for several days. The cooking liquid, once skimmed of fat, makes an excellent foundation for soup or else can be used to warm the haggis for serving. To heat them up, just put some broth or water in a pan and simmer the haggis gently in it for 30 minutes, or else put into a covered dish with some liquid and warm through in the oven. If your haggis looks as though it might burst the second method of warming is safest.

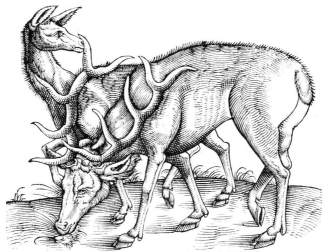

THE HART AND HINDE

Red deer and Salmon
part of a v. fine prehistoric incised bone
carving from Lorthet, s.w. France. Unusual
combination of subjects, esp. so far
south — important food source.?

Juniper
Berries ripe when
bluey black. Trad.
spice for game.
The wood is
very good
for barbecues
as it gives off
a lovely smell.

Rowan
Grows to higher
altitude than any
other British hardwood.
Used for warding off
witches & making bows.
Also rowan jelly — pick
when berries are firm
dry and red.

7
Marinades, Stocks and Sauces

Marinades

To marinade or not? This is a question which seems to bother people more than anything else. Well, like most things in life, the answer lies in what you want the end product to be.

If you are confident that your meat is from a young animal, and farmed venison, squabs, quails and most guinea fowl will be, then there is no need whatsoever to marinade it, if you don't want to. In fact a marinade could interfere with the intended flavour. Many people are discouraged from cooking all game meat in the belief that it is essential to smother everything in wine, making the whole process lengthy and expensive. But a marinade can take the simple form of lemon juice and oil if need be. Michel Guérard recommends, as a slimmers' alternative to oil and alcohol, simply steeping the meat in an infusion of herbs and spices.

However, if the meat is likely to be old and tough, this last process will not be enough. Alternative ways of tenderising meat are discussed on p. 11, but a marinade is certainly among the best. Regarding health and alcohol, I am of the school of thought which believes that alcohol in moderation is beneficial but, if you are unimpressed by this argument, remember that the alcohol will be driven off by cooking, leaving only the flavour and aroma of the wine.

Here's a point to note regarding this wonderful flavour and aroma: I have often heard people say that children don't like game. But provided the game is not too high, most children thoroughly enjoy it. The taste to which they are generally objecting is that of alcohol, used either in a marinade or as part of the cooking process. So when cooking for children keep to simple dishes and don't use alcohol.

There are three purposes of a marinade, and they are not necessarily restricted to game. One is to impart to the meat the *flavour* of the various herbs, spices, and liquids that constitute the marinade. In some cases part of the marinade is cooked with the meat, either as the braising or stewing liquid or else as a baste during roasting. In this case a mild marinade is generally used. Another purpose is to render the meat, particularly old game meat and wild pigeons, more *succulent*. It is the oil in the marinade which performs this task and is particularly effective for steaks, chops, or poultry breasts. However, if a larger piece of meat is to be roasted, rather than cooked in a liquid, then marinading may not be enough; it may also be necessary to lard the meat (see p. 11). A third function of a marinade is to break down the fibres in the meat, to make it more *tender*. This is done by including an acid, which can be cider, wine or spirits, lemon juice or wine vinegar. The choice is determined partly by the desired flavour and partly by the degree of toughness of the meat. Cider and wine are milder, lemon juice and vinegar are stronger, though for reasons of economy diluted wine vinegar may be used in place of wine. A cooked marinade will help old tough meat as it is even more efficient at breaking down the fibres.

Here are a few recipes; there is no need to follow them slavishly. So much depends on what you have in store and on what you like: a pinch of coriander or curry powder can add a spicy note for example. Ingredients such as bay leaves, cloves, cinnamon or lovage should be used in moderation as they can become overpowering, especially if used to cook with as well. If it looks as though there may not be enough marinade to cover the meat, put the meat into a polythene bag, which will draw the marinade around it.

The principles of marinading fish are somewhat different and are discussed in Chapter 2.

general marinade

This is a very general recipe and you may add or subtract as you wish. Red wine suits venison, pigeons and some pheasant recipes. White wine suits guinea fowl, pheasant and quail. The addition of a glass of wine vinegar will make the marinade stronger; the wine could be substituted by 2 glasses of wine vinegar.

¼ pt (150 ml) olive oil
¾ pt (425 ml) red *or* white
    wine
1 onion
1 carrot
2 sticks celery
2 cloves garlic
6 peppercorns
6 juniper berries
1 bay leaf
parsley, thyme

Simply chop the vegetables and garlic, crack the peppercorns, and mix all the ingredients together before submerging the meat. Turn it every now and then. Twelve hours are usually enough unless the meat is very old, in which case it may need two or three days.

light marinade

Suitable for any grilled or sautéed meat, but can also be used for cooking a medium rich casserole. Choose herbs that will complement the recipe or sauce.

3 tablesp olive oil
juice 1 lemon *or*
4 tablesp wine
1 clove garlic, chopped
handful fresh herbs
ground black pepper

Mix all the ingredients and pour over the meat. An hour or so should suffice. Make sure the surface of the meat is wiped dry before cooking otherwise it will not brown.

cooked marinade

This is a stronger marinade used to break down tough meat.

2 onions
2 carrots
2 sticks celery
2 cloves garlic
¾ pt (425 ml) wine vinegar
¾ pt (425 ml) water
¼ pt (150 ml) red wine
¼ pt (150 ml) olive oil
2 cloves
1 bay leaf
6 juniper berries
10 peppercorns (whole)

Chop the vegetables and crush the garlic. Put them into a pan with the rest of the ingredients, bring to the boil and simmer for 5 minutes. When cool, submerge the meat in it in a bowl or plastic bag.

Since this is a marinade for old tough meat, it is likely that it will need a few days to have effect, so it is particularly important that the meat is kept submerged. Put a bowl or plate over the meat and weight it with a jar if necessary. Remember to turn the meat occasionally, and keep it cool.

cider marinade

This is a good marinade for game birds, particularly if they are subsequently to be cooked with cider or apples.

¾ pt (425 ml) cider
2 eating apples
1 small onion
2–3 tablesp walnut oil
2-inch stick cinnamon

Slice the apples and onion and toss them around in the walnut oil until softened. Add the cider and cinnamon and bring to a scant simmer. Cider vinegar (⅓ pt/200 ml) or calvados (3 fl oz/75 ml) may also be used, diluted with a little water if necessary. Let it cool before covering the meat.

beer marinade

This is quite a rich marinade which can be used successfully with venison, pigeon or pheasant. It is excellent when used to baste slow-cooked joints or else as stewing liquor.

1 medium onion
6 cloves or small pinch
    ground cloves
¾ pt (425 ml) brown ale
2 tablesp dark brown sugar

Cut the onion in half and stick the cloves in it. Put them in a pan with the beer and sugar and warm slowly until the sugar has dissolved. Cool before immersing the meat.

grenville foster's yoghourt marinade

This is a particularly good marinade for venison steaks and chops, and for pigeon breasts.

8 fl oz (225 ml) plain
    yoghourt
1 teasp lemon juice
1 dessertsp Garam marsala

Mix the ingredients together and marinate the meat for 4–6 hours. Before grilling or sautéing, pat the meat dry so that it cooks quickly. The marinade can be used to deglaze the pan juices, providing a simple sauce.

ginger marinade

A suitable marinade for pheasant or venison, in which case marinade for 12–24 hours.

2 oz (50 g) fresh root ginger,
    sliced
8 fl oz (225 ml) soy sauce
¼ pt (150 ml) red wine
juice of 1 lemon
3 tablesp olive *or* soy-bean oil
1 whole head garlic
3 star anise
a little fresh thyme

Mix all the ingredients together. If steaks or small pieces are used, a few hours will suffice. Pat them dry before grilling or sautéing.

STOCKS

court bouillon

This is the basic stock for poaching any kind of fish. It can be varied according to whim or the limitations of your store cupboard. Some people add a few mushrooms, some use celery leaves, some a piece of cucumber. If you feel that using a whole bottle of wine is too extravagant, then you can reduce the quantity and put in a larger proportion of white wine vinegar, but be cautious—the court bouillon must not be too acidic. I find it much easier and safer to stick to the real thing. I use parsley stalks or roots in preference to the green tops as they do not discolour the fish.

*Sufficient to poach a
4–5 lb fish*

5 pints (2½ litres) water
1 bottle dry white wine
4 tablesp white wine vinegar
2 large onions
3 medium carrots
2 sticks celery
a bunch parsley stalks *or*
    roots
a bouquet garni, preferably
    fresh herbs
1 dessertsp salt
2 bay leaves
8 white peppercorns

Put everything into a large pot, bring to the boil and simmer for 45 minutes. It is now ready to be used for cooking the fish.

After the fish has been cooked, any discarded bones, skins and heads can be put back and boiled up in the court bouillon, which, once reduced considerably can be used in the same way as a fish fumet (see below).

Further reducing and clarifying will render it suitable for making aspic. To clarify, beat up an egg-white or two, whisk them into the stock, then allow it to simmer barely for 20 minutes. Strain slowly through a linen cloth and then dissolve some gelatine into it —about ¼ oz (6 g) per pint (570 ml).

classic fish fumet and glaze

Almost any sort of fish or seafood can be used, but a large part of it should be sea fish. If you are using fish heads then remove the gills as they will make the stock bitter.

For 1½ pints (scant litre)

2¼ lbs (1 kg) fish
    scraps—bones and flesh
bunch parsley stalks
2 small onions *or* 4 shallots
2 oz (50 g) button
    mushrooms
1 oz (25 g) butter
2 tablesp oil
½ pint (300 ml) dry white
    wine
squeeze lemon juice
pinch salt

On the bottom of a large pan, soften the parsley stalks (parsley leaves will darken the stock and the stalks have more flavour anyway), chopped onions or shallots, and mushrooms in the butter and oil, taking care not to brown them. Add the wine, lemon juice and fish and cover with cold water. Bring gently to the boil and simmer, uncovered, for 30 minutes, skimming once or twice as necessary.

Leave to infuse in the pan until lukewarm and then strain through a fine sieve or cloth. If you should want to produce a pinkish stock, then use some whole crushed prawns and just lightly brown them in the butter and oil before softening the vegetables, and add four or five tomatoes (or a dessertspoon of tomato purée) to the stock.

Fish Glaze
To turn classic fish fumet into a fish glaze, which is invaluable for adding extra flavour to fish sauces or for coating poached or grilled fish, simply simmer the strained stock gently until it has reduced to ¼ pint (150 ml). By this time it will be glossy and syrupy. Season to taste.

pale poultry stock and golden glaze

This should be used for pheasant, guinea fowl and quail recipes where a light coloured sauce is called for. Do not use the badly shot parts of the carcase for this—reserve them for making a Dark Game Stock.

For 1½ pints (scant litre)

2 lbs (1.8 kg) poultry carcases and meaty scraps—use pheasant, guinea fowl, quail or chicken for this, but not pigeon
1 pig's trotter if possible
knuckle-bone of beef *or* veal
2 rashers bacon
8 oz (225 g) minced beef
4 oz (110 g) chopped carrots
1 medium onion
2 sticks celery
2 oz (50 g) mushrooms
2 cloves garlic (unpeeled)
bouquet garni
1 tablesp tomato purée
½ pint (300 ml) dry white wine

Brown the carcases and bones in a moderate oven for 15–20 minutes or until golden, turning once or twice to prevent browning. It is important, when using poultry carcases, not to allow them to burn (and they do quite quickly) as they will impart an unpleasant bitter taste. Covering the dish with foil will help. Add the bacon, beef and all the vegetables, chopped. Turn them around with the bones and return to the oven for 5 minutes.

Put all of this in a large pan with the garlic, bouquet garni and tomato purée. Deglaze the roasting tin with water and add to the pan. Add the white wine and enough cold water (about 3 pints/ 1¾ litres) to cover. Bring slowly to the boil and simmer gently, uncovered, for 3–4 hours, skimming off the fat and scum as it surfaces. If you don't do this, the scum makes the stock a little bitter. Strain off the stock and it is ready to use. You can remove every trace of fat by letting it cool completely, by which time the fat will have solidified on the surface.

Golden Glaze
To make a tawny meat glaze, simmer the pale poultry stock, once it has been skimmed of all fat, slowly reducing until it is syrupy and darker in colour. When it is ready, it will be about ¼ pt (150 ml) and it will coat a spoon with a delicious-looking film. Do not season until it has reduced.

Small Iuniper of the Alps.

dark game stock and rich meat glaze

This is the stock to use with venison, pigeon, pheasant and other game birds, where a brown stock is needed. It is also the essential ingredient for a Brown Sauce or Sauce Ragoût (p. 166), from which port or red wine sauces and others of that ilk are made. The red wine is optional—obviously it makes it darker and richer. None of the game should be too well hung, particularly poultry, or the stock will become bitter.

For 1½ pints (scant litre)

2¼ lbs (1 kg) venison bones
    and meat, pheasant or
    pigeon legs and carcases,
    beef scraps and bones etc.
a little dripping
2 oz (50 g) ham *or* bacon
2 small carrots
2 small onions
1 large celery stalk
1 leek
½ pint (300 ml) red wine
2 cloves garlic
a bouquet of juniper berries,
    sage, thyme, bay leaf and
    2 cloves

Brown the meat and bones with some dripping in the oven or under a gentle grill, turning once or twice and making sure that any poultry carcases don't burn. Remove them if they brown too quickly. Add the ham and vegetables, which should be chopped, and return to the oven for about 5 minutes, turning them around with the bones and fat.

Put all of this into a large pan and rinse out the roasting tin with water, scraping up all the caramelised juices. Add this to the pan with the red wine, garlic and the bouquet of herbs. Cover with more water, bring to the boil and simmer uncovered, for 3–4 hours, topping up with a little water if it gets too low.

Strain through a fine sieve or cloth. It is better to leave the stock unseasoned at this point.

Rich Meat Glaze

Remove all traces of fat from the stock and gently simmer until it has reduced to about ¼ pint (150 ml). By this time it should be dark and glossy and rather syrupy. Be careful at this point not to burn the glaze as the bitterness which will appear cannot be got rid of. This is the time to season the glaze. You are now armed with an invaluable commodity which can turn a rather characterless sauce into something special, or just be used as it is.

The great Iuniper tree.

brown sauce and sauce ragoût

To turn Dark Game Stock (p. 165) into the thickened and richer brown sauce which is the basis for many traditional game sauces, you more or less repeat the stock procedure, this time adding a small amount of flour. The game scraps turn it into sauce ragoût. To produce the genuine article it is necessary to simmer the sauce for a minimum of 2 hours, but this undoubtedly produces the best results. However, if time is lacking, you may need to use the quick version which produces reasonable results.

For about 1 pint (570 ml)

1½ pint (850 ml) Dark Game Stock
4 oz (110 g) diced mixed vegetables
2–3 rashers mild lean bacon *or* ham
4–6 oz (110–170 g) game scraps and bones (optional)
butter *or* fat for browning
rounded tablesp flour
1 tablesp tomato purée
bouquet garni
a large glass red wine

In a large saucepan, brown the vegetables, bacon and game scraps if used, in the butter or fat over a medium heat. Take them out temporarily and scatter the flour over the remaining fat, stirring into a smooth roux. Add the stock (preferably boiling, but if not, add slowly to eliminate lumps), the tomato purée, herbs and wine and replace the browned vegetables and meat. Simmer gently for 2–3 hours, skimming occasionally. Once strained and seasoned the sauce is ready.

quick version for busy people

For about ¾ pint (425 ml)

¾ pint (425 ml) Dark Game Stock (p. 165)
4 oz (110 g) finely diced mixed vegetables
a large glass red wine
a few herbs: parsley, bay leaf, thyme, juniper berries
2 rashers mild bacon
1 dessertsp cornflour

Simmer the vegetables in most of the stock, a little more briskly this time, with the wine, herbs and bacon. Half an hour should suffice, then strain off the stock. Dissolve the cornflour in a tablespoon or two of cold stock and whisk in the hot stock. Simmer gently for 5–10 minutes, or until it has cleared and thickened a little.

Hollandaise Sauce

Everybody has their own method of making hollandaise sauce. At its simplest it is made from egg yolks, butter, salt and lemon juice only. This is fairly mild and best suited to the delicate flavour of fish. However, the smooth creaminess of this type of sauce goes extremely well with most roast game, venison in particular. In this case I prefer to make it less bland by using a foundation of reduced vinegar with garlic or shallots. This is where Hollandaise Sauce merges into Béarnaise, which has tarragon stirred into it. Both have variations which will suit different dishes.

There are a few points worth noting. The most important is that it must be thickened over a gentle heat, and the butter added gradually. There is simply no point in rushing it along and ending up with scrambled eggs. Hollandaise Sauce is meant to be served warm, not hot. It is worth having a pan of cold water handy to cool the bowl quickly if it should get too hot.

Once used to the process, more butter can be incorporated if desired. But if you are not familiar with it, and particularly if it has to wait around a little, then stick to the given quantities. The butter should be slightly warm.

basic hollandaise sauce

Serves 4–6

3 egg yolks
6 oz (170 g) butter
1 tablesp lemon juice
salt

Beat the egg yolks together in a small bowl that sits nicely over a pan of warm water (or use a bain-marie). Cut the butter into 8 slices and put one into the bowl of egg yolks. Put the pan over a low heat and stir with a wooden spoon until the butter shows signs of melting. Immediately put in the next slice and stir until the butter is absorbed. The sauce will begin to thicken. Add the other slices one by one, stirring all the time and allowing the sauce to thicken in between each one. If at any time during this process, the sauce starts to stick to the edge of the bowl, whip it off the pan at once and cool it in cold water. Keep stirring and add the next slice of butter.

When all the butter is used, beat in the lemon juice. If salted butter was used it may not be necessary to add more salt—taste and see. Keep the sauce warm over a pan of tepid (not hot) water or on the side of the stove, and give it a stir every now and then.

john purser's hollandaise with cucumber

I think this is the most delicious sauce to have with poached salmon.

Serves 6

½ cucumber
salt
Hollandaise Sauce
  (see page 167)
fresh dill leaves (optional)

Two hours in advance, wash the cucumber and slice it paper thin. Put it in a bowl and sprinkle a few pinches of salt over the top. Mix well and leave for 2 hours. Then rinse the now floppy cucumber under the cold tap. Taste to check the cucumber is not too salty. If it is, soak in cold water, then drain thoroughly.

Make the Hollandaise as described previously, but omit the salt. Stir in the cucumber and, if desired, a teaspoon of chopped dill leaves. Now check the seasoning.

sauce mousseline

This is just a lighter form of Hollandaise Sauce, most suitable for simply cooked fish or soufflés.

Serves 6

Hollandaise Sauce
  (see p. 167)
¼ pt (150 ml) whipping
  cream

The cream should be chilled. Whip it up until soft peaks are formed. Then fold it into the hollandaise sauce. It may be necessary to add a drop or two more lemon juice.

béarnaise sauce

Traditionally made with tarragon, there is no reason why other herbs cannot be used instead. With venison try lovage, though use it in moderation for it is a strong herb. Try dill or fennel with salmon and trout. If a herb predominates elsewhere in cooking, then use the same one in the Béarnaise so that meat and sauce are married together. With dried herbs, use just under half the volume.

Serves 6

1 shallot and/or garlic
5 tablesp white wine vinegar
3 egg yolks
6 oz (170 g) butter
2 tablesp fresh tarragon
salt, pepper

Chop the shallot, and a garlic clove if used, very fine and simmer in the wine vinegar until it has reduced to 2 tablespoons. Let it cool a little, then transfer to a bowl. To be correct, one should discard the shallots, but I like to leave them in. Beat the egg yolks into the reduced vinegar, add a knob of butter and proceed as for Hollandaise Sauce (p. 167). Stir in the herb of your choice before seasoning with salt and pepper.

béarnaise with glaze

Serves 6

Béarnaise Sauce
2 tablesp meat *or* fish glaze

As well as choosing an appropriate herb for your dish, sometimes it is good to bring them together even closer by stirring in a little concentrated essence of goodness.

Since we are not always organised enough to have little cartons of meat glaze tucked in the freezer, it might just take the form of pan juices from the roasting joint, especially when there isn't enough to make decent clear gravy.

With fish poached in a good fish stock, a ladleful could be quickly reduced to a glaze. Simply stir into it the Béarnaise Sauce once it has cooled slightly.

Port and Red Wine Sauces

Used for grilled or roast venison and game birds, generally speaking, this is a thin type of sauce, smooth and full of concentrated flavour. The exception is when meat is slowly cooked in wine and the resulting gravy thickened (as on p. 140). The thin types of wine sauces are made by boiling down the wine so that the flavour is concentrated and the sauce becomes syrupy in texture. Simplest of all is the recipe on p. 123 for venison steaks. However, if you prefer to grill your steaks, then the flavour has to be added in the form of stock. Here are three variations.

traditional port wine sauce

To make a classic port wine sauce, you first have to make some excellent stock, and, from that stock, a brown sauce. This is a lengthy procedure unless you use the cheating method, but of course the end-result will be a concentrated essence of goodness. If made from game meat and bones, it will be the perfect accompaniment. Since brown sauce is slightly thickened, so will the sauce.

Serves 6

¼ pt (150 ml) port
¾ pt (425 ml) brown sauce
   (p. 166)
1–1½ oz (25–40 g) butter

Boil the port rapidly until it has reduced to 3 tablespoons. Then add the brown sauce and simmer for a minute or two. If you have a tablespoon or two of roasting or pan juices, add those too. Taste, adding a little more port if necessary, and adjust the seasoning. Take the pan off the heat and whisk in the butter, bit by bit. This makes the sauce smooth and velvety.

port wine sauce for cheats

Cheating sauces are never going to be so good as the real thing, but this one is reasonably acceptable if you are caught short. If you have a reputation for doing everything the hard way, nobody will believe that you have just opened a tin, but they will love you all the more if you confess. The extra port is necessary to drown the 'flavour enhancers' that some tins have. If possible find a tin without additives.

Serves 4–6

7 fl oz (200 ml) port
½ pt (300 g) tin concentrated consommé
1 oz (25 g) butter (optional)

Boil the port until it has reduced by half, then add the tinned consommé and bring to simmering point. Check the seasoning. It is unlikely to need salt, but a splash more port might be necessary. Draw the pan off the heat and whisk in the butter if wished—it certainly makes the sauce a little smoother.

red wine sauce

This sauce, which is suitable for roasts and grilling, is slightly less clear because of the mustard, but it is extremely good. Once again, the better the stock, the better the sauce. If you have to resort to a tin, use about 7 fl oz (200 ml) of concentrated consommé, but dilute it with the same amount of water, otherwise it will be far too strong.

Serves 4–6

¼ pt (150 ml) dry red wine
¾ pt (450 ml) Dark Game Stock (p. 165)
1 tablesp rowan or redcurrant jelly
2 tablesp French mustard
4 tablesp brandy
1 dessertsp lemon juice

Boil the red wine and stock together until they are reduced to ¼ pt (150 ml). Then add the rowan jelly and stir until melted. In a cup, dissolve the mustard in the brandy (the mustard stays in lumps if added straight to the sauce). Stir it into the sauce with the lemon juice, taste, and adjust the seasoning if necessary.

basic mayonnaise

Make sure that your bowl, oil and egg yolks are at blood temperature. In the winter olive oil can become grainy, in which case warm it until clear once more, or the mayonnaise will curdle. Suitable oils are olive, peanut (arachide), safflower or the various nut oils.

Serves 4–6

2 egg yolks
lemon juice *or* wine vinegar
½ teasp mustard
up to ½ pt (300 ml) oil
pepper, salt

Beat the egg yolks hard till slightly thickened, then beat in the mustard and a teaspoon of lemon juice or white wine vinegar, till thick and smooth again. Drop by drop, start beating in the oil. When the mayonnaise has thickened you may pour in the oil a little more quickly. If it becomes terribly stiff add a drop or two more lemon juice, then continue adding oil. Season to taste with salt, pepper, lemon juice and more mustard if desired. Curry powder and other flavourings can also be beaten in when appropriate.

cold green sauce

This is a flavoured mayonnaise made in a liquidiser or food processor. It is thinner than ordinary mayonnaise but goes very well with fish and cold game. Herbs and flavourings can be varied according to the dish they are to accompany, but spinach or Swiss chard leaves make the best foundation.

Serves 4–6

2 shallots *or* garlic cloves
2 oz (50 g) spinach leaves
1 oz (25 g) mixed herbs
1 large egg + 1 egg yolk
8 fl oz (225 ml) oil
white wine vinegar,
    seasoning

Chop the shallots or garlic very fine. Boil a little water and throw in the shallots and any herb that has tough stalks. Boil for 2 minutes, then add the spinach and other herbs. Boil one more minute (the herbs are to be softened, not cooked), then drain and refresh in cold water to keep the colour green. Squeeze all the water out.

Put the prepared herbs into the liquidiser with the egg and yolk and blend until all the herbs are puréed. Then, with the machine running, add the oil very slowly indeed until the mayonnaise reaches a good coating consistency. Season to taste.

For a quick cheating method, prepare the shallots and herbs as above, then liquidise with 2 tablesp bought mayonnaise. Add an egg yolk and some lemon juice if too stiff.

warm green sauce

This sauce goes extremely well with soufflés, quenelles, roulades, savoury pastries and fish.

Serves 4–6

1 shallot *or* ½ small onion
½ oz (12 g) butter
¼ pt (150 ml) dry vermouth
1 oz (25 g) spinach leaves
1 oz (25 g) parsley and herbs
  to taste
1–2 egg yolks
¼ pt (150 ml) whipping
  cream
salt, pepper

Chop the shallot and soften it slowly in the butter till translucent. Add the vermouth (a medium dry vermouth can be used if more appropriate), bring to the boil and reduce by half.

Meanwhile, plunge the spinach and herbs into a little boiling water and boil for 2 minutes. Drain, run them under cold water, then squeeze out as much water as possible. Put them in a liquidiser with the reduced vermouth and shallot and blend to a purée.

Return the purée to the pan and stir in the egg yolk. One yolk gives a fairly runny sauce suitable for pastries, two gives a coating consistency. Add the cream and stir over a very low heat until thickened.

Then rub the sauce through a metal sieve, leaving behind a large part of the greenery. Season with salt and pepper.

yoghourt and cucumber sauce

For fish when served cold. This is also good when made with mayonnaise instead of cream.

Serves 4–6

yoghourt
cream (whipping)
cucumber *or* gherkins
dill, seasoning

You will need equal quantities of cream and yoghourt. Whip the cream lightly and stir in the yoghourt. The cucumber may either be sliced paper thin or else finely diced. The more cucumber the better as far as I am concerned. If the stronger gherkins are used, chop them finely and use more sparingly. Stir them into the cream with a little dill and seasoning. I think dillweed (the leaves) is preferable, but the seeds may also be used.

yoghourt sauce

Suitable for any type of grilled or pan-fried game, this is the one to use with the flambéed venison chops.

Serves 4–6

8 fl oz (225 ml) plain
   yoghourt
1 dessertsp rowan jelly
1 teasp chopped mint

Blend the ingredients together. In order to make the rowan jelly blend properly it may be necessary to warm it slightly.

jens berg's dill sauce

This is the sauce designed for Gravadlax but it is also good with marinated fish.

Serves 4–6

2 tablesp pale soft brown
   sugar
2 tablesp Swedish mustard
   (this is extremely mild)
1 tablesp corn oil
fennel seeds
fresh dill—a lot

Stir the sugar into the mustard until it has dissolved, and then beat in the corn oil. Next, take just the tip of a teaspoon of fennel seeds, crush them to a powder, and mix them in. Then add a very heaped tablespoon of finely chopped dill. This should be a fairly stiff sauce but it may be thinned with more oil.

lemon sauce

For steamed or poached fish.

Serves 4–6

2 eggs, size 3
4 oz (110 g) cream cheese
1 clove garlic
2 tablesp double cream
zest and juice 1 lemon
pinch salt

Separate the eggs and put the yolks in a blender with the rest of the ingredients. Blend to a soft paste. Whip the egg-whites stiffly and fold them into the paste. Put this in a bain-marie and stir over a gentle heat. The sauce will thin at first, and then gradually thicken to a smooth coating consistency. Avoid overheating or keeping warm for too long once thickened, or you risk curdling the sauce.

two tomato sauces

The first sauce is a traditional unthickened sauce which can be left fairly chunky, or else strained through a fine sieve to produce a clear coulis. The choice of herbs will depend upon whether it is served with meat or fish: fennel, basil or tarragon, perhaps, for fish; and thyme, rosemary or what you will with meat. Be sparing with the herbs, particularly if dried, and give them time to infuse before adding any more.

The second sauce is smooth and buttery, excellent for poached salmon or trout. Again, the herbs can be varied.

Recipe 1

Serves 3–4

4 ripe tomatoes
2 cloves garlic
2 shallots
1–2 tablesp olive oil
fresh herbs to taste
seasoning

Peel the tomatoes by dropping them into boiling water for a few seconds. The skins will then come off easily. Cut them in half and discard the seeds and core. Chop the remaining flesh. Crush the garlic and chop the shallots very fine.

Heat the oil over a moderate heat. If the sauce is to be strained afterwards, use only 1 tablespoon. Sauté the tomato, garlic and shallots gently until soft and pulpy. Then add salt, pepper and the herbs to taste.

Recipe 2

Serves 3–4

2 ripe tomatoes
1 shallot
½ glass white wine
4½ oz (120 g) butter
1 teasp fish glaze (optional)
2 teasp fresh basil
pepper, salt

Peel and de-seed the tomatoes as described above. Chop the shallot into tiny pieces and simmer them in the white wine and a knob only of the butter. When the wine has all but disappeared, add the pulped tomatoes and a teaspoon of fish glaze if you have any. Reduce again until it is quite syrupy. Add the basil. Then, a little at a time, beat in the rest of the butter. Make sure the sauce does not get too hot otherwise is may go oily. Season to taste.

roman honey sauce

Best used as a basting liquid for a small roast, when it will amalgamate with the meat juices, it is admirably suited to a slow-roasted joint.

Serves 4

6 black peppercorns
½ teasp cumin seeds
dessertsp pine kernels *or*
    flaked almonds
teasp chopped lovage
sprig of parsley, chopped
pinch of salt
2 tablesp honey
dessertsp wine vinegar
dessertsp olive *or* walnut oil

Crush the peppercorns and cumin in a pestle and mortar, then add the pine kernels or almonds and crush them roughly. Scrape these out into a bowl and add the lovage, parsley and salt. Beat in the honey (easier if slightly warmed) and then the wine vinegar and oil.

Apples of loue

francatelli's venison sauce

Francatelli was Queen Victoria's most famous chef, who wrote down many of his recipes for posterity. The vast majority of Victorian sauce recipes (which were frequently named after illustrious men of the time) are rather difficult for most of us to execute at home since they rely on a huge larder groaning with various fundamental sauces and glazes, ready to have a quart of this and a ladleful of that removed. However, this one is atypically simple, which may account for its continued popularity. There is no need to restrict it to venison though, it can be used with other grilled or roasted game very successfully.

Serves 4–6

1 small cinnamon stick
2 tablesp port wine
8 oz (225 g) redcurrant jelly
thinly pared rind 1 lemon

Bruise the cinnamon stick and put it in a pan with the port, redcurrant jelly and lemon rind. Heat slowly, stirring until the jelly has dissolved, and then simmer for 5 minutes. Strain into a hot sauce boat.

cumberland sauce

Everybody has their own way of making Cumberland sauce; here is mine. I like to have it hot, with a raised game pie, but it was originally designed to be a cold sauce, which thickens as the jelly cools. If you like added sharpness, substitute a lemon for one of the oranges.

Serves 6–8

2 oranges
8 oz (225 g) jelly (rowan,
    redcurrant *or* port wine)
2–3 teasp French mustard
5 tablesp red wine *or* port
pinch ginger
salt, pepper

Pare or grate the citrus peel and blanch it. Put the jelly, mustard and blanched peel into a small pan and dissolve the jelly over a low heat. Then add the rest of the ingredients and stir them together till hot.

white butter sauce

White butter sauce is one of the greatest classic accompaniments to fish. It is not difficult to make, but it doesn't like to wait around for too long after it's made. Reheating is not successful as it reverts to mere melted butter, but any left-over sauce can be used in place of butter to cook fish (or game for that matter).

Serves 8

4 tablesp dry white wine
4 tablesp white wine vinegar
2 *or* 3 shallots
at least 8 oz (225 g) butter cut into knobs and chilled
lemon juice
salt, white pepper

Chop the shallots very finely indeed. They should not appear as great lumps in the sauce. If shallots are not available, use spring onions instead, but bear in mind that they are a little more powerful. Boil them in the wine and vinegar and reduce the whole to about 1 tablespoon.

Remove from the heat and allow to cool a little, then whisk in a couple of pieces of butter. Once it has softened and looks creamy, beat in the rest of the butter gradually, setting the pan once more over a very gentle heat. It is essential not to overheat the sauce and let the butter melt completely. The end-result should have the appearance of really thick unbeaten cream. Once all the butter has been used, season delicately with a hint of salt, white pepper and lemon juice. Serve as soon as possible.

brown (or black) butter sauce

For sautéed breasts of pheasant or guinea fowl and grilled trout, as well as the classic dish of brains.

4 oz (110 g) butter
2 tablesp chopped parsley
3 tablesp lemon juice, *or* tarragon vinegar
salt, pepper

It is necessary to clarify the butter first so that the buttermilk doesn't burn. Melt the butter in a small saucepan and strain it into a bowl. Carefully pour it back into the rinsed-out pan, leaving behind all the milky fluid at the bottom.

Then heat the butter again until it is nutty brown. Add the chopped parsley and remove from the heat to prevent further cooking. In another pan, reduce the lemon juice or vinegar to barely a tablespoon and then add it to the butter and parsley. Season to taste.

mushroom purée

For roast game, trout quenelles, or quails (p. 113).

Serves 6–8

½ lb (225 g) mushrooms
2 oz (50 g) butter
¼ pt (150 ml) thick white
    sauce
salt, pepper, nutmeg

Wash and peel the mushrooms and then chop them extremely small. It is actually better to rub the raw mushrooms through a metal sieve or mouli. Then squeeze this semi-pulp in a cloth to remove some of the moisture.

Melt the butter in a thick pan till sizzling and stir in the mushrooms, stirring them around constantly until all wateriness has gone. Turn the heat down and gradually add the white sauce. Beat hard until it is nice and smooth, and then season.

savoury chestnut purée

For roast or grilled game.

Serves 6–8

1 lb (450 g) chestnuts
water or stock to cover
2 sticks celery
butter, cream or milk to taste
salt, pepper

Peel the chestnuts by your favoured method, then simmer them gently in stock with a good pinch of salt and the celery. When they are nice and tender (after about 1 hour), pulverise them. If you leave the celery in, you will need to sieve the purée to get rid of the fibres. Purists will remove the celery but it can be appropriate.

Ideally the final stage is done just before serving to keep its lightness, but if you add a little extra milk and keep it hot in a bain-marie it will last fairly well. Put the chestnut pulp into a heavy pan and set it over a low heat. Beat it very hard, gradually incorporating some of the butter, cream, or boiling milk, until you have the desired consistency. Season to taste.

bread sauce

Bread sauce has been the subject of much cruel derision from those who love to knock traditional British cooking. Well, I am not going to join them—I think bread sauce is marvellous. I can only suppose those unfortunates tried to make it quickly, and with frightful sliced bread. Of course it wouldn't taste good. Proper bread sauce is made slowly so that it becomes rich with creamy milk, and so that the spices can impart their flavour. Either white or fine brown bread may be used, but full wholemeal gives a rather solid sauce. In any case it should be real bread. You are well advised to use a non-stick pan or bain-marie for bread sauce.

Serves 6–8

½ pt (300 ml) milk
1 oz (25 g) butter
1 onion
4 cloves
4 peppercorns
3 oz (80 g) fine breadcrumbs
4 tablesp single cream
salt, pepper, nutmeg

Put the milk, butter, onion (chopped), cloves and peppercorns into the pan and bring slowly to just under the boil. Keep them hot, but not actually simmering, for ½–1 hour to infuse. Strain the flavoured milk and discard the onions and spices. Add the breadcrumbs to the milk and bring to just below simmering point for 30 minutes, stirring from time to time. If it becomes too thick, add a drop more milk. Just before serving, stir in the cream and season with salt, pepper and nutmeg.

rowan jelly

Once you have had rowan jelly you will never want to return to any other—they will be insipid by comparison. Unfortunately, since I know of only one firm producing rowan jelly commercially (Moniack Wines in Inverness-shire), you will probably have to make it yourself.

I am a purist and don't favour diluting rowan jelly with apples. As long as you pick the berries as soon as they are ripe and don't overcook them, there should be plenty of pectin to set the jelly. If you wait till the frost has touched the berries, not only does it destroy pectin, but you will find that the birds have swiped them all.

rowan berries
sugar

Pick the berries on a dry day and strip off the longest stalks and leaves. Cover the rest with water and bring to the boil. Thoroughly mash them and leave them to rest for 1–2 hours. This will release more pectin. Then strain the rosy pink juice thoroughly and add 1 lb (450 g) of sugar to every pint (570 ml) of juice. Dissolve the sugar and bring to a rolling boil, skimming every now and then. In order to let it boil thoroughly remember to use a huge pan. Test for setting in the usual way, and the jelly will be the colour of vintage port. If you should have a disaster, a bottle of pectin should remedy it without altering the taste, but purists frown upon this!

Celery &
fennel both
excellent
for game

juice of fennel stalks
restored or strengthened
sight.

seedy bud

the "little excrescencies"

17th tulipmania
- digbie's tulip
pease clearly
venja la mode.
- also v. delicious!

Carrots for eyesight
- spinach for strength.

Shaggy cap
(Lawyers Wig) - pick
when young before
it auto digests

8
Vegetables

I was once criticised for including a vegetable section. I'm afraid that was a typical indication of some people's attitude to vegetables. They may lavish endless care and attention on the main dish and its sauce but, for some reason, when it comes to vegetables they think it is fine just to chuck whatever is to hand into a vat of water and boil it to oblivion.

Well, I don't agree. Vegetables need not be cooked in a complicated way, they need not be cooked at all, but they do need to be considered as part of the dish every bit as much as the accompanying sauce or wine. The fact that in Britain we eat our vegetables with our meat means that choosing complementary vegetables, as well as methods of cooking them, is even more important. These recipes were chosen because they go particularly well with game and game fish. Some are meals in themselves and are useful when there are vegetarians present.

However, I have not included some of the most obvious but nevertheless delicious of all —namely, plain-boiled or steamed vegetables. Cooked well they will grace any banquet. Generally speaking, any vegetable that is to be steamed or boiled briefly should be cut into thin strips or slices so that they cook to an even *al dente* firmness. Vegetables that are slowly simmered should be left whole or in large pieces so that they don't break up. Quick cooking retains vitamins and is undoubtedly healthier, but I, for one, find winter carrots, slowly simmered to a soft melting sweetness that requires no sugar, very hard to resist on a cold day.

braised celery

In my view, the best possible vegetable to go with game.

Serves 4–6

1 large head celery
3 oz (80 g) butter
water
salt, pepper, mace
beurre manié (p. 15)
    (optional)

Cut the celery into ½ inch lengths. Melt the butter in a pan and throw in the celery. Add a good splash of water and a pinch of salt and simmer gently until the celery is tender. Do not let it brown, so add more water if necessary. Season to taste.

This is how I usually serve it but, if the dish requires a less watery version, stir in about 2 oz (50 g) of beurre manié to thicken.

carrot and spinach parcels

These are quite rich and very delicious and make a perfect foil to game dishes. These quantities will make six parcels which ought to be sufficient for six people. If you feel that it looks a little mean, then serve another vegetable with them rather than increasing the quantity.

Serves 6

1 lb (450 g) carrots
2½ oz (70 g) butter
1 tablesp chopped fresh
  chives
juice ½ orange
squeeze lemon juice
6 large *or* 12 small spinach
  leaves
salt, pepper

Prepare the carrots and cut them into chunks. Cook them in a little salted water until tender and then drain and purée them. Melt the butter in a pan and stir in the purée, adding the chives, orange juice and lemon. Stir over a low heat until some of the moisture has evaporated and the mixture is thick and creamy, and season.

Blanch the spinach and remove the stalks, if necessary cutting away the thick part which extends into the leaf so that they can be folded without breaking. Divide the carrot mixture evenly among the leaves and fold them into little parcels, laying them loose end down, in a steamer or colander. Steam for 5–10 minutes. They are rather fragile to lift out, so beware. A double layer of leaves would overcome this and the flavour will not be drastically altered, but I rather like the paper-thin green layer.

fennel al grattinato

Because this sauce is thickened with flour and egg it is a very much plainer dish than those cooked *au gratin*, and I think makes it all the better for savouring the fresh taste of the vegetable. It is a wonderful accompaniment to poached fish. The cheese should be Parmesan, but Gruyère or a sharp Cheddar will do.

1 lb (450 g) bulb fennel
3 oz (80 g) flour
pinch salt
1 large egg
½ pt (300 ml) water
2–3 oz (50 –80 g) cheese

Remove the stalks and tough outer parts from the fennel and slice thinly lengthways. Simmer in salted water until tender (10–15 minutes), then drain.

Put the flour and salt into a pan, make a well in the middle, and break the egg into it. Beat the egg into the flour, gradually adding up to half of the water, until smooth. Then set the pan over a low heat. The sauce will quickly go lumpy, but beat or whisk it until smooth and thick, then beat in the remaining water by degrees.

Pour a third of the sauce into a wide serving dish, lay the cooked fennel on top, and cover with the remaining sauce. Dredge with grated cheese and bake in a moderately hot oven (Mk 5, 375°F, 190°C) for about 15 minutes when the cheese will be cooked. It is better to finish the cooking in an oven rather than under the grill, because the flour needs time to cook and lose that pasty flavour.

braised chestnuts

For grilled or roast game.

Serves 4

1 lb (450 g) chestnuts
good stock *or* consommé to
    cover
1 stick celery
a little meat glaze (p. 165)
    (optional)
salt
butter

Peel the chestnuts thoroughly and then pack them neatly into a shallow dish. They should make a layer, one chestnut deep all over the bottom, and be fairly tightly packed. Tuck pieces of celery to fill up any gaps, and then just cover the layer with the game stock.

Sprinkle a good pinch of salt over the top and cover the dish with a buttered paper. Cook them in a very moderate oven (Mk 3, 325°F, 170°C) until they are tender. This will take 1–1½ hours. When cooked correctly, the chestnuts will remain intact and will have just absorbed the stock. To keep them firm and attractively glossy, spoon a little meat glaze over them.

vegetable soufflés

This is a very useful accompaniment to roast game—light and creamy but quite filling. In other words it is an ideal way to stretch a meal when the meat may be a little too sparse for comfort. In theory any vegetable may be used, but in practice one with a pronounced flavour is best. Broccoli, spinach and Florence fennel are all good—the last two also go well with poached fish.

Serves 4

8 oz (225 g) broccoli heads
    or 6 oz (110 g) spinach *or*
    12 oz (340 g) bulb fennel
½ oz (15 g) butter
1 tablesp flour
¼ pt (150 ml) milk
1½ oz (40 g) good grated
    cheese
2 large eggs
salt, pepper, nutmeg

Prepare the chosen vegetable: discard any tough stalks from the broccoli. Trim off the stalks and any coarse outer leaves from the fennel and slice it very thin. Cook the vegetable until tender. Broccoli and spinach may be steamed, fennel is better boiled in a little salted water. Then drain and blend to a coarse purée.

Make a thick white sauce from the butter, flour and milk and stir in the grated cheese. Edam or Gruyère are ideal. Remove from the heat and add the pulped vegetable. When it is slightly cooled beat in the two egg yolks and season with salt, pepper and a pinch of nutmeg. Beat the egg-whites stiffly and fold them in. Turn it into a 1 pt buttered dish (or individual ones if you like) and bake in a moderately hot oven (Mk 5, 375°F, 190°C) until well-risen and brown on top (about 15–20 minutes for a large soufflé).

Whilst no soufflé likes to hang around for too long, this one will stand quite happily while the meat is carved though still having a moist interior. If cooked too rapidly the soufflé collapses at once.

mrs harrison's vegetable terrine

This is what Mrs Harrison served with Venison in Blackberry Sauce for her winning menu (see p. 123), and very good it is too. My thanks to her for permission to reproduce it.

Serves 8

1 lb (450 g) carrots
12 oz (340 g) peas
1 lb (450 g) parsnips *or*
    celeriac

Peel, core and chop the carrots and parsnips. In separate containers, steam all the vegetables until just soft—3 minutes for the peas and 10–15 minutes for the root vegetables. Purée them, also separately.

Line a 1 lb loaf tin with cling film and then layer the different coloured vegetable purées into the film, smoothing the surface of each layer nicely. Cover the tin with cling film and put it in a tray of hot water in a low oven (Mk 2, 300°F, 150°C) until the mixture sets (about 10–15 minutes). Turn out the mould very carefully and serve in slices to show off the attractive colour combination.

Since one of Mrs Harrison's briefs was to produce a low salt menu, she uses none, but the unconverted may care to add a small amount to the purées.

pease of the seedy buds of tulips

I found this curious little recipe in a seventeenth-century book *The Closet of Sir Kenelme Digbie Opened*. As the son of one of the notorious Gunpowder Plot conspirators, Sir Kenelme started life in a less than enviable position, but his boundless charm and insatiable enthusiasm for learning eventually won him respect and admiration in many eminent quarters. He was particularly interested in the art of healing, concocting many potions with which to cure his family and friends.

It is typical of the Renaissance generation that such a scholarly and well-travelled man should take an interest in everyday cooking. He does not say whether the following recipe has any curative powers, but I imagine that, after a long winter, some esoteric fresh vegetable would certainly tempt the palate as well as the mind. In any case, I thought that these Tulip Pease would make a delightful, if somewhat pretentious, accompaniment to quail—surely the epitome of frivolity?

'In the Spring (about the beginning of May) the flowry-leaves of Tulips do fall away, and there remains within them the end of the stalk, which in time will turn to seed. Take that seedy end (then very tender) and pick from it the little excrescencies about it, and cut it into short pieces, and boil them and dress them as you would do Pease; and they will taste like Pease, and be very savoury.'

vegetables à la grecque

The oily moistness of vegetables cooked à la grecque complements cold game and fish dishes excellently—choose one that is sympathetic, and bear in mind the flavour of the main dish when choosing herbs. I think that they are improved if made a day in advance.

Serves 6

Basic Recipe
1 lb (450 g) vegetables
¾ pt (450 ml) water
2 shallots
herbs and spices to choice
parsley, peppercorns
juice 2 large lemons
5 tablesp olive oil
fresh chopped herbs to serve
salt

Chop the shallots and tie them in a cloth with the parsley, herbs and peppercorns. Put this bouquet in a pan with the water, lemon juice and oil. Add just a tiny pinch of salt, bring to the boil and simmer for 10 minutes, then add the prepared vegetable of your choice. Individual simmering times are given below. Then remove the vegetables to a bowl and discard the bouquet. Boil the liquid until it has reduced to ¼ pt (150 ml), correct the seasoning and pour it over the vegetables. Leave them to cool slowly, mixing them round from time to time. Stir in some chopped fresh herbs before serving.

Cucumber
Slice into manageable strips and sprinkle with a good pinch of salt. Leave for 2 hours, then rinse under cold water. Omit salt from the basic recipe. Simmering time: 10–15 minutes. Herbs: parsley, dill, thyme, melissa.

Celery
Discard tough outer stalks. De-string if necessary and chop into 2 inch (5 cm) sticks. Simmering time: 45 minutes. Herbs: parsley, lovage or fennel.

Bulb Fennel
Discard stalks and tough outer parts. Cut lengthways into ¼ inch (6 mm) slices. Simmering time: 30 minutes. Herbs: parsley, melissa, lovage.

Mushrooms
Tiny mushrooms can be left whole. Larger ones should be thickly sliced. Simmering time: 15 minutes. Herbs: thyme, parsley, basil, melissa.

Leeks
Wash thoroughly. Discard any tough green leaves and trim. Cut into 2 inch (5 cm) lengths. Check there is no grit left in them. Simmering time: 40 minutes. Herbs: parsley, thyme.

potato pancakes

It is generally accepted nowadays that potatoes form the mainstay of many of our meals—and why not? They are stuffed with vitamin C and roughage, even though we may doubt an eighteenth-century claim that they 'provoke lust, causing fruitfulness in both sexes'. But potatoes were not always so well regarded. After Sir Walter Raleigh demonstrated their virtues on his Irish estates, they were hotly denounced by some priests as 'a dangerous thing of a dangerous race (referring to the Incas)—to be avoided by saint and sinner alike'. However the potato won in the end and was added to the already vast list of culinary and medicinal plants in contemporary herbals.

It is well worth serving potatoes in an unusual way; people really do seem to appreciate the effort. I find these potato pancakes a perfect foil to any game—like Lear's tiger, it 'well repays the trouble and expense'. Although the potatoes may be peeled in advance and kept in cold water, the rest should be done just prior to cooking or the mixture will discolour.

Serves 4–6

1½ lb (675 g) peeled
  potatoes
4 oz (110 g) low-fat soft
  cheese
2 oz (50 g) sharp cooking
  cheese
1 tablesp flour
1 large egg
salt, pepper
spices and/or herbs to taste
milk or cream if necessary
butter or fat for frying

Grate the potatoes coarsely and immediately rinse them thoroughly in cold water to eliminate excess starch. If you don't, the potatoes rapidly turn pink and then black, which is not particularly sightly. Drain and squeeze out as much water as possible.

In a large bowl, mix together the two cheeses, the flour and the egg. Season with two pinches of salt and some pepper. Add the grated potatoes. If appropriate, stir in some other spices and herbs. Chives are good; so are crushed garlic or juniper berries, but I wouldn't overdo them especially if they appear elsewhere in the course. The plain variety is perfectly good.

It may be necessary to add a splash of milk or cream to moisten the mixture. Remember that flour and eggs thicken as they cook and the pancakes want to remain moist in the centre. I usually add a couple of tablespoonfuls.

Heat some fat in as large a frying-pan as possible. When the fat is hot, give the potato mixture a final stir and put heaped tablespoonfuls into the pan. Keep them apart from each other and press into round shapes. Let them brown on the bottom, then carefully turn them over to brown the other side. Lower the heat and keep turning them over and over so that the centre cooks through. They will take about 10 minutes in all.

If by chance your initial mixture was left lying around, it will almost certainly have become too runny and the pancakes will stick to the pan. In this case add a little more flour and keep on turning them over. They will come right in the end.

The pancakes are at their best served straight from the pan, but don't worry if you have to do them in batches—they are still good if kept warm and can even be reheated. They should be nicely crisp on the outside with a moist interior, and the potato shreds, though cooked, have an interesting bite to them.

celeriac and potato purée

This is a classic accompaniment to any sort of game. Being a little lighter than mashed potato, it is particularly good with very rich dishes.

Serves 4

1 lb (450 g) potatoes
1 lb (450 g) celeriac
3 oz (80 g) butter
salt, pepper

Boil the celeriac and potatoes in separate pans until cooked. This is necessary to make sure that they cook evenly. Purée them together with the butter, and season well with salt and pepper.

clapshot

Clapshot is a Scottish version of the above, and is good with haggis. Sometimes, instead of mashing, the vegetables are hashed or shredded which gives an interesting texture.

Serves 6

12 oz (340 g) potatoes
1¼ lb (560 g) turnips
bunch of chives
good meat dripping, salt,
    pepper

Cook the potatoes and turnips and either mash or flake them. Add the chives and the dripping and season to taste.

juniper potatoes

I was introduced to this excellent way of cooking potatoes by Elizabeth David in her classic *French Provincial Cooking*. It should certainly be more widely known because juniper berries are such a perfect foil to game. It is too easy to over-emphasise them in the cooking of the meat, but this is the ideal solution. This recipe works very well with other root vegetables too.

Serves 4–6

1½ lb (675 g) potatoes
 (peeled)
1½ oz (40 g) butter
tablesp well-flavoured oil
salt, black pepper
12 juniper berries

Shred the potatoes on the coarsest hole of your grater and then wash the excess starch out of them by rinsing in a colander under the cold tap. Dry them thoroughly on a cloth. Heat the butter and oil (this stops the butter burning) and softly fold the potato over and over in it. Add a good pinch of salt, some fresh black pepper and the juniper berries which have been well crushed into small grains.

Now you have a choice. The potatoes can be served when the shreds are separate and still have a little 'bite' to them. Or, continue folding until you have a soft cohesive mass. Or, if you turn up the heat and brown them, the potatoes come out rather like American brownies. Each way is good and offers a contrast appropriate to different recipes.

savoyard potatoes

This is one of the best ways of serving potatoes with a game dish. Although for daintiness's sake they can be cooked in individual portions, I think it tastes better done in a large shallow dish. Gratin Savoyard, as it is properly called, is very similar to Gratin Dauphinois, but uses meat stock instead of milk or cream and I find it a little less rich. There is also an advantage, particularly if the meat recipe requires last-minute attention, in having the potatoes already cared for. Swiss cheese is the most authentic kind to use but, rather than give up in despair, use the best substitute you can find. It will still be good.

Serves 4–6

2 lb (900 g) potatoes
3 oz (80 g) butter
4 oz (110 g) grated cheese
½ pint (300 ml) good dark
 stock
salt, pepper, garlic

Peel the potatoes and cut them into thin slices about ⅛ inch. Rinse, and keep them immersed in cold water until ready to use. Rub the bottom of a large shallow earthenware dish with garlic and grease with a little of the butter. Pat the potato slices dry and put half of them in the dish. Sprinkle a small pinch of salt, a few turns of a pepper mill, and half of the cheese over them. Cut the butter into small dice (this is easiest if the butter is well chilled) and sprinkle half of them over the potato layer. Then spread the rest of the potatoes on top, making an even layer. Heat the stock and pour it gently over the potatoes. Sprinkle the rest of the butter and cheese on top with another pinch of salt and pepper.

Bake in a hot oven (Mk 6, 400°F, 200°C) for about 30 minutes. The potatoes are done when they have absorbed the stock and are golden brown on top. If it is more convenient, you can bake them in a slower oven (Mk 3, 325°F, 170°C) for 3 hours, increasing the heat to brown the top just before all the stock has been absorbed. Waxy potatoes will give much more satisfactory results than the floury type, which tend to disintegrate.

Virginian Potatoes

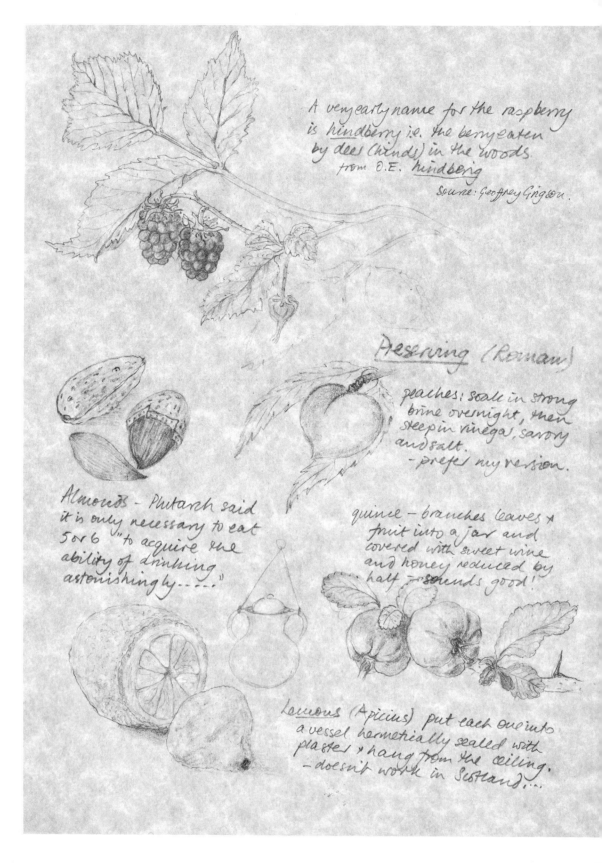

A very early name for the raspberry is hindberry i.e. the berry eaten by deer (hinds) in the woods.
from O.E. hindberg
Source: Geoffrey Grigson.

Preserving (Roman)

peaches: scald in strong brine overnight, then steep in vinegar, savory and salt.
- prefer my version.

Almonds - Plutarch said it is only necessary to eat 5 or 6 "to acquire the ability of drinking astonishingly....."

quince - branches leaves & fruit into a jar and covered with sweet wine and honey reduced by half - sounds good!

Lemons (Apicius) put each one into a vessel hermetically sealed with plaster & hang from the ceiling.
- doesn't work in Scotland...

9
Desserts

I should hate you to think that we sit down, Billy Bunter-style, to these puddings every night. Far from it. When asked 'What's for afters?' the answer is usually 'W.T.I.F.' (Well that's it folks) and the fruit bowl is brought on. But sometimes the reply is 'W.A.S.' (Wait and see), and then everyone gets a very greedy look in the eye. Health fanatics will shudder—but they already know that superb desserts consist of making simple use of what is in season. They will stick to a bowl of fresh cobnuts with a fresh cheese, or strawberries with pepper on them. They might possibly approve of the Maharani's honey and gold leaf tonic.

My feeling is that, since we eat so much venison and other game, which is very low in cholesterol, we can afford to have the occasional blow-out with a really sinful pudding. Certainly our many foreign visitors are delighted by our pudding ritual, and I hope you will enjoy them too.

cranachan with red berries

Cranachan is to my mind the epitome of a Scottish pudding: perfect in its simplicity and using the best of ingredients. The addition of whisky is a modern adulteration devised by people who think that putting whisky into food instantly transforms it into a 'Taste of Scotland' recipe. Cranachan is perfect without it and I prefer to keep my whisky and drink it another time. Traditionally raspberries are used, but I like it even better with redcurrants' sharper tang.

Serves 6

4–5 oz (110–140 g) medium
    oatmeal
¾ pt (425 ml) double *or*
    whipping cream
12 oz (340 g) raspberries *or*
    redcurrants
tiny amount caster sugar

Put the oatmeal on to a baking sheet and toast it gently for 5–10 minutes until tawny brown. Once oatmeal has dried out it burns quickly, so stir it occasionally. Allow to cool completely.

Whip the cream softly—the oatmeal stiffens it up so don't be too zealous. It should barely hold a soft peak. Fold in the berries with a little caster sugar. The amount will depend on the sharpness of your berries but it should hardly be sweet at all. Lastly, fold in the oatmeal. Exactly how much you use will depend on the thickness of the cream, but the mixture should be of a dropping consistency. Turn it into glasses and serve immediately because if left for any length of time the oatmeal will draw moisture from the cream and lose its crunchiness, leaving the rest as a solid heavy affair.

In case you think this a horrendously sinful pudding, allow me to reassure you by mentioning the fact that both oatmeal and pectin are known to reduce cholesterol levels. Thus, with protein and calcium, roughage and cereal, vitamin C and pectin, Cranachan is a remarkably balanced food, bound to be terribly good for you.

peaches in brandy

We have been preserving peaches for years now, they easily repay a few sticky days' preparation. They improve with keeping, are invaluable for an impromptu meal, and make excellent presents.

Wait until there is a glut of peaches—the flavour is often better then. It is worth buying a whole tray since it takes very little longer than making just a few. But before investing in a tray, do try one to check that they are firm but juicy. Don't use dry, stringy or unripe fruit. Sometimes nectarines have a better flavour. Buy medium to large fruits as they shrink quite a lot. It makes no difference to the flavour whether brandy, kirsch or vodka is used, so buy the cheapest.

An excellent by-product is the excess of peach syrup which we call 'trésor de cuisine'. It keeps indefinitely with brandy, and for about a month without, and can be used to lift up any fruit pudding from the good to the sublime.

2 lb (900 g) peaches
2 lb (900 g) sugar
8 fl oz (250 ml) water
½ bottle brandy

The only tiresome task is peeling the peaches. Don't be tempted to skip it as the skins impede the process then break up, looking most unsightly. Put a pan of water on to boil, then throw in the peaches two or three at a time. Leave for 10 seconds, then remove with a slotted spoon. The skins come off easily while they are still hot. Continue with the rest, then weigh the fruit and measure out the other ingredients in proportion.

Boil up the water again, throw in the peaches and quickly return to the boil. Lift them out into a large clean non-metal bowl.

Chuck out the boiled water and put the measured sugar and water into the pan. Dissolve, then boil until it reaches 230°F (112°C). This is the pearl stage when it bubbles with little pearl-like beads. Add the peaches, and as soon as they have come to the boil (do this rapidly so that the fruit is not over-stewed) pour the whole lot into the bowl. The peaches will bob up to the surface. They must be kept submerged, so weight them down with a plate. Leave for 24 hours.

Then lift out the peaches. They will have shrivelled considerably. Return the syrup to the pan and bring to a rolling boil. Throw back the peaches, bring quickly to the boil, then return to the bowl, weighting as before. Leave for a further 24 hours.

Then lift out the fruit again and pack them into clean preserving jars, filling them ⅔ full. This gives the correct proportion of syrup to fruit when serving. Keep them covered for the time being.

There will be considerable amounts of syrup. Boil it until it has reduced to two-thirds of its original volume and is thickened, then strain if necessary and leave till cold.

You now have a choice. Either mix the full amount of brandy thoroughly with the syrup and fill the peach jars to the rim, pouring the rest into screw-top bottles as your 'trésor de cuisine' or, if you want to economise, mix half of the brandy with half of the syrup and use this to fill the jars. The rest is plain peach syrup which will keep for a few weeks if kept cool, but eventually goes fizzy.

Leave the peaches for a minimum of 3 months if you can bear it. They will go on improving for another 6 months and keep indefinitely if given the chance. They are very rich and need only plain cream and perhaps a simple biscuit.

the maharani's honey and gold-leaf tonic

When I was at art college, somebody gave me a book of gold leaf. Every now and then I would take it out, admire the fragile sheets, wonder what to do with it, and put it carefully away again. Then one day, in a radio programme about the Maharajahs of India, I learnt that their wives used to make a tonic out of gold leaf and honey. I immediately decided to eat my gold leaf. I can vouch for its remarkable properties. The first time I had this tonic I am told that I danced the Highland Fling. On the second occasion I was a little more sedate, but after both I woke up with nothing like the hangover I deserved.

You need something very simple to go with this tonic. Sheep's yoghourt is excellent, or petit-suisse cheese (fromage blanc), or natural set yoghourt. Even plain junket with a few curls of lemon rind instead of sugar is good—directions are on the rennet bottle. I sometimes use half-cream and half-milk, but for a real tonic both should be unpasteurised.

Rennet can be bought at independent chemists' shops. Gold leaf can be bought at a few specialist artist's suppliers, otherwise you'll have to visit the bullion dealers.

Serves 8

12 oz (340 g) excellent clear honey
4 sheets gold leaf
8 portions cheese, yoghourt *or* junket etc

Nature's finest wild flower honey is what you should use. Warm it until it is very runny. Marvel at the delicate sheets of gold leaf, then roll them up and break them up into tiny flakes with your fingers. A pestle and mortar is not much use unless you want it gold-plated. Stir the flakes into the honey and keep it well warmed in a plain porcelain bowl.

Put the cheese, yoghourts, etc, neatly into exquisite individual dishes and chill. Junkets should be poured into individual bowls to set. Decorate with a tiny flower.

Pass the glistering gold tonic round separately so that everyone can have the pleasure of ladling it out.

fairy butter

Scotland's Age of Enlightenment in the late eighteenth and early nineteenth centuries produced, as well as an outpouring of architecture, philosophy, and so on, a great upsurge of elegant cuisine, as immortalised in the affairs of Sir Walter Scott's 'Cleikum Club'. This delightful pudding is typical of the period. The original recipe came from Mrs Dalgairn's *The Practice of Cookery* published in 1829. She recommends serving Fairy Butter with Naples biscuit. I must confess I find this rather heavy, having very little to recommend it bar its ability to soak up prodigious quantities of alcohol. I prefer to serve it on a good home-made sponge biscuit (which also has that admirable quality), or else in little lacy baskets made from brandy snap mixture.

Fairy Butter

Serves 6

1½ oz (40 g) sweet almonds
rose water
1–2 drops almond essence
   (optional)
3 oz (80 g) unsalted butter
4 hard-boiled egg yolks
peel of ½ lemon
tablesp brandy
dessertsp caster sugar

Blanch the almonds and pound them to a smooth paste with a little rose water. If you use ready-ground almonds a drop or two of almond essence may be necessary, but add this to taste at the end. Soften the butter, then beat in the ground almonds and crushed hard-boiled egg yolks. Add the finely grated lemon peel and the brandy and beat until smooth and creamy, adding sugar to taste. Chill to firm the butter.

When your chosen base is ready, put the chilled fairy butter into a conical sieve or a Mouli and press it through, making feathery heaps 'as high as can be raised'.

Naples Biscuit

Serves 6

2 small eggs
2 teasp rose water
4 oz (110 g) plain flour
4 oz (110 g) caster sugar
6 tablesp sweet wine

Beat the eggs together with the rose water, then 'mix flour and sugar, then wet it with the eggs and as much cold water as will make a light paste; beat the paste very well then put the biscuits in papered tin pans. Bake in a gentle oven.' This is enough for six biscuits which should be 1 inch (2½ cm) deep in their little tins. When nearly cool, soak them in the wine. Cutting off the base helps the absorption of the wine. Madeira, Muscat, or sweet sherry are all suitable.

Lacy baskets

Serves 6

2 oz (50 g) sugar
scant 1 oz (20 g) butter
1 tablesp golden syrup
1 tablesp flour
pinch ground ginger

Cream together the sugar, butter and golden syrup. Then stir in the sifted flour and ginger. Make this mixture into six balls and place them far apart (for they will spread) on to a greased baking sheet. Bake in a cool oven (Mk 2, 300°F, 150°C) until they are a rich golden brown colour.

Have ready three upturned and oiled jam jars. When the biscuits have cooled a fraction, remove them one by one with a metal spatula and flip them in turn on to a jam-jar base, leaving just long enough to set before continuing with the others. If the others should harden as they wait, return them to the oven to soften. Fill with chilled Fairy Butter.

jackson pollock pudding

This pudding never fails to delight. It is a variation on crème brûlée, but the addition of the fruit makes it a more refreshing dish to eat. The spun caramel top looks delightful and crackles wickedly when you eat it.

Serves 6

8 oz (225 g) redcurrants
4 egg yolks (size 2)
2 oz (50 g) sugar
1 teasp cornflour
¾ pt (425 ml) cream
2 teasp vanilla essence
sugar and water for caramel

Take a dish 8 inches in diameter and at least 3 inches deep and line the base with redcurrants. You can use individual dishes if preferred but not your best glass ones in case the caramel should crack them.

Beat the egg yolks and sugar until they are pale yellow and the sugar has dissolved. Then scatter on the cornflour and beat it in. Cornflour is not essential, but it makes the custard less likely to separate and is a good safety precaution if you are not accustomed to making egg custards.

Take a pan with a very heavy bottom and heat up the cream until it is nearly boiling, but not quite. Pour it slowly on to the yolks and sugar, beating all the time. Return it to the pan and over a very gentle heat stir until it is thickened. Don't let it reach simmering point or it will separate. Remove from the heat, add the vanilla essence and stir it occasionally until nearly cool, to prevent a skin from forming.

Spoon the custard over the redcurrants, taking care that they remain on the bottom. Tap the side of the dish to remove air bubbles and then chill.

The caramel should not be applied more than an hour before serving, particularly if the atmosphere is damp, otherwise it will become tacky and lose its interesting texture.

Make a caramel out of 3 tablespoons of sugar and 5 of cold water. Heat gently until the sugar has dissolved. Failure to do this will result in a most interesting powdered sugar but no caramel. Then increase the heat and boil until you have a tawny caramel. Remove from the heat immediately, as it can go on cooking by itself, and allow it to cool for a moment. If the caramel is too hot, it will disappear into the custard in a bubbling fury of scrambled eggs.

Holding the pan over the dish of chilled custard, dip a warm metal spoon into the caramel and whirl it gently off the spoon in a random fashion on to the surface of the custard. Continue to do this with the rest of the caramel until the hectic pattern of blobs and trails resembles a Jackson Pollock painting.

caramelised pears

One of Osgood MacKenzie's earliest memories is of pears. He recalls being taken to Jersey in 1842, where a Colonel Lecoutier gave a dinner. 'The dessert consisted of pears only, there being thirty dishes, each containing a different variety'. He doesn't tell us what the dishes were, but it is quite likely that this would be one of them, as both apples and pears are cooked this way in Normandy. Sadly, we have far less choice nowadays, but my recommendation would be Conference pears, ripe and juicy but firm enough not to disintegrate. John always cooks this for us, so I'd better leave him to tell you how it is done:

'If, like me, you find the ritual of prising raw fowl off shattered, needle-sharp bones the exemplification of frustration then I suggest the following recipe. I find it useful to prepare while the rest of the company are still busy with their cavemen impressions. The exercise provides a release from the disappointment of failing to dislodge that crumb of game bird, and the spirits soothe wounded gums. We eat in the kitchen so that the diners are obliged to admire the sheets of flame.

Serves 6

9 pears
butter
syrup or 'trésor de cuisine'
 (see p. 192)
spirits
cinnamon

'Pears are essential as their curious crunchy stone-cells add texture and disguise the fact that you have not bothered to peel the fruit. Melt a knob of butter in a heavy frying pan while you slice the pears longitudinally into six slivers and remove the cores. Add the fruit to the butter and, if you have one, put a lid on the pan. Use plenty of heat. After two or three minutes add the secret ingredient. For this I use our "trésor de cuisine" produced by preserving peaches but I suppose any syrup would serve; pour in a good dollop. Add some cinnamon. Quite a while before caramelising has progressed too far add some spirits. I choose one of an array donated by a Swiss deer farmer friend and distilled from apples, pears or the roots of the gentian. Add a wine glassful or so and, standing well back, ignite, having first made sure no clothes of value are drying above the stove. As soon as seems decent quench the blaze with the lid, thus preventing all the alcohol being wasted, and immediately serve with plenty of liquid cream to the impressed and by now intoxicated diners.'

luxemburg rhubarb tart

This is actually a classic Alsace tart, but since I was first introduced to it by my Luxemburg friend Maggy, to me it remains Luxemburg Tart. It is best eaten cold in large quantities.

The amount of sugar used depends on the rhubarb—early forced rhubarb can be a bit bland for this and will need less. Early garden rhubarb is ideal as it is tender and colourful but whilst not being too sour it has a good sharp flavour which contrasts well with the smooth custard.

Serves 6–8

12 oz (340 g) sweet pastry
6 oz (170 g) juicy red rhubarb
1 dessertspoon sugar
1 little water
2 eggs (size 2)
1 tablesp caster sugar
  + 2 drops vanilla
  essence
⅓ pt (200 ml) double *or*
  whipping cream

Line an 11-inch diameter flan case with the pâte brisée and bake blind. Cut the rhubarb (don't peel it) into ¾-inch lengths and put them into a small pan with the sugar and a small amount of water. Cook them gently with the lid on until just soft but well before they break up. Drain very carefully.

Beat the egg yolks and sugar together until the sugar has dissolved. Bring the cream to the boil in a heavy-bottomed saucepan and beat it into the eggs and sugar. Return this to the pan, and over a gentle heat (use a double boiler or heat diffuser if you don't have a heavy pan), thicken the custard until it coats the back of the spoon.

Put it into the flan case and then arrange the rhubarb pieces, standing on end, in concentric circles in the custard. If the small amount of syrup produced by the rhubarb is nice and tart, brush it round the pastry edges—this tastes good but does make it rather sticky to eat with fingers. Bake in a slow oven (Mk 1, 275°F, 140°C) for about 2 hours to finish setting the custard, then allow it to cool before serving.

The Katherine Peare tree

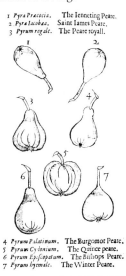

1 *Pyra Præcocia.* The Ienneting Peare.
2 *Pyra Iacobæa.* Saint Iames Peare.
3 *Pyrum regale.* The Peare royall.

4 *Pyrum Palatinum.* The Burgomot Peare.
5 *Pyrum Cydonium.* The Quince peare.
6 *Pyrum Episcopatum.* The Bishops Peare.
7 *Pyrum hyemale.* The Winter Peare.

The great Choke Peare

chocolate pots

I can't decide which nuts I prefer in these very rich puddings. Almonds and walnuts have their own characteristic flavour and give some texture to the pudding. Chestnuts are softer, and I use an extra ounce as they are blander. Whole chestnuts obviously need to be cooked and peeled first, and then crumbled, but tinned chestnuts are also good; they are so soft that only a light mashing is necessary. When the pudding has cooked you may find they have separated so that the chocolate mixture with crumbs of chestnut is on top, and a sort of chestnut paste is at the bottom.

Serves 8

4 oz (110 g) bitter chocolate
1 tablesp very strong coffee
2 tablesp brandy or rum
4 oz (110 g) nuts
2 oz (50 g) butter
1 oz (25 g) caster sugar
3 eggs

Break up the chocolate and melt it in a pan with the coffee and brandy. Chop the nuts. For once, a food processor or blender is good for this job as ideally there should be a mixture of chopped and ground nuts. Beat the butter and sugar together till very soft and stir in the nuts. Then beat in the melted chocolate.

Separate the eggs and beat in the egg yolks. Whip the whites till stiff and fold them in. Butter 8 small dishes and fill with the mixture. Bake in a slow oven (Mk 2, 300°F, 150°C) for 2 hours, then leave to cool. Serve at room temperature with icy cold single cream.

lemon mousse with almonds

Here is a really good lemon mousse which is nicely sharp and light. For my own preference I would make it slightly stronger, cutting down a little on the cream, and missing out an egg-white, but the proportions given here seem to please everyone else. The toasted almonds are essential—so don't burn them!

Serves 6

2 lemons
1 oz (25 g) butter
4 eggs (size 4)
2 oz (50 g) sugar
½ pt (150 ml) double *or* whipping cream
2 oz (50 g) flaked almonds

Wash the lemons and grate the peel. If you like a little texture then use a lemon parer to bring it off in thin curls. Put this in a bowl with the lemon juice, butter, egg yolks and sugar. You may like to start off with a little less sugar and add more to taste.

Stand the bowl over a pan of simmering water and stir, scraping round the edges from time to time, until you have a curd. It should taste pretty sharp since it will be diluted, but if it brings tears to your eyes you may add a little more sugar. This procedure can take a while, and to begin with it can be quite safely left as long as the water isn't simmering too hard and as long as it gets an occasional stir. It will thicken about halfway through a daydream.

Allow the curd to cool completely, then whisk the egg-whites till they are stiff, and then whip the cream till it is light and fluffy and will plop gracefully off a spoon. Then beat the lemon curd until it is pale and creamy. Retrieve the lemon peel from the beaters and pop it back in, then fold in the cream and lastly the egg-white. Keep chilled.

Toast the flaked almonds till they are golden brown and once they are cold, scatter them over the mousse. It is best to eat this within a day or so of making it since there is no gelatine to give everlasting life. Put the almonds on top just before serving.

ginger meringue

I am not the person to proffer advice on making perfect meringues, those feather-light crisp shells with a moist interior that nineteenth-century cooks called 'cream cakes'. No, mine come out hard and dry whatever I do, the sort that other people scathingly refer to as plaster of Paris or concrete. But mine do have the advantage of keeping excellently in a tin where they become powdery and softer, and they also make this excellent sweet. As you will see, if the meringues break up when removed from their baking sheet, it doesn't matter in the least. If you do make perfect meringues, then assemble the dish at the last moment so that those wonderful puffs don't dissolve in the cream.

Serves 4

2 large egg-whites
4 oz (110 g) caster sugar
pinch ground ginger
2 tablesp crystallised ginger pieces
1 tablesp brandy *or* rum (optional)
½ pt (300 ml) whipping *or* sour cream

Warm a baking sheet, and smear it with a thin layer of butter. When this is cold, dust lightly with flour. Alternatively, line a tin with Bakewell paper. Beat the egg-whites till stiff. Beat in ¼ of the sugar for a few seconds, then fold in the rest with a pinch of ginger. Pipe the meringues on to the baking sheet, making them about 2 inches in diameter. Bake in a very cool oven (Mk ¼, 225°F, 110°C) for about 2–2½ hours, until dry. If necessary, turn them upside down and return to the oven for another 30 minutes, to dry the underneath.

Meanwhile soak the crystallised ginger in the brandy. If you are using large pieces in syrup, this is not essential, since the ginger will be moist, but I often use those small flakes which can sometimes be a little hard. Cut large pieces of ginger into small dice.

When the meringues are cold, whip the cream until it holds soft peaks. It shouldn't be too hard. Break up the meringues and fold them into the cream with the crystallised ginger. I prefer to drain the ginger if it has been soaked, because the liquor dissolves a lot of sugar and I find it makes the whole thing too sweet. I think the contrast between the sweet meringue and the plain cream studded with ginger is more interesting. The choice is yours.

pineapple pudding

'Pineapple Pud' is always greeted with a cheer in our household. I have stopped being ashamed of the fact that the main ingredient comes out of a tin, because I have tried it with fresh pineapple and it doesn't work half so well. I must say I am usually put off by recipes that use tinned produce, but all I can say is that I sympathise but recommend that you try this one. It's not the healthiest of puddings (the best ones never are), since you need a lot of cream to go with it.

Serves 6

1½ lb (675 g) tin pineapple chunks
1½ oz (40 g) butter
2 tablesp flour
a little milk
sugar to taste
4 eggs
8 oz (225 g) caster sugar
loads of thin cream

Make a roux with the butter and flour and stir in the pineapple juice to make a thick smooth sauce. Add a little milk if necessary, to thin it to a good coating consistency once the flour has cooked. Then stir in the chunks of pineapple. Add a small amount of sugar—the sauce should be barely sweet otherwise it will be unbearable. Stir in the egg yolks and reduce the heat while the custard thickens once more. Turn it into a large soufflé dish and bake in a slow oven (Mk 2, 200°, 150°C) for about 45 minutes so that it is a little thicker but certainly not solid.

Beat the egg-whites till stiff and fold in the sugar. Cover the pineapple custard with this meringue and bake in a moderately hot oven (Mk 5, 375°F, 190°C) for about 20 minutes, or until the meringue has puffed up and is brown on top.

And there you have it—a puffy meringue with a crisp top covering a smooth flavoured custard with tart pieces of pineapple just waiting to soak up the cream. You must of course serve this immediately or else the meringue will collapse.

almond soufflé

This is more of a cake than a soufflé since it doesn't really collapse when you take it out of the oven, but it must be eaten hot, when it has a lovely crispy crust. One egg-white per person gives them a helping, but usually they want more. Serve only runny cream with this, in unbelievably unhealthy quantities.

Serves 4

4 egg-whites
4 oz (110 g) sugar
8 dessertsp water
4 oz (110 g) ground almonds
4 dessertsp brandy

Dissolve the sugar and water and bring them to the boil in a heavy-bottomed pan (not enamel). Add the ground almonds and stir with a wooden spoon. To begin with, the mixture will be runny and will brown on the bottom if you stop stirring for a few seconds. Stir this in and keep going. Gradually it will become lumpy and dry. It is done when it resembles speckled brown breadcrumbs. Do not attempt to make it all as fine as ground almonds; the larger grains give the pudding its character.

This is hot work and invariably makes me bad-tempered, so you might like to make double quantities and keep some in an airtight jar for next time. Freshen it up before re-using.

When the almond crumbs are cool, stir in the brandy, whip up the egg-whites till stiff, and fold in the almonds. Turn into a buttered dish 2 inches (5 cm) deep and bake in a moderate oven (Mk 4, 350°F, 180°C) for ½–¾ hour. It will not rise much.

You can also make a superb ice-cream by stirring the brandied almond crumbs into whipped cream and freezing.

orange and oatmeal meringue

Knowing my fondness for oatmeal, friends collect recipes for me. This is adapted from one of them—my thanks to the anonymous author. It is extremely rich and rather fragile, but I think you will be excused a perfect appearance for once. The fruit that goes inside must be nicely sharp to act as a contrast to the sweet meringue. Redcurrants or raspberries are good.

Serves 6

1 oz (25 g) medium oatmeal
1 oz (25 g) almonds *or* hazelnuts
3 egg whites
pinch salt
6 oz (170 g) caster sugar
rounded dessertsp cornflour
3 drops vinegar
zest ½ small orange
¼ pt (150 ml) whipping cream
fresh fruit

Chop the nuts as fine as breadcrumbs and stir them with the oatmeal in a small dry frying pan until nicely brown and crisp. Allow to cool.

Line two 7 inch diameter cake tins with foil. Whip up the egg-whites stiffly with the salt. Beat in ¾ of the sugar and then the cornflour and vinegar. Then with a metal spoon, fold in the remaining sugar, the toasted nuts and oatmeal, and the grated orange peel.

Divide this meringue mixture between the two tins, smoothing the surface of one and raising peaks with the spoon on the other (the top). Bake in a moderate oven (Mk 4, 350°F, 180°C) for 40–45 minutes. Halfway through, check that the oven is not too hot (ovens do vary a lot). If the peaked meringue is browning too fast, reduce the heat a little. When done, remove from the oven. If the meringues should show signs of imminent collapse, return them quickly to the oven for another 10 minutes or so. Then very carefully turn them out on to a cooling rack. The tin foil will peel off quite easily if the meringue is cooked.

When the meringues are cool, whip the cream. Put the smooth-surfaced meringue on a plate and spread it with half of the cream. Put the fruit on top (it should make a solid layer) and cover it with the remaining cream. Place the peaked meringue on top.

mount vesuvius

We tend to push the boat out a bit at Hogmanay. Last year I thought it would be a good culinary joke to bring in what appeared to be a flaming Christmas pudding. In fact it was a sinfully rich iced chocolate terrine with flames coming out of the top. The basic recipe is Antony Worrall-Thompson's which I read about in *À La Carte* magazine, and that should be sufficient recommendation for anybody. The flamboyant method of presentation is my only contribution.

Serves 8

4 oz (110 g) prunes
4 tablesp cold tea
4 tablesp brandy
12 oz (350 g) good dark
   chocolate
3 eggs
1 oz (25 g) caster sugar
3 oz (80 g) unsalted butter
1 oz (25 g) cocoa powder
½ pt (300 ml) double cream
1 large orange, sugar
sherry glass brandy

Soak the prunes overnight in the cold tea and brandy. Then drain off the liquid and keep it aside. Stone the prunes and chop the flesh.

Melt the chocolate in a cool oven or a double boiler. In the meantime, separate the eggs. You will only need two of the whites. Beat the three yolks with the sugar until they are light and fluffy, then fold into the melted chocolate. Beat the butter and cocoa powder till soft and light and add to the chocolate. Then fold in the chopped prunes with about 3 tablespoons of the brandy/tea marinade. You should now have a fairly stiff purée.

Whip the egg-whites to soft peaks, and the cream, separately, until light and fluffy (ribbon stage). Fold the cream into the chocolate mixture and then the egg-whites. Turn the mixture into a 1½ pint (900 ml) pudding basin or bombe mould and freeze for at least 6 hours.

This on its own is a great dessert but to turn it into a volcano, proceed as follows. While the terrine freezes, remove the zest (but no pith) from an orange and cut into thin strips or use a lemon zester. Squeeze the juice from half the orange into a small pan with 2–3 teaspoons of sugar. Add the orange zest and simmer gently until the peel looks transparent. Leave it to steep for 1 hour then drain off the liquid. This candied peel is your boiling lava.

When the terrine is frozen turn it out of the mould by dipping it in hot water or wrapping around it a tea towel wrung out in hot water. Scoop out a little hole in the top about an inch deep. Line the hole with foil and arrange the orange peel around the edge. This is to contain the brandy.

When you are ready to serve, warm the brandy and quickly pour it into the foil. Ignite the brandy immediately (for it will cool quickly) and carry it in at once. You could stick little sparklers into the crater as well if you want.

Seasons for Game

Any game that is bound by close seasons may legally be sold fresh only during the open seasons listed below, and for 10 days afterwards. Frozen game, provided it was legally caught, may be purchased throughout the year from licensed game-dealers.

Farmed deer are exempt from close seasons and so fresh farmed venison can be legally obtained at any time of year.

OPEN SEASONS FOR WILD DEER

	England	*Scotland*
Red stags	August 1–April 30	July 1–October 20
Sika stags	August 1–April 30	July 1–October 20
Fallow bucks	August 1–April 30	August 1–April 30
Roe bucks	April 1–October 31	April 1–October 20
Red hinds	November 1–February 28/29	October 21–February 15
Sika hinds	November 1–February 28/29	October 21–February 15
Fallow does	November 1–February 28/29	October 21–February 15
Roe does	November 1–February 28/29	October 21–March 31

Pheasant open season: October 1–February 1.
Guinea Fowl, pigeons and quail have no close seasons.

Salmon and trout fishing are bound by local water authorities' open seasons, which vary. Farmed salmon and trout are available all year round.

Index